THE GLOBALIZATION OF WAL-MART

ELLEN ISRAEL ROSEN

The Workers Press

Table of Contents

1

The Imperial Supermarket

Ever since the 1970s, there has been a movement in the United States by the very wealthy, to make the society work for them. They have been reshaping the rules of business and society to their own ends, to change or destroy much of the legislation that passed the Congress in the New Deal—The Social Security Act, The Fair Labor Standards Act, and especially The Wagner Act. They have been remodeling the world in an image which suits them. They are replacing it with a society which has only the very rich and the very poor. This 40-year political movement of the very wealthy has restructured the world for the "one percent."

One of the strategies in doing this is the derailment of unions. The legal structure must be made void of regulation, and Government must defend this. Wal-Mart has helped make this happen often around the world. And Wal-Mart has violated the law as it stands, in many countries. It has not paid workers for their labor, has used child labor and sweated labor. Generally this plan suits Wal-Mart very well.

Wal-Mart may say it "accepts" unions in any country where they are part of the culture. But that is to say it is like a chameleon—it changes its behavior as it moves from country to country. Such a framework has a global dimension. Wal-Mart is part of a very large chain of global linkages that tie it into the world market. One of these places is the Inland Island Empire of Riverside, California and, indeed, throughout the United States and the world, wherever there is a large seaport or a port, or where there is a railroad, a hypermarket or a supermarket, or a myriad number of sweatshops.

Mr. Ylan K. Mui of the *Washington Post* wrote, "in the United Kingdom, Wal-Mart touts a growing roster of union employers and has negotiated contracts with entrenched labor groups for decades." But as this book will show, Wal-Mart has **never** negotiated a labor union contract in North America.

Mr. Mui then adds, "In some countries, such as China, recognition of unions is required by law. Wal-Mart has said about 70% of its employees in China are members of the All China Federation of Trade Unions." But in China the company hasn't signed a true and binding contract with any companies or corporations yet—and has certainly not for Wal-Mart employees. As to the managers, once they have begun their career with Wal-Mart, they know that their job is to make the name of Wal-Mart something to be feared—that is, if they want to keep their jobs as managers of Wal-Mart.

In the course of my research I spoke to a young man who was a manager. I asked if he ever wanted to do something else with his life other than to be a manager at Wal-Mart. He said, "How could I do something else? Wal-Mart is all I know." He had been trained from a very young age, when he was about 16, to be a manager of a Wal-Mart supercenter. It was, in truth, all he knew, and of course he knew nothing about unions.

I chose to look at Wal-Mart's unions abroad, first because I care about unions. A union gives people who work for a living a sensibility that they have some rights in the workplace. I chose to study unions in a place where they are least likely to flourish—in a Wal-Mart store. In each country where there was a Wal-Mart I saw a union trying to do its best to avoid Wal-Mart's worst.

Today, Wal-Mart has stores in 16 countries, including the United States. There are unions in Mexico where the government also has "protection contracts."

But Wal-Mart changes its behavior to deal with each country's vision and practice of unions. Wal-Mart's goal is to control union or-ganization, so that the union becomes emasculated. Wal-Mart cloaks its policies in such a way that Wal-Mart will seem reasonable and hon-est. Often its anti-union ploys don't work and people get angry, and protest.

Wal-Mart is a place where unions are <u>least</u> likely to flourish. In each country I saw a union trying to do its best to avoid Wal-Mart's worst. Wal-Mart is now seen as the "new way to do business," and its norms are becoming the way business is done—in all forms of corporate en-terprise. Insofar as this is the case, the future of unions for Wal-Mart does not look promising.

Some see Wal-Mart as a predatory colossus, as the "Beast of Bentonville." Wal-Mart's rapid expansion and tremendous profitability has allowed it a market power unequalled by any of its large corporate competitors, a power which is reshaping the nature of America's and the world's industries. A new kind of America, and global capitalism, has been born.

Wal-Mart is the most highly rationalized, centralized retail chain in the world, a company managed from the top down, and controlled directly from its home office in Bentonville, Arkansas. From there, ex-ecutives have the ability, perhaps unequalled by any other corporate executives in the world, not only to control the flow of goods, but to monitor, coordinate, and control the work of the company's 2.2 mil-lion employees in the more than 11,000 Wal-Mart stores and distribu-tion centers throughout the world. (1)

Wal-Mart is also a traditional "bureaucracy," where the CEO and his closest associates make decisions for the entire company. All direc-tives and policy changes decided at this level flow through the employ-ment pyramid to all Wal-Mart stores and distribution centers, from the store managers to those at the very bottom of the pyramid, where "sales associates" unload merchandise and deal with customers, and cashiers check out merchandise. Managers of stores and distribution centers must send data directly to the home office. The technology is specifi-cally designed to allow corporate headquarters to constantly be abreast of information about its suppliers and its stores, so top management can respond to any event that affects Wal-Mart stores. Today at corporate headquarters a newly reformulated Wal-Mart culture reaches into each store, designed to motivate employees to work to the rhythms of the "machines"—both the technology and the logistics—without increasing, and sometimes even reducing, their wages. At Wal-Mart, there is an authoritarian form of "management by intimidation" and shame. We will see how Wal-Mart's current labor abuses, abuses of law, stem from management practices, a company culture geared to intensify work, and a leadership that only gives "lip service" to government labor law.

The New Global Wal-Mart, has approximately 11,000 stores and 2.2 million workers in 16 countries throughout the world (see Table 1), with subsidiaries in 15 countries. I will deal with those in this book. Wal-Mart is in England, India, China, and Mexico, and previously was in Germany until 2006 when it left that country. Wal-Mart didn't make a profit in Germany, and it was not able to deal with the strong unions there. Wal-Mart also has strength in South America. It owns stores in Argentina, Brazil, and Chile. Wal-Mart has stores in five countries of Central America—in El Salvador, Honduras, Nicaragua, Guatemala, and Costa Rica. And it has most recently acquired stores in South Africa. Wal-Mart has them in Puerto Rico, which is accounted for in the United States figures. It was also exploring retail business opportunities in Russia, despite its post-Communist practice of graft.

This book will leave readers with an intimate knowledge of the working lives of the company's employees in American stores—what they want from their jobs, what they get, and how they deal with the work and authoritarian relationships they face from those above them. Secondly, it will also demonstrate how Wal-Mart, this great leviathan, functions in the world; how it acquiesces to the ways of foreign countries, to provide what they want, when it must. But in each country, it tries to make its stores a copy of the American stores as much as possible. It does so by "cooperating" with the powers that be. But Wal-Mart, as the world's largest company, and a company with the most interest in its own global power, has learned to **pretend to** genuflect to the wishes of other countries.

Unlike in Germany, where it spoke boldly of its anti-union stance and its aversion to the way Germans did business, over the years it has learned to portray itself as a flexible business partner, that will treat its unions any way the culture of the country does. But it uses its negative practices on consumers, and the people who work in its stores. It does its underhanded deeds to women, in the interests of its own success. And the more success it has, the more it can exercise its global power.

Unlike Enron or WorldCom, Wal-Mart does not appear to have mismanaged its funds. Nor has it engaged in any of the more bizarre accounting shenanigans that have taken place in some of America's financial firms, so as to doom itself to great losses of money. But it has used its money to bribe others, especially those in Mexico, to its own ends. Its infamous bribery scandal there may have reached India, where Wal-Mart has allegedly invested illegitimately. But its fiscal base is sound; its sales and stock prices continue to rise and fall at a relatively modest level.

Wal-Mart's dramatic success, its profitability and spectacular growth over the years, has now reached a point in history where it makes its own "laws", though, of course, there are also public laws which it violates. Its ethos and its morality are based on the principle that people whose rights it violates, employees and suppliers, are extraneous, and even its consumers are dependent on Wal-Mart. Surprisingly, both the U.S. government and business see this as legitimate, as merely the "ins and outs" of business competition. Other businesses admire it greatly; they are awed by its rising stock prices, its mammoth size, and its efficiency.

Wal-Mart: Work and Technology

I start with a discussion of Wal-Mart in America. Then I will compare its practices to those of other countries where it has its subsidiaries. Most importantly, I will examine how it deals with its unions in the countries and stores abroad. Examining the unions in most countries,

I will show that unions, in and of themselves, can do little more than moderate the exploits of Wal-Mart. Often governments can do little to step in and ensure Wal-Mart's compliance with the law.

Next, I will examine its political and social structure in the context of the norms and values that influence people: its "human resource" strategies. If business analysts explain Wal-Mart's efficiencies as "ideal," a result of advanced technology, they often ignore how technology is actually used in Wal-Mart stores. Wal-Mart is hardly a workplace where employees do mindless work with a touch of a button. In many ways Wal-Mart's retail stores resemble industrial workplaces. Wal-Mart is not like McDonald's, where pictures tell the staff just what the customer wants; Wal-Mart's technology doesn't "deskill" the work, it make it harder. Many Wal-Mart employees do hard physical labor. They lift and stack heavy merchandise all day.

There is little regard to the hours of work and the health, the fatigue, and, especially, the stress of employees. To get the job done faster, better, and more effectively, a vast use of computer technology is employed. Even before modern computers, Wal-Mart sought to centralize authority and operations. It was standard practice to send managers out to visit each and every store in their territory, to discover its flaws, report on its ability to make profits, and make this report to headquarters. At the same time, new technology speeds communication, making it easier for corporate headquarters to transmit directives more rapidly.

Wal-Mart employees are taught to sing the Wal-Mart song; to be cheerful all the time. They must feel it is "my Wal-Mart." And the work must always get done, on time. Wal-Mart creates an environment in which it is supposed to be functioning properly at all times.

The story of Wal-Mart can only be told from the perspective of the culture on which it is based. The culture begins in the foothills of Arkansas, where Sam Walton opened the first Wal-Mart store. Hard work and frugality were lessons taught at the dinner table and from the pulpits, with evangelical fervor. Within this framework the "common man" was seen as the repository of virtue, but only if he worked hard and accepted the values of the patriarchal community and the "women's" roles within it. This mix of values created a moral arithmetic that guided the pattern of human relationships, defining a virtuous way to live and do business, in a society where success in business was itself the major virtue.

Employees were expected to be loyal and hard-working, and to work even harder in a business emergency—without concern for compensation. As team players, employees were expected to cooperate with one another, to go the "extra mile" to ensure the well-being of the enterprise. As the patriarch of the large Wal-Mart "family," it was Sam's responsibility to "take care of his people."

Today such values, embedded in Wal-Mart's early culture, have been perpetuated and formalized by his successors. But they have not been formalized on the other side of the equation—taking care of the people. They have been carefully distilled into rules and regulations designed to shape the behavior of Wal-Mart "sales associates"—clerks and cashiers—as well as its management. Wal-Mart's "human resource strategies" are fundamental to the company's competitive strategy, a way to promote employee loyalty and reduce wage costs, and increase productivity. Despite the apparent down-home folksiness of the Wal-Mart culture, the firm's human resources, or "people policies and practices," are today steeped in a form of the Protestant Ethic—more like the views of Ebenezer Scrooge than Benjamin Franklin. And the goal is to vastly increase the amount of work employees do, while reducing their compensation, without the complaints that are usually heard. Building Wal-Mart was Walton's vocation, as he believed it should be for all his employees—those at the highest levels of management and the most humble retail clerks. There is a fine line between the workers' loyalty and their exploitation. Sam Walton was always anti-union.

Yet even today, as the patriarch of the Wal-Mart "family," Wal-Mart management still claims it "takes care of its people," just like Sam did. Managers are taught that even the simplest things are a "fireable offense." Status barriers are muted by a paternalism and sexism "and a good-ole-boy" ideology. The elite have power and privilege, and have the right to manage. Such a mixture of southern culture, paternalism, and a religion tied to the work ethic, created a moral arithmetic that guided the pattern of human relationships. The only part of this equation which is often left out is that management was supposed to "take care of its people," a myth which defied the need for unions.

Wal-Mart's down-home folksiness is not a fiction created by Madison Avenue or a public relations gimmick designed to promote the company image. It is designed to extract the most cash from the workers. But Wal-Mart's public persona is also a direct outgrowth of the private beliefs that shaped Sam Walton's vision, a vision he promoted with missionary zeal as he built his retail empire. Since Sam Walton died, Wal-Mart has established a special "People Division," with business analysts to monitor that Wal-Mart's vision endures.

One of the worst ways Wal-Mart exacts "a pound of flesh" from its workers is through its practice of sex discrimination. In 2011 they sued, and lost, a case of class action of sex discrimination in which it was alleged that Wal-Mart pays its women employees 72 percent of what full-time hourly male workers earn, and hardly ever promotes them to management positions. In countries around the world, Wal-Mart has the same sexist practices, although women make up its vast proportion of employees in the store. Wal-Mart has developed a unique company culture, one which in American stores encourages workers to identify with Wal-Mart's goals, generating work practices that allow management to "steal time" from them in both legal and illegal ways.

Many will say that other retail employers often do many of the same things. It is true that companies are often exploitative of their workers. But Wal-Mart's store managers are given the responsibility each year for saving more and more on labor costs. The consequence is a labor budget that leads to all stores being seriously understaffed—even when labor costs are unusually inexpensive compared the American model. "Sales associates" are asked to "do the work of three people."

The company is no longer solely in the United States; it has 15 other subsidiaries in other countries, so it promotes itself as a company of multinational value. It has great worldly expertise, which means it can do as it wishes. Wal-Mart looks all over the world to find new places in which to invest. The message is "nothing can stop Wal-Mart."

Where Wal-Mart leads, others follow. A new generation of managers in large and small companies are now learning how Wal-Mart operates as they try, in their effort to compete, to reproduce the Wal-Mart model. Business school professors use case studies of Wal-Mart to educate their students. Not only retailers, but also other enterprises, must follow its lead, or risk failure. Inevitably, more and more companies are beginning to behave like Wal-Mart. With an unequalled degree of market power, Wal-Mart is setting the rules, and becoming the new model for efficiency and growth. Yet my research has shown that Wal-Mart may actually impoverish families, as well as the whole community in many of the 15 countries, by driving out and impoverishing the once middle class. Indeed, it does this in India, where the government is debating whether to permit "foreign direct investment" of retailers like Wal-Mart. Wal-Mart, they say, will put millions of kiranha workers and small store retailers out of business. Those are some of the people whose work is defined by "Main Street" values in India. Conversely, the one hundred million Americans who shop at Wal-Mart every week are the ones who contribute to the 40 percent of stock owned by the Walton family—literally the richest family in America.

Many of the 1.3 million Wal-Mart employees in America now lack health insurance, since the company has decided to pare it back from its variety of fringe benefits. With the coming of "Obama Care," the corporation refuses to pay for it for those who work "part time." Wal-Mart encourages employee turnover, to reduce the number of employees, even when the stores are understaffed. They try to force out older workers whose pay is "too high", and workers who are injured on the job. These people are seen as disposable. They are usually added to Wal-Mart's turnover numbers. And a large preponderance of them work part-time in U.S. stores and in stores abroad, as well. Wal-Mart's retail stores are becoming America's new "sweatshops." They are, in fact, similar to the Chinese factories, but in America people don't work for 16 hours a day.

Why pick on Wal-Mart? Other companies are guilty of the same "sins," but Wal-Mart is different. First,, it is the largest company in the world and the company is tremendously profitable. Its market expansion throughout the world has given this firm a degree of leverage unequalled by any of its large global competitors.

Anti-Unionism

Perhaps the practice that Wal-Mart is most guilty of is denying workers the right to join unions. There are other companies who do this, as well, but Wal-Mart breaks this labor law in more than the usual ways. Wal-Mart has a panoply of anti-union practices, written down in a specialized anti-union handbook. The Human Resource people have learned them, from the boldest uses of the psychology. And they use these methods in a way that demoralizes, depresses, and is emotionally destructive to workers. (See subsequent chapters.)

The ostensible reason is to save costs. But the most important thing contemporarily is to ensure that management has ultimate control of the enterprise, and its funds. When the only union formed at Wal-Mart, at the Jonquiere store in Canada, Wal-Mart closed the store down. Wal-Mart executives said that they wanted to change the way the store worked. Yet, the executives really closed the store to get rid of the union, and to make sure that other stores did not see Jonquiere as model of a new, free Wal-Mart. (2)

Wal-Mart Abroad

The first chapter of this book that follows is the story of Wal-Mart at home, in the United States; the nature of its organization, its culture, and the way it affects workers. The rest is about the way it operates abroad. Does it use the same techniques abroad? Does it have the same consequences? Wal-Mart initially tried to make one of its first organizations abroad function like its organization at home. It was hostile to unions and defied them in Germany. They soon learned that was a foolish thing to do, especially in a country where the union was highly institutionalized and strong. Not even when the union in Germany challenged Wal-Mart in the courts, for trying to lower its prices on food. But, when Wal-Mart lost in court, it challenged the union in a higher court. It lost again! It soon realized it had created a fiasco: this was not the way to make Wal-Mart be appreciated. Besides, it was not making any money, but, instead, losing it. It soon relinquished the game and cleared out of Germany, losing $1 billion on the way. Bentonville wondered what it was doing in Germany.

After the German fiasco, Wal-Mart learned to modify its anti-union "hubris" to make it "fit" the people it serves better, but it hasn't changed its *modus vivendi.* Rather than being a pariah, it has learned to modify its ways, and makes its employees work even harder and pays them poorly.

Recently, Wal-Mart had some setbacks in the United States. After an "inferior" performance due to the economic crisis, many stores were closed, and 12,000 people were laid off—an extraordinary thing for Wal-Mart. But as far back as 2007, it was clear its new stores were "cannibalizing" the profits of its old ones: Wal-Mart built too many stores, too close together. At home in the U.S., its executives wracked their brains trying to find out where all its consumers had gone.

Nevertheless, Wal-Mart continues to grow—internationally. In fact, its prospects internationally are better than its prospects at home. Wal-Mart's sales have slowed, at home, between 1 and 3 percent per year on average, over the last three years, down from 5 percent, nationally. Internationally, however, it is doing well. Its foreign stores account for about 25 percent of its total earnings. It was not a bad idea to go abroad.

When Wal-Mart decided, in 1992, that its American stores were "oversaturated," it started to build an empire overseas. In almost two decades, a relatively short time, it has built or bought a major part of that empire. It continues to open new stores in the countries where it operates, and "scours the world" looking for new sites and countries in which to invest. It has the funds, and whenever and wherever it finds a "good place," it buys stores. A "good place" is where: 1) there are not too many supermarkets; 2) there is a potentially "free market" for

Wal-Mart to expand; and 3) there are no "impediments to growth," i.e., no regulations. When it finds a country that has all those attributes, it buys the company and all its stores—or as many as it can get. It buys or builds stores as if it were playing Monopoly. But somehow there was never a problem with a scarcity of funds. Wal-Mart always has enough, given how little it pays its workers. Thus, it can afford to pay a heavy price for a chain of supermarkets. It can "cut out" another supermarket, if the store chain has some strategic capability.

It is only by having more and more stores that Wal-Mart makes such a large profit. Wal-Mart prefers to buy a whole chain of supermarkets, and have a "partner" to share the "ins and outs" of the country in which it invests. Then it buys more stores, or builds them until there are a great number of them. The more stores Wal-Mart has, the more likely that it will have a ruling share. Sometimes it can't buy additional stores because there are no more to buy, or because there is no one to sell it to them, or because there are rules which do not allow it to buy. Then it leaves the country, or changes direction. Only in India could it open only one store alone, and India has, as of this point, a cloudy outcome.

I have written about all but two of the countries where Wal-Mart has stores. Perhaps there will be more in the future. For the executives at Wal-Mart never stop. They are even now in Peru.

The Countries

I have chosen most of the countries because with each I found a story too interesting to pass up. Each one was different in the forces at play. At the same time, each one is a story of Wal-Mart's strategies—against unions. The countries are: Germany, in which the system has failed because Wal-Mart was too rigid; England, where it struggled against the law, with the union, and has not given up in its fight for stores; and India, a country that is in the process of rethinking its laws, perhaps changing them to make it more hospitable to Wal-Mart. But India is fighting within itself about the changes. I chose China because it is very different from America. Wal-Mart decided to open its stores there, and was surprised that there was a large and powerful union. Mexico, was chosen because it is so corrupt, and because it was the "jewel in the crown," with so many stores in Wal-Mart's empire. Chile is a land bridge for imports. Then there is Central America, which has a drug war and a war over land, which may never be settled. And finally there is South Africa, which is fearful of Wal-Mart because of its supply chain. I made a decision to include Chile and South Africa because, in the course of writing this book some of these countries were newly incorporated in Wal-Mart's empire.

Wal-Mart is growing mostly in Latin America, from Mexico where it first got its start. As early as 1992, when the American company decided to expand and go abroad, the initial free trade agreement, NAFTA, was beginning to take shape. That was a treaty between Canada, the United States, and Mexico which was ostensibly intended to make it easier for business to eliminate trade tariffs and investment barriers between these three countries. President Bill Clinton and his administration claimed that it would increase trade between the three countries, and it certainly did that. NAFTA has managed to impoverish Mexico, despite making parts of the U.S. richer. But Ross Perot, a conservative, a candidate for President, and a billionaire, said NAFTA would "make a huge sucking sound" taking the jobs (and livelihoods) from the United States. And, despite what the administration said, he was right. (4)

Indeed, as a result of NAFTA which was passed in 1994, many corporations decided to go "offshore" since "Overseas investment [was] rising at twice the rate of exports. And from each dollar earned from exports by American companies the companies could take in nearly $2 from the sale of what they produce." (1) Wal-Mart is now counting on "rapid global growth", **not on domestic store openings**, to fuel growth over the next five years." (3)

South America is now selling commodities to China and that is making South America richer. That is one reason why countries in South America are developing. In South America there is a need for supermarkets. Hence, Wal-Mart will have a new market in South

America. Wal-Mart is a company which has found a way to domi-nate South America. It started with NAFTA, with Mexico and Canada, and then found its way to Brazil, to Argentina, and then to Central America. It has opened stores in Chile as well. Wal-Mart also is scout-ing out Peru and Colombia for new investments, as business is encour-aging free trade agreements with most of the Latin American countries. The free trade agreements are, like NAFTA, initially designed to allow Mexico and the United States to trade and invest with other partners in this hemisphere. But it has led to a colonized Mexico. Indeed, it isn't merely investment, after the bribery scandal in Mexico. Ultimately, Wal-Mart now has investments on four continents; with the new in-vestment in South Africa, and with its vast supply chain, it is getting ready to colonize the world.

How I Did It

A small part of this book was written with the help of more than 70 current and former Wal-Mart workers. They were salesclerks and store managers, and they came from all over the U.S. These individuals agreed to speak with me about their work lives, about the conflicts they faced, and the ways in which they tried to resolve these conflicts. I also spoke with trade union leaders and attorneys about Wal-Mart. While the United Food and Commercial Workers were very cooperative and helpful in assisting me in finding these people, unfortunately Wal-Mart would not agree to participate in this endeavor, or let me see the stores.

I spoke with each of these people on the telephone for an average of about two hours. Those who wanted most to tell their stories often had a "bone to pick" with Wal-Mart. Some had initially been opti-mistic about their jobs at Wal-Mart, having heard good things about the company—its health insurance, 401K plans, and bonuses for good work. Many Wal-Mart workers like their jobs and thrive on Wal-Mart's ordered setting and family culture. Yet, the stories of those with whom I did speak, and their experiences with management practices, were consistent with each other, along with what they said about the tales of reward and punishment.

In conducting this second part of my research, I have examined carefully the news media from each country separately. I looked at the newspapers, journals, and reports from many sources, and the reports from many NGOs. However, the many journals, newspapers, and reports I have read, in English, tell you what kind of strategies Wal-Mart uses, and their importance to the company.

Many people have documented phenomena from newspapers or even from "blogs" or web sites, in a sociological inquiry. Anita Chen is a case in point. She searches the newspapers for articles or web sites. In looking at China, she has learned things which were unknown, and ferrets out the story behind the official story. She uses this technique because there is no other way of finding out the hidden information, or that which is a secret in China, and can't be known any other way. (5) What she does, to get access to Wal-Mart, is remarkable.

There was no way I could learn first hand about Wal-Mart in all the countries I have written about, because Wal-Mart is as closed as the CIA. It is a very secretive company. Finally, I could not speak the many languages of the countries I wrote about, such as Urdu in India. Thus, I needed to use the news media and articles that were translated into English.

Wal-Mart is creating a new kind of capitalism in the world. It is a capitalism that covers the world, with its massive ships and great supply chains, and the almost 11,000 stores to which they go. What that kind of business is like, we shall see in the pages ahead. Any mistakes or errors in judgment are mine.

Table 1. Approximate Number of Wal-Mart Stores in the World

Country	Number of Stores
Argentina	88
Brazil	532
Canada	333
Chile	325
China	374
Costa Rica	201
El Salvador	79
Guatemala	200
Nicaragua	74
Honduras	69
India	17
*Japan	426
Mexico	2,147
South Africa	309
United Kingdom	544
United States	5,733
World (approximately)	11,451

Source: Wikipedia (December 2012)

Footnotes

1. Louis Uchitelle. "US Corporations Expanding Abroad at a Quicker Pace," *The New York Times*, July 25, 1994.

2. Doug Struck, Wal-Mart Leaves Bitter Chill, Washington Post (Foreign Service), April 14, 2005.

3. Miguel Bustillo, "With US Saturated, Wal-Mart Looks Overseas," *The Wall Street Journal,* February 2009.

4. Looks Like Ross Perot Was Right About "The Giant Sucking Sound", The Business Insider, February 11, 2011.

5. A good analysis of this method is her book *China's Workers Under Assault: The Exploitation of Labor in a Global Economy*, M.E. Sharpe (2001) and article, China's Troubled Workers," by Anita Chan and Robert A. Senser, in *Foreign Affairs*, (March 1997).

2

How Bad Is Wal-Mart in America?

As you can see from the sky as you fly over it, the Inland Island is a vast flat space with miles and miles of distribution centers. It is the first destination for the goods of large seagoing vessels and their containers, which come into the ports at Los Angeles and Long Beach on ships from Southeast Asia. There, in Mira Loma, you can see the merchandise for chain stores all over the country. The ships carry the large containers that hold merchandise destined for the stores in all the countries in North and South America. More than 80 percent of Southeast Asian imports come into America by these two ports. It is a truly bi-continental powerhouse. Much of this merchandise is for Wal-Mart stores.

This is just one of many inland ports. There are others in the nation; for example, where the railroad system meets in Chicago. In Will County, Illinois, there is a vast woodland space near Chicago. "Located South of Chicago, with access to railroads, highways, and airports and an abundance of undeveloped land, the county has attracted companies looking for a strategic location for warehousing and distribution functions of supply chain management . . . . It is the only place in North America where six Class I railroads meet, creating links between all corners of the continent. It the largest U.S. inland port in the country and has 88 million square feet of warehouse space." (1) There are others, too: in Kansas City, in Houston, and in the Port of New York where the warehousing is in New Jersey. And they are all projected to grow.

According to the U.S. Census, Wal-Mart alone imported about 75,000 Twenty-Foot Equivalent Units (TEUs) of cargo in 2009. Each new cargo ship "holds more than 4,000 containers." Wal-Mart imports the largest amount of freight to the United States, larger than any other retailer—more than twice as much as Costco, Home Depot, and Target. (2) The sheer volume of cargo has caused problems, so that the supply chain is over-stressed. It is most over-stressed at the Los Angeles/Long Beach Ports, which handle 43 percent of America's imports. But as manufacturing continue s to be outsourced to China and places in Southeast Asia, the capacity of the nation's ports "is nearing its breaking point." Everything takes longer and longer to be delivered to the appropriate store, and the costs are higher—from $4,000 by train and $40,000 by plane. If a supplier misses the time for delivery, he can suffer fines, or lose the contract altogether. (3) So, some shippers are using the Seattle and Tacoma ports. Some are waiting for the expansion of the Panama Canal. The canal currently is undergoing a $5.3 billion expansion so it can accommodate larger cargo ships but it will not be ready until 2014. (4)

Some companies are thinking of a cheaper way of getting their merchandise through—by shipping containers of goods through the port on the Southwest of Mexico, the Port of Lazaro Cardenas, up through the San Antonio, Texas by train, and from there to Kansas City. Rather than American workers, Mexican workers, who earn much less than International Longshoremen Workers Union (ILWU) workers, would be hired to ship goods from Southeast Asia to Mexico and the U.S. Mexican truck drivers, who earn much less than the American Teamsters, would be used for driving the trucks on the North American Superhighway.

With the surge of imports, the ports of America are a relatively new business, and a growing one. The U.S. Department of Transportation tells us that the "total freight moved through U.S. ports will increase by more than 50 percent from 2001 to 2020." (5) Corporations are gearing up for this. Not only are they planning to expand the ports, they are planning to expand and build new logistics centers. Citing one ad from Jones Lang La Salle on "the perspectives of the global supply chain" they write, "About 40 miles from Chicago . . . is the Ridgeport Logistics Center. [It] contains 14 million square feet."(6) There may well be a new surge of people working at these ports—and perhaps a whole new wave of protests.

In this chapter on the American Wal-Mart, I will first discuss the distribution centers. Second, I will discuss what Wal-Mart has done in the past in America which demeaned its workers. And last, I will describe a big problem today for Americans: how to keep Wal-Mart's supermarkets and hypermarkets out of the "big cities"—Chicago, New York, Boston, Washington, and Los Angeles.

The Newly Exploitable

In what used to be called a distribution center is now an "inland port." The distribution center used to be located right near the ports, at the point of disembarkation. Today, because the cost of land is so high, and the amount of product to be distributed is so much greater, the distribution centers are a distance from the ports, on cheaper land, inland. The "distribution center," as it is called, is the place where the containers are trucked from the ship. Then they are sorted, loaded on trucks once more, and sent to their destinations—the retail stores. These stores are owned by any one of the myriad retail chains in America: Target, Kohl's, Costco, Sears, etc. Since America now outsources its products instead of making them "onshore," this is the way to get the goods to the stores. It is a new development for most of the retailers. But the only retailer that gets news coverage is Wal-Mart. For in this new set-up Wal-Mart has discovered a new way to take advantage of workers. Wal-Mart doesn't actually employ the workers who move the goods from the trailers to the trucks. Retailers and consumer goods manufacturers will often contract with third-party logistics companies, or warehouse companies. The warehouse managers often hire another firm, and that firm hires the employees indirectly. The workers do not "officially" work for Wal-Mart; they work for the warehouse company.

This firm is obligated to pay for the wages, and sets the working conditions. Thus, the workers in these distribution centers are their employees. So, although the company whose goods they handle is Wal-Mart, Wal-Mart is not legally responsible for their wages, or the working conditions.

Wal-Mart formerly had its own distribution center. While the working conditions weren't wonderful, to say the least, at least the workers were paid well; they got about $14 an hour—good money for a three-day-a-week, and 12-hours-a-day job. But now they have a different system—they pay California's minimum wage, which is $8 an hour, and hire "temporary" workers, as well. If workers are lucky they get the minimum wage; but sometimes they get below the minimum wage from the private contractors.

At Schneider Warehouse there are 100,000 employees. On May 28, 2011 all the workers staged an act of civil disobedience at Inland Empire, "in the heart of the largest concentration of warehouse space on the planet, issuing an urgent national call for dignity and respect of the rights of warehouse workers." (7) After that, they filed a lawsuit in October, 2011. The low pay, below the minimum wage, is what led the workers at Schneider Logistics. But it is actually Rogers-Premier Leasing Company who employed them. They filed a class-action lawsuit against both of these firms, Rogers-Premier Unloading Company Services and Schneider Logistics.

The workers claimed they "load and unload products destined to go to Wal-Mart Stores" . . . contending that their "employer," Rogers-Premier Unloading Company Services and Schneider Logistics, the company's that together contracted with Wal-Mart to run the warehouse, didn't pay either the legal minimum wage or overtime. What's more, workers were threatened with termination if they complained—and their employers lied to them and kept a fraudulent record of their wages as well. The workers were told that they would receive $9.25 to

$10 per hour and that they would receive a "productivity bonus." They never received any of it.

Dickerson, an employee, explained further. Although they spent their work days performing "strenuous, unskilled physical labor in an environment where the temperature often exceeds 90 degrees," she said she was paid by a new system that was recently introduced, similar to a piece-rate system,

"She was paid not by the hour but by the trailer—a stressful pay scheme meant to encourage her and her colleagues to work faster and faster, and one that the labor movement worked hard to abolish in many industries in the 20th century. Each paycheck was different than the last and most of them were disappointingly low. She says, at her year at the warehouse, she never had health benefits, sick days or vacation days. If she didn't unload containers, she didn't get paid." (8) Jorje Soto works for a contractor where, in addition to routine jobs, "he also had been ordered to perform an illegal task." He was asked to falsify employees' time sheets to cheat them out of getting the minimum wage," and "to severely understate workers' hours. He said the purpose was to cover up the widespread practice of paying well below the legal minimum, which is $8.in California. (9)

Lopez says, "They only got paid when they 'loaded and unloaded' the trucks" and not when they did auxiliary tasks, like sweeping the floors. And "There were times when he worked double shifts, several days in a row" and he didn't get overtime either. The workers were told they would be fired if they even questioned their wages. When they finally filed the suit in October, the workers found out that the California Labor Commissioner had agreed with their cause. She had issued "additional citations" totaling over $600,000 to Premier Warehousing Ventures, for "failure to provide itemized wage statements to workers." (10)

As Bonacich and Wilson have said, "the motivation of the warehouse owners is to clearly save wages, and prevent the warehouse workers from forming a union. And they also save money by not paying for workmen's compensation." (11) But accidents do happen, not occasionally, but once out of five times. It is extremely hot in the warehouses, plus the constant pressure for speed creates safety problems, which is why the California Division of Occupational Safety and Health accused the three warehouses that serve Wal-Mart of more than 60 workplace safety violations, and why it sought $256,445 in penalties.

"There is heat in the summer, over 90 degrees, and stifling conditions in containers and the warehouses themselves; exposure to hazardous dust, fumes, mists, vapors, and gases; no hand protection to prevent punctures; cuts and burns; no safety harnesses for work in cherry pickers; and danger from falling cartons and slippery floors." (12) There is a small percentage of good jobs in the warehouse industry, but the industry relies on a large percentage of low-wage workers.

In another study of a warehouse, in Will County, Illinois which is near Chicago, there is much of the same thing. Only 1.4 percent are managerial jobs, compared to 63 percent who are temporary workers—they are called "temps." The median hourly wage for a temp was $9 an hour—$3.48 an hour less than the direct hires. One in four warehouse workers had to rely on government assistance to make ends meet for their families. Only 5 percent of temps had sick days and 4 percent had health insurance. Twenty percent of warehouse workers had been hurt on the job. Of those, one in three were disciplined or fired when they reported their injury. And finally, 37 percent of current warehouse workers had to work a second job to provide for their families. (13) Naturally, most of these workers would rather have good-paying jobs, with pensions and health-care benefits. But the managers hire people as "temps," and workers hold these jobs for a long period of time. In a time of high unemployment, good jobs are scarce. No one says they discriminate by age and racial status, but the managers usually do. The workers they hire are mostly young; 63 percent are under the age of 35. A full 89 percent are non-white; 84 percent are either African/American or Latino. Indeed, 81 percent were hired by a temp agency.

The following was somewhat of a victory for the workers in the

Mira Loma warehouses. "A federal judge in Los Angeles issued a temporary restraining order on October 31, 2011, requiring three Inland Empire warehouse employers that service retail giant Wal-Mart immediately to begin complying with state and federal payroll record-keeping and disclosure law." (14)

More recently, in California, another grievance has appeared. Warehouse Workers United, has filed a complaint to Cal-OSHA and the NLRB for causing "repetitive-motion injuries" at the cross-dock facility at the Roadlink facility. The claimants say that "the workers who do this are required to perform up to 100 pounds of lifting" from shipping containers. Workers "must move between 200 and 250 boxes per hour . . . under the pressure of managers who aggressively pressure workers to meet this quota with threats and harassment," despite temperatures of 100 degrees. And "the cross-docking fits into the Wal-Mart system of 'just-in-time delivery'." The men walked off the job. They subsequently had a "six-day, 60-mile march from the Inland Empire to the steps of the Los Angeles City Hall," to show what this meant to them. (15)

Immediately after that, workers at the Ellwood facility near Chicago, who were "connected" to the United Electrical Workers, also filed a claim. The Elwood facility is a distribution center similar to the one in Los Angeles. It was the sixth claim they filed with the local office of OSHA. And finally, they got "settlement payments "out of three claims. And they had the same kind of wage complaints! The Elwood workers ultimately delivered a petition with 37,000 signatures from the California workers to Wal-Mart's corporate offices in Chicago.

Although they have filed numerous requests with Wal-Mart, the company has turned a deaf ear to them. Yet now, with so many complaints, it seems Wal-Mart is about to listen—but silently. Even though it signed no agreements with them, and made some of the working conditions better, and although there were a lot of problems that did not change, workers are getting more angry and feisty. They are beginning to feel "The prospect of working theses low-paying jobs for long hours became scarier than risking losing the job to improve it." (16)

Presumably, in the larger statement that the Department of Labor in California issued, one can tell that they are likely to be assured of the minimum wage. At least all the workers will get $8 per hour, and will be paid for the time they are not loading or unloading the trucks, as federal law requires. It is certainly a better law than they have in Mexico.

Santos Castaneda describes a warehouse "with unmaintained fork-lifts and temperatures of 115 degrees inside the containers." After he filed a complaint with Cal-OSHA and was successful at it, "workers got new forklifts, safety mirrors in the aisles, a clean warehouse, and safe water to drink." (17)

Last October The Inland Island Empire near Los Angeles, the Elwood Workers, in the southeast of Chicago, and workers from the New York and New Jersey Port Authority shared a videoconference about common problems. Each had a lawyer to help him get through legal claims. Things have changed to the benefit of Wal-Mart's workers in the past two years. Since then, they found that all the goods were shipped to Wal-Mart Stores. Wal-Mart, requested that it be removed from the lawsuit. But the plaintiff's attorney, Theresa Taber, said that she had submitted evidence to support Wal-Mart's contention they were "the employer of record." Now Wal-Mart will have to answer the claims of Wal-Mart Workers United in court. (18)

Quite interestingly, Costco, a competitor of Wal-Mart, actually does not use temp workers; it does not outsource workers. "Costco's well-earned reputation for treating its employees well carries over to its warehouse. The Costco warehouse does not rely on temp workers. It hires employees directly, it pays pretty well, and it has a safety representative and even stretching classes." Says Richard Galanti, Costco's Chief Financial Officer, "We tend not to outsource even if we could save money by doing it . . . we recognize it's the right thing to do." (19)

The Port at Lazaro Cardenas

It was President George W. Bush who had the idea that they should build a "NAFTA Superhighway." It was he who called together Paul

Martin, Prime Minister of Canada; Vicente Fox, President of Mexico; plus himself and 30 CEOs of the largest corporations from each of the three respective nations. Thus was founded Security and Prosperity Partnership (SPP) of North America. With SPP's working groups, they planned to establish a new transportation conduit from Mexico to the U.S., via Texas and Kansas City, and north to Canada.

This "partnership" was developed for several years and then President Bush was out of office, with the plans still intact. This project was met with opposition from Congress. First the Montana legislature voted against it. Then, negative resolutions have been "introduced in 18 other states as well as the House of Representatives," where it picked up 27 co-sponsors. It wasn't voted upon by Congress and, ultimately, there was a great deal of resistance to it. By 2008 it was "dead." (20)

But it didn't die in the minds of some people. What kept it going was a partnership, in 2006, between Wal-Mart and Hutchison-Whampoa Ltd. They joined forces to set up a new $300 million partnership in the Mexican Pacific port of Lazaro Cardenas, a deep seaport in the Pacific, on the southwest coast of Mexico. U.S. goods were coming from China, and they were clogging the ports of the Pacific coast—the Los Angeles and Long Beach terminals. Hutchison-Whampoa is a Hong Kong shipping company and it is run by Hong Kong billionaire, Li Ka-shing. (21)

The reason for this urgency was the time it takes to get to market. It is the biggest cost that all importers have. It costs as much for shipping and ground transportation as it does to make the product in China. That is why speed to market is of the utmost importance to retailers, and U.S. ports are overcrowded. The Los Angeles and Long Beach ports operate at 130 percent of capacity, so when a ship arrives it has to wait to be unloaded—sometimes for hours, sometimes the next day. When a ship arrives in a Mexican port it is unloaded immediately.

Both Wal-Mart and Whampoa Ltd. were looking for a new port to handle their expanding volume of trade. Home Depot and Target were also looking for new ports, and the Mexican ports were only too happy to take on this load. All of the "big-box" stores began using the ports in

Mexico—Lazaro Cardenas, Manzanillo, Vera Cruz, and Altamira; the growth of Mexican ports was surging. Because these imports were going largely to Mexican stores in 2005 and 2006, rather than to American stores. This, after all, was the time of their Mexican bribery scheme, as they got to build more and more stores, and their stores in Mexico were booming. The goal was to reduce the cost of importing by as much as 50 percent through the use of Mexican ports. (22)

But, this could happen only because Mexico privatized their ports in 1999. This made it possible for Danish and American capital, and Wal-Mart, to take advantage of the cheap labor in Mexico, because it allowed Mexico to have competing ports.

"A Danish Shipping terminal operating company in 2011 has won the right to build a new deepwater container terminal at the Mexican port of Lazaro Cardenas," costing $900 million. This latest phase of the construction will be ready around 2015, when the Danish shipping terminal, a division of Denmark's Moller-Maersk Corporation is finished. It "is scheduled to complete the first phase of the four-berth terminal in 2015." (23) The Moeller-Maersk Corporation is in the process of developing trading ports all over the world.

At Lazaro Cardenas the new seaport will permit imports from Southeast Asia to go to the United States as well as to Mexico. The ports of Lazaro Cardenas and Manzanilla are on the southwest coast of Mexico. And "the lion's share of new products from the Pacific Rim is flowing now through Lazaro Cardenas and Manzanilla." The port will have, when it is completed, a more efficient "on-dock rail yard which is designed to allow shipping lines to pre-stow inter-modal cargo for direct transfer to rail, "which is not an option presently offered at other terminals." (24) The law was changed through the privatization of the seaports, to not have the shipments be inspected by customs as they pass through Mexico, if their final destination is the United States. The shipments are first inspected in China. Then, when they arrive at Lazaro Cardenas in Mexico, they pass "through multiple X-ray screenings upon [their] arrival in Mexico. The cargo then, in containers, is transported via rail to Monterrey, Mexico, where it is transferred to trailer trucks for the northbound journey." (25) It's easy to do, simply a change in the law privatizing these companies. Mexican dock workers earn one-fourth of what the Americans in the International Longshore and Warehouse Union (ILWU) earn. And from Lazaro Cardenas and Monterrey, the merchandise connects, by railroad, to Kansas City in 36 hours, through the Kansas City Railway.

Mexico's port workers are "unionized" but they lack a union's ability to struggle for their rights. That makes them a "good" port for the importers. The West Coast dock workers, in the American strike in October 2002, "crippled" the West Coast when they all went out on strike. But the Mexican dock workers haven't struck for 85 years. The Mexican truck drivers, who were able to drive the trucks through to Kansas City, undercut the Teamsters—just as the Mexican railroad workers undercut the American members of the United Transportation Union (UTU).

Because it saves time and money, Wal-Mart can keep its prices low, one of the lynchpins that is extremely important to Wal-Mart. Wal-Mart is based on keeping prices lower than any other store. This is part of what is meant by "Wal-Mart's exceedingly good supply chain." They are not solely about technology, but the ability to keep the prices low by having Mexico change its laws; i.e., letting Mexicans allow the cargo to pass through Mexico without customs inspection. And the lower cost of Mexican workers has the potential to decimate the American West Coast ports. What could not be accomplished by government capital will be accomplished by private capital. Wal-Mart, rather than George Bush, will have its "NAFTA-Superhighway."

The Panama Canal

At about the time the Lazaro Cardenas Terminal will be finished, the new widening of the Panama Canal will also be finished, around "late 2014." This terminal will be able to handle container ships up to 18,000 TEUs, designed to support more than 2 million TEUs in the initial performance, with future expansion capabilities." According to the "advertisements" this port is the "mother of all ports." Because "the ports on the West Coast, in the Gulf of Mexico in the United States, the East, South America, and the Caribbean do not have the capacity to receive vessels of this size." And it will cost $600 million to build.

And with all of this, the Panama Canal Railway Company is teaming up with the Kansas City Southern to build a terminal link—to let ships from the East and West pass through, simultaneously. What is planned is that mostly the ships from Southeast Asia will pass through the Canal and go on to New York and New Jersey ports, instead of having to make the trip overland.

The faster time and the lower cost of the Mexican ports affect the temporary workers who work for Schneider Logistics in California. They are likely to face increased unemployment, and layoffs may start to occur in just a few years, when the Lazaro Cardenas port is fully complete. It will happen slowly. It is as if the United States and Mexico were "sending" a whole industry to Mexico, again, just as they "sent" the apparel industry to Mexico with its lower costs. That is what the benefit is to Wal-Mart.

Workers at Wal-Mart

From the workers in the deposition depots to the workers in the stores, from the stockrooms to the shop floor, the corporate model of Wal-Mart is one and the same. (26) The leaders of Wal-Mart, today, make the assumption that its "Associates" are innately submissive; but more likely, the work environment will make them submissive, in the process of learning the rules.

When they first step in the door as new recruits, they are subjected to training videos, and the trainers who prepare their entrance "inform" them in a not so subtle a manner, that no union will ever dare to raise its ugly head in this store. The low wages, publicly and privately, lead them to believe that Wal-Mart is a place to work only if you are poor, and have no other alternative.

But Wal-Mart seeks not to notice or respond to the malignant consequences that this approach has on employees, managers, and everyone else in the company. The heavy hand of the bureaucracy makes everyone in its purview quake with fear—even some of the executives. Wal-Mart workers have been fired, or threatened with the loss of their jobs. They have lost their benefits. Fear has been used with an "arsenal" of legal and illegal practices to prevent employees from joining unions.

The common understanding is that Wal-Mart doesn't want any unions because having a union would mean higher wages. But, that is not the sole reason. Wal-Mart doesn't want a union because it would mean the loss of its control. It could not get what it wants done, when it wants it to be done, at the lowest price. Wal-Mart could not run its store as it does, or outsource the work as it does, in a store that was unionized. Before it was outlawed, Wal-Mart could not have had the wage abuse, or later have workers go home and miss hours in their working day. It could not have managers speak with such disrespect to Associates (another tool for making the workers feel frightened for their jobs). And, of course, they could not pay such low wages.

But Wal-Mart worker are waking up. They are beginning to see what Wal-Mart management is about. Since they have been thwarted in forming a union, they have created an organization that is not a union. It is called Organization United for Respect at Wal-Mart, or "OUR Wal-Mart," has members from the store managers to those at the very bottom of the pyramid, where "sales associates" unload merchandise and deal with customers, and cashiers check out merchandise.

Carol Pier, who is an activist, and trade researcher for Human Rights Watch, notes, "Our major finding is that Wal-Mart is a case study of what is wrong with U.S. labor law." (27) She means that which is wrong with the U.S. law is the fact that it has never been improved since the 1930s, about 75 years ago. The infractions that used to be enough to stop an employer from violating the law against unions which were effective then, are minor today, like the small fines. Wal-Mart, with all of its more than $400 billion in sales, can pay them and ignore them.

But worst of all is the fact that the Employee Free Choice Act (EFCA) did not pass the Senate in 2007. And neither was it introduced again, when Barack Obama was President. Then, and now, is the time when Congress was overloaded with Republicans, to say nothing of the Tea Party, who wanted nothing to do with labor reform. The EFCA is a newly proposed legal act "which would change Federal law with regard to the rights of workers to form unions by signing cards authorizing union representation, establishing higher penalties for employees who violate employee rights when workers seek to form a union, and instituting new mediation and arbitration processes." (28)

That the "1 Percent" is possible in America is attributable to this, as described by Sylvia Allegretto, a labor economist at the Center on Wage and Employment Dynamics at the University of California-Berkeley, who found that the money had by the six richest Waltons was equal to $102.7 billion for the family. This was equal to the 30.1 percent of U.S. families—that was in 2007. The very richest of the rich are having their day. And Wal-Mart's owners, the Waltons, are among the richest in the country. Until the EFCA or an equivalent to that is passed, the 1 percent will not change. The power that Wal-Mart exerts, the control it exerts from its persistent agressiveness, and the forcefulness of its strategy may, in reality, destroy the right of "freedom of association." That is the major problem! Other companies are choosing to follow Wal-Mart's example. And as Nelson Lichtenstein says, the new American businessman is following the way of Wal-Mart.

The Wal-Mart "Crimes" in the Past

Wal-Mart has always believed that a penny saved is a penny earned, but it acts much less like Benjamin Franklin and more like Ebenezer Scrooge. Here is how they used to do it; Wal-Mart workers worked "off-the-clock." When an "associate" was just about to go home after a day's work, he (or she) was asked to stay late, for sometimes several hours, without pay. She was not given lunch breaks or work breaks, either. This type of wage abuse probably still exists today in some of Wal-Mart's stores. But Wal-Mart was sued all across the country in each state, and fined $78 million for doing this.

Now this old form of exploitation has been changed to a form more legal. Workers are not asked to work "off-the-clock" any more.

They are asked to arrive and leave—at Wal-Mart's discretion. Now, when associates find no work to do because it is a slow time at the stores, they are sent home early, without any pay. There is of course no overtime, and certainly no overtime pay. When they reach their limit of 40 hours a week, their hours are transferred to the following week. No one has thought of suing Wal-Mart for this.

Wal-Mart still has a "workers' hot-line" in the store, on which workers are required to call at any time, when one wishes to accuse another of breaking one of Wal-Mart's rules. And then the "guilty party" is "coached" (given a warning), or Wal-Mart simply fires the person if he or she is a "troublemaker." If this "troublemaker" starts to "talk union," Wal-Mart sends in a "labor relations team" and "starts to have meetings with the workers, showing them anti-union videos in which unions are depicted as antiquated organizations, and union representatives shown as aggressive and unsavory characters." (29) Wal-Mart found out that it was facing a class-action sex discrimination suit. About one million women all throughout the United States were systematically earning lower wages than men, for doing the same jobs. They were not promoted, because they were women. They finally lost their case because the Supreme Court made the decision that they worked in over 4,000 stores, and whether they were discriminated against on a class-action basis could not be decided in a class-action suit. The women were treated differently in all the stores. Today they are pursuing that case in California. (30)

Wal-Mart: Into the Big Cities—
Washington, Chicago, New York, Boston, and Los Angeles

For decades, Wal-Mart's strategy of putting huge stores in small towns, free of exposure to unions, has been Wal-Mart's main strategy for keeping unions out. Now, after all the "site fights," and the saturation of these towns, they are trying to penetrate the cities. For this they are "trying" smaller stores, and no parking lots. It will rely on smaller, "more efficient stores" to drive the future U.S. expansion, and help it penetrate yet untapped urban markets.

At its analyst meeting on Thursday, October 22, 2012 Wal-Mart said it, "feels the sting of too much competition," (31) as they felt a slight drop in business. As Wal-Mart sees it, they are "losing money," because for eight straight quarters they have not seen a rise in sales in its U.S. stores. Other stores in the United States, such as Family Dollar, Target, Kohl's, and even Macy's, have taken Wal-Mart's sales with even lower prices. (32) All their profitability comes from abroad. As a result, Sam's Club has outsourced personnel, and its stock has declined about 7.5 percent. Wal-Mart has shuttered 10 Sam's Clubs and 1,500 workers have been laid off in the process, as well as 800 employees from Bentonville—a total of 2,300 workers. (33)

In the years 2009-2010 Wal-Mart was also feeling the heat from the recession. The stores were so close to each other in proximity that they were "cannibalizing" each other. As a solution to the problem they decided to market their wares in the big cities—Chicago, New York, Boston, Washington D.C., and most recently Los Angeles. Wal-Mart was desperate to open urban stores. But Wal-Mart had problems.

Today, Wal-Mart is bad-mouthed by information that Wal-Mart puts smaller stores out of business, which leads to unemployment. This, in a time of recession and high unemployment, is enough to make people dubious about Wal-Mart. And of course, there is the bribery scandal in Mexico. Exacerbating the problem for Wal-Mart is the fact that cities have stricter zoning laws and property is more expensive. And, once a site is selected, the company often faces stiff opposition from neighborhood associations concerned about traffic congestion, or labor groups who turn out against Wal-Mart's union-free policy. (34) Since Wal-Mart will have no unions, cities, with their large urban, often unionized labor force, have generated resistance to the new expansion policy of the world's largest retailer. Labor activists and leaders are opposed to Wal-Mart's move to the city. Protests against Wal-Mart have been everywhere, in every city where they have tried to gain entry, not withstanding New York City.

Given this kind of opposition, Wal-Mart has decided on a new strategy. Its response is to open small Wal-Mart stores—one-fourth smaller than the original stores—in places where real estate values have declined. Taking up such spaces does not require consultation with a building code review board, so the mini-stores may be able to bypass angry citizens and groups that want to stop the retail giant from coming to their towns. (35) Certainly, in the past, it has used its Neighborhood Market or its Supermercado de Wal-Mart, both small stores, to see how they worked. However, in areas "where real estate has declined," in neighborhoods where the poor have lost their homes, the reviews are not very good. But Wal-Mart, at this point, will use this strategy anyway. It will try to build a store anywhere it can.

Second, Wal-Mart has increased charitable giving, donated money to various political campaigns, and created jobs and opportunity zones in an effort to improve its image. (36) In Chicago, Wal-Mart gave $13 million to non-profit organizations in the city—that is how desperate Wal-Mart has become. In the summer of 2011, it gave $4 million for summer jobs.

Washington, D.C.

In Washington, Wal-Mart has said it would locate its stores in the Northeast district, in areas where supermarkets are scarce, where the population is mostly poor and Afro-American. When Wal-Mart breached Washington D.C., it signed a community benefits agreement. In cities like New York, Chicago, and Washington, Wal-Mart is courting the same "low-income communities." They are frequently heavily minority and they hold out the promise of jobs—but poverty jobs. They are poor, and Wal-Mart tries to keep them poor, by paying them low wages, and its policies give "associates" little respect.

This means Wal-Mart will entertain large requests from the city. It has given $25 million dollars to fund Washington D.C.'s summer youth program, while it has also entertained projects from citizens. (37) For example, the Living Wages, Healthy Communities Coalition can ask for anything it wants—and that Wal-Mart wants to grant. The Living Wages Committee asked for a great number of things like the demand for a living wage of at least $12.50 per hour. (38) But they know that such "high" wages are "pie in the sky."

However, it will not appease the city's vocal anti-Wal-Mart contingent, because the citizens know Wal-Mart will never give in. As it stands, Wal-Mart could easily afford to do this. But Wal-Mart will never pay $12.50 an hour, all around. For it would have to give that much to its employees in 4,000 other stores. And, to be honest, it could easily afford it—if it didn't need to make over $400 billion in profits. Even at over $400 billion of profit, Wal-Mart could still pay its workers better wages. At Berkeley's Center for Labor Research and Education, Dave Jamieson points out that this wage would only cost the shoppers 46 cents per trip, or $12.49 a year, if "the brunt of the increase was passed on to the consumers," (39)

Wal-Mart has agreed with the city to build four stores; two more stores were added to their plan, bringing it to six. But in Washington, one critic says the stores "will not happen." Yet, talking with one Wal-Mart analyst, "who has covered Washington politics for several years," he says, "There is significant pushback from local communities in D.C. that they don't want to see a Wal-Mart in their backyard." (40)

At Costco, which is unionized, the workers earn $44,000 after three years, and workers at Wal-Mart only earn $18,500—a lower than poverty wage. And at Target, two studies showed that prices were even lower than Wal-Mart's. (41) After having satisfied its critics by giving them better packages on their health care in recent years, Wal-Mart, for all workers in all stores, cut its health care benefits. To be exact, "all future part-time employees, those who work less than 24 hours a week, no longer would qualify for any of the company's health insurance plans." According to this, some of the Wal-Mart workers will become "eligible for Medicaid." (42) Wal-Mart, once again, puts workers at risk for rescue by the U. S. government.

Chicago

To get into cities like Chicago, Wal-Mart has planned a war to "end all wars." It fought "dirty." Wal-Mart had a five-year struggle with former Mayor John Daley over wages in the supermarkets. Daley wanted to have workers paid more, and Wal-Mart said "no." Two months later,

Mayor Richard M. Daley used his veto power for the first time in 17 years to kill the bill, arguing it was anti-competitive.

Then Wal-Mart did "a divide and conquer" act with construction unions. It offered them the right the build the stores at a union wage. But Wal-Mart workers in the stores, "associates," would get nothing but the hourly wage that Wal-Mart currently paid $8.50 an hour. Thus, it was a split between men and women in Chicago among the labor unions, since 70-80 percent of Wal-Mart workers in the stores are women. (43) After getting clearance from Chicago, without Mayor Daley's approval, the City Council unanimously approved Wal-Mart's deal, Wal-Mart opened a new store on Chicago's South Side in Austin, and is planning "dozens" more, including in upscale neighborhoods.

Wal-Mart does it again, causing jobs to be lost in Chicago. David Merriman, a professor of Economics at the University of Illinois, said "the second Wal-Mart in Chicago . . . caused a net loss of 300 full-time jobs in the area, and that the retailers closer to the Wal-Mart have been disproportionately more likely to go out of business." (44)

New York

Wal-Mart tried to build a store in New York City as early as 2004, in Rego Park, Queens, at the corner where Queens Boulevard meets the Long Island Expressway. But a team of unions, politicians, and the local population voiced a loud protest, and it was never built. Wal-Mart tried again some years later, in Brooklyn, but that effort failed again. For the third time, in 2010, they tried to open a store. They searched for potential sites for a store. At this time it could be anywhere at all in the five boroughs. But all they could come up with was a place for a small store in Brooklyn, in East New York. But for a small store, the company doesn't need any "city council or zoning laws changed." Despite all the angry protests and the fierce opposition to it, Wal-Mart made a bid for the store. (45)

Wal-Mart was then having a very difficult time selling itself to New York City. There was opposition from the City Council, community officials, elected officials, and a vociferous public who didn't want a Wal-Mart in their backyard.

But Wal-Mart made the same agreement with New York construction unions as it had in Chicago. It would build Wal-Mart stores with union labor, but not give the workers in the stores a raise. This time, the United Food and Commercial Workers (UFCW) supported this agreement. It said, although the union wants to unionize Wal-Mart, we "understand the economic pressures our brothers and sisters in the building trades are facing. We support them getting whatever work they can get." (46) The construction union has no work, due to the housing collapse, and the unemployment is phenomenal, more than New York City's 9 percent, with the poverty that follows.

It's hard to imagine New York City as "the poorest city in America." Actually, New York City "shares the bottom with Mississippi." According to a study by Council for Community and Economic Research (C2ER), a company that produces cost-of-living data found that someone earning $51,000 in Chicago and $63,000 in Washington D. C. enjoys the same standard of living as a New Yorker making $100,000, due to the "astronomical" cost of housing. Everything costs more in New York City than anywhere else in the United States, even food. And Wal-Mart pays low wages and offers poor benefits. (47)

And the report says, "What is not in the interest of New Yorkers is more low-paying jobs, especially when that means the poverty jobs in other places will follow." Adjusted for inflation, Wal-Mart wages have fallen 35 percent since 1970, and Wal-Mart has actually shifted high numbers of lower-paid employees to Medicaid, without any heath care benefits in its package. (48) Certainly it would make sense for Wal-Mart to pay wages according to the standard of living across cities and towns. But it will not do that. It pays a flat $8.50 an hour—for store "associates."

A new report published by the labor affiliated Murphy Institute, reported that more than 159 Wal-Mart Express Stores would have to be built for Wal-Mart to get a 21 percent share of the New York market. That is the share that the company typically gets in the rest of the

U.S. So many stores in New York City, in all the boroughs, would lead to thousands of jobs lost rather than gained. (49) Some say that is a fantasy; they will never get so many stores. But some say that if you let them into the city, what if they do? (50)

Indeed, several studies have shown that Wal-Mart is wanted in the communities. A poll by Quinnipiac College found that 57 percent of the people in New York City believed that Wal-Mart "should be allowed to open stores in the city." (51)

Then there was the Mexican scandal. Wal-Mart had allegedly given $24 million dollars to Mexican officials, in order that it would be permitted to build more stores. Wal-Mart now has half as many stores in Mexico as it does in the U.S. and some Americans were worried that the bribery also took place in many of the other countries where it has stores. The Department of Justice and the Security and Exchange Commission were looking into the charges that Wal-Mart had breached the Foreign Corrupt Practices Act. This Act prohibits American corporations from bribing foreign countries. Wal-Mart said it would cooperate with the investigation.

But, alas, Wal-Mart didn't cooperate with the investigation. On August 14, 2012, Congressmen Elijah J. Cummings and Representative Henry A. Waxman wrote a letter to Michael T. Duke, Chief Executive Officer of Wal-Mart, saying the committee had found that, "although you have stated on multiple occasions that you intend to cooperate with our investigation, you have failed to provide the documents we requested, and you continue to deny us access to key witnesses." In addition there were "internal company documents including internal audit reports from other sources suggesting that Wal-Mart may have had compliance issues relating not only to bribery, but also to questionable financial behavior including tax evasion and money laundering in Mexico." (52)

Wal-Mart, it seems, was not complying; it was withholding documents which would let the committees proceed with the investigation. Maybe it had also bribed officials in other countries as well as Mexico? The New York City Council held a hearing on Wal-Mart, but they needed a larger hearing room because so many had something to say about Wal-Mart's bribery scandal. So the hearing was postponed.

In the midst of this crisis Wal-Mart kept negotiating with Related Companies, who owned the site on which Wal-Mart wanted to build in Brooklyn. Wal-Mart had plans for a small store to open in Brooklyn, East New York, at Gateway II. (53) It would open the store in an impoverished neighborhood. Wal-Mart does not need any City Council or zoning laws changed to do that, so it secretly proceeded with its negotiations with Related Companies.

Wal-Mart lost the bid with Related for the site. Instead, Related signed a deal with Shop-Rite, a supermarket unionized by the UFCW (54). At the end of these negotiations a statement was issued by Steven Restivo, the Senior Director of Community Affairs for Wal-Mart in New York, saying, "Wal-Mart was unable to agree on economic terms for a project in East New York." (54) Although it seems that Wal-Mart was out of the picture in New York City, who knows when Wal-Mart will be back?

Boston

In Boston, Wal-Mart was more clever. Though Boston Mayor Thomas Menino reportedly criticized the Company, and there were large protests from the "We Want Good Jobs Coalition," Boston's protest movement, in Roxbury. (55) Wal-Mart decided not to come to Boston, but it would not be stopped in environs. It had planned to come to places like Saugus and Watertown, two Boston suburbs. It couldn't fight the city, but it could win in the suburbs. Possibly as a result of the scandal in Mexico—Wal-Mart was too busy fighting off attempts to deal with the bribery scandal—it decided not to spend time fighting the two suburbs that opposed it. They subsequently withdrew; they are not going to locate in the Boston area.

Los Angeles

Several years ago an "Interim Control Ordinance" was passed by the citizens of Los Angeles, to keep Wal-Mart out of the city. It was not only issued for Wal-Mart, but for all "formula retail stores." This prevented stores which kept "standardized facades, color schemes, décor, employee uniforms, and standardized merchandise" from setting up stores in Los Angeles. The interim control ordinance would keep Wal-Mart and many other stores, including banks, grocery stores, and fast–food locations out of Chinatown in Los Angeles. It would keep Trader Joe's, Starbuck's and Fresh and Easy out of Chinatown, too. Ultimately, there was a request by Chinatown's residents to keep Chinatown the way they wanted it, the way it had been for a long time. Yet, despite all this, Wal-Mart sought to open a large market in Chinatown, in the city. And Wal-Mart couldn't care less.

It was discovered in February, 2012 that Wal-Mart had signed a lease back in 1991, for a 33,000-square-foot space, which Wal-Mart was holding on to for the long term. (56) The City Council had "unanimously approved" the motion to ban Wal-Mart stores from Chinatown. But the ban was overturned "when the city building authority and safety department representative told the council that Wal-Mart had obtained building permits to begin construction." (57)

Aiha Nguyen, who is senior policy analyst for the Los Angeles Alliance for a New Economy, a group that favors blocking Wal-Mart, says, "It is an outrage that they managed to pull a number of permits at 5 p.m." the night before they said Wal-Mart was to begin its building effort. (58) Then on October 4 , for the first time in history, all the workers at Wal-Mart, in Mira Loma, California, went out on strike, not only those who were warehouse workers, but also, the women who worked in the supermarkets, as "associates." So did those at Elwood, Illinois.

The warehouse workers are backed by the United Food Workers of America, and in Chicago, by the United Electrical Workers of America. In the past their efforts have generated some improvements, but they have also generated "waves of retaliation," as well.

As we can see, there have been many spectacular protests against Wal-Mart in the cities, and at suburban sites too. And though there are protests and demonstrations, Wal-Mart, with its aggression and persistence, has just kept pushing, until it finally builds its stores or gives up. Few have been built yet in Los Angeles, but it comes back, year after year, to create more havoc and misery, all over the country, and beyond. Always it comes back, with promises—and low wages, and with no respect for a union, and no respect for its workers. To date, there are very few stores in American cities.

Wal-Mart Workers Plan "OUR Wal-Mart"

Despite the difficulty in forming a union to have collective bargaining, the current workers at Wal-Mart have formed a substitute. It is not exactly what they want, but it will at least give workers a chance to know each other's problems, and that others are suffering on Wal-Mart's low wages, and the disrespect they get from their superiors at the store. As they meet other workers from around the country who work at Wal-Mart, they have been learning that it is not just their store where they are treated so badly, but there are 2.2 million workers around the world who suffer as they do.

"OUR Wal-Mart" it is called—Organization United for Respect at Wal-Mart. It was started with the help of the UFCW. The problems they face include: 1) scheduling that isn't predictable or stable; 2) being "coached" for speaking up about an issue; 3) favoritism or discrimination; 4) unavoidable or no health care options; and 5) understaffing, disrespect and, of course, low wages.

In October of 2011, one hundred members of OUR Wal-Mart made a trip to the "Home Office" of Wal-Mart in Bentonville, Arkansas. As the company hosted Wall Street analysts and investors for a whole week of discussion on the company's financial health, they demanded an "open-door" meeting with Mike Duke, the President of Wal-Mart, to deliver the organization's Declaration for Respect.

In that Declaration the following things were mentioned, that Wal-Mart was an objectionable place to work, and suggested ways to make it better, and expressed the need to be heard. They said, "And to honor the hard work and humanity of Associates, Wal-Mart should allow Associates to join OUR Wal-Mart freely, without fear of negative company action." Wal-Mart claims that the earnings should be $13 per hour, when most of us work for $10 an hour or less, and are scheduled for part-time hours.

Wal-Mart should also expand the number of full-time workers, who can't be sent home early. Wal-Mart should honor our Constitutional rights, rights to freedom of speech, and company policies that support dialogue and resolution. Wal-Mart should do more to ensure that managers are properly trained on how to evenly and equitably enforce Wal-Mart's written policies, and to provide all Associates with a policy manual. Wal-Mart should provide affirmative action policies to all Associates regardless of, race, disability, sexual orientation, or age.

And finally, with respect to wages: "Far too many of us have to rely on government assistance for our basic needs. Wal-Mart should provide wages and benefits that ensure that no Associate has to rely on government assistance." These are the main things, but not little things. With a union they know they could ask for so much more.

Mike Compton was an Elwood worker. He told Amy Goodman: "You know, we finally just had enough, and we started to organize. We started a petition, just asking for some basic rights. And our managers refused to take it. So that was kind of the final straw. We decided that that was it, and we walked out that day." (59)

There was a recent decision that all of the workers at all of the Wal-Mart's around the country should take another day and strike. The day that was decided on was "Black Friday," the day after Thanksgiving. That's the busiest shopping day of the year, the day everyone begins their search for Christmas presents.

Wal-Mart is "taking its first legal step to stop months of protest and rallies outside its stores." It filed an unfair labor practice charge against the United Food and Commercial Workers, asking the National Labor Relations Board to halt what the retailer says is an attempt to disrupt its business. But, Jill Cashen, UFCW Communications Director, says there's nothing in the law that gives an employer the right to silence workers and citizens. (60)

Fortunately, the National Relations Labor Board (NLRB) now "has authorized legal action against Wal-Mart Stores for allegedly retaliating against workers who participated in strikes against the company..." Wal-Mart will answer these charges. The case is ongoing. But if the NLRB is successful, that sends a shot across the bow to all employers across the line—Wal-Mart is the largest employer to face such a complaint in years. (61)

Footnotes

1. Warehouse Workers for Justice (WWJ), Bad Jobs in Goods Movement, Warehouse Workers in Will County, Illinois, August 16, 2010.
2. Jean-Paul Rodrigue and Markus Hesse, "North American Logistics," in Global Logistics: New Directions in Supply Chain Management, 6th edition, London, Kogan Page, October 2009.
3. Barney Gimbel, "Yule Log Jam," Fortune Magazine, December 13, 2004.
4. "Studying Seaports: Industrial Investment Opportunities Exist Near Ports, Recapitallink, 2008.
5. Ibid.
6. Jones Lang Lasalle, The Emergence of Inland Port, Spring 2011.
7. "Inland Empire Warehouse Workers Shut Down the Warehouse District," PR Newswire, May 28. 2011.
8. Dave Jamieson, "The New Blue Collar: Temporary Work, Lasting Poverty and The American Warehouse," The Huffington Post, December 20, 2011.
9. "Many Paid Below Minimum Wage, Suit Claims; State Proposes Fines." MSNBC.msn, March 5, 2012.
10. Ibid.
11. Edna Bonacich and J. B. Wilson, Getting the Goods: Ports, Logistics and the Logistics Revolution, Ithaca N.Y.: Cornell University Press.
12. CAL-OSHA Reporter, Inland Empire's Giant Warehouse Safety Spotlight, December 2, 2011; and see Lilly Fowler, Many Paid Below Minimum Wage, Suit Claims; Proposes Fines, MSNBC. msn, March 12, 2012.
13. Warehouse Work in Will County—Bad Jobs in Goods Movement, n.d.
14. See Federal Court Issues Temporary Restraining Order Requiring Wal-Mart Warehouses to Comply with Law, October 31, 2011.
15. Cal-OSHA Reporter, "New IE Warehousing Complaint," September 28, 2012.
16. David Moberg, "As One Wal-Mart Warehouse Strike Ends, Another Snowballs," In These Times, October 1, 2012.

17. Jane Slaughter, "Supply Chain Workers Test Strength of Links," Labor Notes, March 29, 2012.

18. Federal Court Rejects Wal-Mart's Bid to Escape Liability, Bet Tsedek (Justice For All, January 15, 2014)

19. Kenneth Quinell, Wal-Mart Workers Abused By Wal-Mart and Others, UFCW 1167, n.d.

20. Christopher Hayes, "The NAFTA Superhighway," The Nation, August 9, 2007.

21. Jerome R. Corsi. "Red China Opens NAFTA Ports," Human Events on Line, July 26, 2006.

22. John Gillie, "New Terminal Could Mean More Competition for West Coast Ports," Tacoma News, The Tacoma Tribune, January 4, 2012; see also "APM Terminals Wins Lazaro Cardenas Contract," Eye for Transport, n.d.

23. "APM Terminals Wins Lazaro Cardenas Bid," The Journal of Commerce, December 29, 2011.

24. Human Rights Watch.

25. Labor, Immigration and Retirement Policy, U.S. Congress, 110th Congress.

26. Report: "Wal-Mart Violates Worker Rights, Fosters 'Culture of Fear' to Prevent Employees From Forming Unions," Democracy Now, May 1, 2007.

27. "Discounting Rights: Wal-Mart's Violation of US Workers Rights to Freedom of Association," Human Rights Watch, Volume 19, No. 2, May 2007.

28. Bernie Sanders, "Bernie Sanders Says Wal-Mart Heirs Own More Wealth Than Bottom 40% of Americans," PolitiFact of the Tampa Bay Times, July 22, 2012.

29. Nicole Maestri, "Wal-Mart Shrinks U.S. Supercenters, Sees Tepid Sales," October, 2010.

30. Reuters, "Wal-Mart Seeks to End Re-filed Gender-Bias Lawsuit," January 17, 2012.

31. Anne D'Innocenzio, "Profit Up, but Sales Down as Wal-Mart Feels Sting, of Competition," Delaware County Times, February 19, 2010.

32. Jack Neff, "Wal-Mart to Lay Off Up to 800 Employees at Headquarters," Advertising Age, February 11, 2009.
33. Joseph De Avila, "Why Wal-Mart Needs Help," CNET Network Business, 2007.
34. "Wal-Mart Has Plans to Go Mini," American Consumer News, May 11, 2010.
35. Wal-Mart in Crisis: How the World's Largest Retailer Lost Its Way, A Wal-Mart Watch Report, June 2007.
36. Jonathan O'Connell, "Where Wal-Mart Donated in 2010," Capital Business, December 20, 2010.
37. Michael Niebauer, "Wal-Mart D.C. Foes Release Reports," Washington Business Journal, April 21, 2011.
38. Marina Streznewski, Commentary: "Wal-Mart's Philanthropy Doesn't Make Up for Lack of Fair Wages," Washington Post, October 2, 2-11.
39. Dave Jamieson, "Wal-Mart Wage of $12 Wouldn't Drive Up Prices," Huffington Post Business, October 6, 2012.
40. Food Trade, Food Trade News, September 2012.
41. Brigid Sweeney, "Hard Hats Criticize Wal-Mart's Chicago Union Deal", Crain's New York Business.com, February 10, 2011.
42. Steven Greenhouse and Reed Abelson, "Wal-Mart Cuts Some Health Care Benefits," The New York Times, October 20, 2011.
43. Leslie Patton and Matthew Boyle, "Wal-Mart Cracks Chicago by Splitting Union, Non-Union Workers," Bloomberg News, July 22, 2010.
44. Kari Lydersen, "Wal-Mart Opponents Oppose New Crop of Chicago Stores," In These Times, October 31, 2011.
45. MarketWatch, "Wal-Mart Abandons a New Store In Brooklyn," September 15, 2012.
46. Joseph Grosso, "Drawing a Line in the Sand: Wal-Mart and New York City," Counterpunch, October 28, 2010.
47. Bill Hammond, "It's the Cost of Living, Stupid: 58,000 pages of rules and regs make everything in N.Y. expensive," The Daily News, April 10, 2010 From the Cost of Living Project.

48. Josh Kellerman and Stephanie Luce, "The Wal-Martization of New York City," CUNY, The Murphy Institute.

49. Chris Bragg, "Wal-Mart Foes Predict New York City Invasion," City Hall News, September 21, 2011.

50. Samantha Sleevi and Monee Fields-White, "Wal-Mart Backers Rally for Second City Store," Chicago Business, July 29, 2009; Elizabeth A. Harris, "Wal-Mart Tries a Refined Path into New York," The New York Times, March 25, 2011.

51. Courtney Gross, "The Wonkster," The Gotham Gazette, March 18, 2011.

52. Congress of the United States, House of Representatives, to Michael T. Duke," August 14, 2012.

53. Laura Kusiato, "Brooklyn Wal-Mart Deal Falls Apart," The Wall Street Journal, September 14, 2012; Andrew J. Hawkins, "Shop-Rite Deal Means No Wal-Mart," Crain's New York Business, September 14, 2012.

54. Mary Moore, "Showdown Looming—Mayor Menino Objects as Wal-Mart Sharpens Focus on Roxbury," Boston Business Journal, July 11, 2011.

55. Jobs With Justice, "Greater Boston Community Wins Fight Against Wal-Mart Expansion," June 15, 2012; "Sustainable Watertown Wal-Mart Abandons Plan for Watertown," 2012.

56. "Wal-Mart Battle Takes a Turn," Los Angeles Downtown News, March 21, 2012.

57. Kathleen Miles, "Chinatown Wal-Mart Wins Building Permits as LA Council Readies Chain Store Ban," Huffington Post,(Los Angeles), March 23, 2012.

58. Ibid.

59. "Wal-Mart Workers in 12 States Stage Historic Strike, Protests Against Workplace Retaliation," Democracy Now, October 10, 2012.

60. "Wal-Mart Takes Legal Action in Labor Battle," Business on NBC News, November 16, 2012.

61. Analysis: Wal-Mart Case Seen A Key Test in a Struggle Over Labor Rights, Reuters, January 16, 2014.

On 24 July, 2000 the world's largest retailer, Wal-Mart, opened its first American-style Supercenter in the U.K., placing it on the outskirts of Bristol. As queues of cars choked the July sunshine, clamoring to squeeze into the 1.000-space car park, both the local and national media, with a disturbing unanimity of message, warmly welcomed the behemoth's arrival. "Store wars as U.S. giant offers 60% off," blazed the approving headline of the Daily Mail. "Shoppers set out for cut-price bonanza," yelled the Bristol Evening News. ("Why Britain Can't Afford Wal-Mart," The Ecologist, September 2000.)

3

Wal-Mart: In Piccadilly Circus

In the early 1990's Wal-Mart desired to be a global retailer; the megalith had aspirations to penetrate every part of the world. Then John Menzer is quoted as saying, "The United States is 37 percent of the world's economy, which leaves 63 percent for international. If we do our job, international operations should someday be twice as large as the United States. That's a big challenge, but that is the opportunity in front of us."

Wal-Mart was facing a dilemma. U.S. operations were slowing, and it was becoming more and more difficult to find places for stores. "Site fights" grew as Americans began to learn more about Wal-Mart, and soon decided they were opposed to having one in their community. Wal-Mart was having difficulty maintaining its super-duper growth rate. Its culture and its stock prices were both built on the expectation of double-digit sales, and profit gains year after year. It was getting increasingly difficult for Wal-Mart to record those double-digit returns. Though Wal-Mart then opened "a new store every 42 hours, it [was] suffering from soft sales, rising inventories, and languishing sales at its famous Sam's Club division." It was finding it more and more necessary to expand abroad. (1)

Wal-Mart seemed eager to spread its wings farther. By 1999 when it moved to England, it would begin to expand its corporate presence in Europe and could, by its investment first in England and then in Germany, expand its stores all the way from England to Turkey.

Just before it left Germany in 2006, there was a strike brewing among Asda's truckers and carriers in the north of England. There was conflict between Asda's depot workers (the distribution centers) and the corporate management. But, the trade union which represents many types of British industrial workers (the GMB) resisted rather than give in. They were Wal-Mart's depot workers: the men who drove the trucks to the depots before they were trucked to the stores and the men who worked inside the depots as well, carting around the heavy loads.

The GMB had a strong presence when the "old Asda" was in charge, when it represented all the workers in the company. It was weakened when Thatcher and New Labour took power. In Britain most unions had fallen away from the old militancy; the old diehards of the Labour Party were sunk in a period of inaction and the labor movement was relatively quiescent. It was certainly not doing any organizing, and the percentage of union members vis-à-vis the population had dropped from 11 percent to 7 percent in the years 1970 to 2002, a bit lower than in the U.S., where it was 12.5 percent of the working population. (2) But, despite the small number, when a laborer or laborers had a problem in the company, the problem was resolved through the union norms—and peaceably. Not everyone was a member of the union, but no one doubted that everyone had labor rights. But when Wal-Mart took over the new Asda, and made their anti-union feeling clear, the GMB had to rethink its position. From what they had heard about Wal-Mart, they knew that its anti-union position called for a new militancy, as well as for a new regime of collective bargaining. Wal-Mart made it clear that it would recognize the union, the GMB, but there would be no collective bargaining. They would be a union—but without a voice!

The first thing the GMB wanted was a bargaining agreement; and second, an end to the 1,400 pound quota of lifting each day, upon which a £250 bonus was to be paid. They wanted the bonus that was promised to them, despite the fact that they had not reached the

1,400-pound work limit. Second, and related to this, they wanted a requirement that an outside agent be hired to ascertain that safe work rates were established.

When Wal-Mart took over Asda in England, it was not a good time. Asda's margins were down for four quarters in a row—a whole year. Asda was also feeling competitive pressure from its two rivals, Tesco and Sainsbury. And finally, England's Asda Essentials clothing stores were failing. It had to act, and it had to act now. Things between the union, GMB, and Asda/Wal-Mart came to a head in June of 2006.

Asda had done fairly well since 1999 when it was purchased by Wal-Mart. In only seven years it had grown, substantially. It was twice as large as other superstores, 89,500 square feet vs. the 42,300 square feet of Tesco's supercenters. Asda sold similar goods and operated in a similar way to Wal-Mart in the United States, only it did so a little more tactfully.

Asda had the same business practice as its U.S. Wal-Mart's, ruthlessly lowering prices in order to get market share. It was rapacious towards its suppliers, as it is in the U.S. Its goal was to be the number one supermarket in the U.K. Fortunately, the U.K. is more sympathetic to unions than the U.S. When labor rules are violated the workers' blood stirs.

The United Kingdom is a country with a strong working class, with unionists who believed they would always be in the working class. It was working class that had its own traditions, loved its football, and had a sense of being just like their parents before them. They knew that when "push came to shove" men should have a union behind them. They were not held hostage to an ideology of giving deference to their employer, as some are in the South of the United States where the ideology was born.

The battle between the workers in the depots and Asda started when the British War on Want, a European NGO, suddenly found a leaked document entitled "The Warehouse Chip-Away Strategy, 2005." This document showed how Wal-Mart senior management planned to undermine labor standards in the depots, in order to drive down wages and keep the difference in profits.

For example, the leaked document said, "Work breaks will be cut, grievance mechanisms are to be removed, and health and safety conditions are to be weakened. Also, the right to take individual grievances to external arbiters is to be stopped. Single–man loading [is to be required], and line managers are not to take breaks lest they provide an example to the workers." And at the time the wages were 20 percent lower than the industry standard. (3)

Asda ran an anti-union campaign much as it did in the U.S., and it used similar strategies to break unions in the U.K. as it used in its American stores. It tried to buy off the union. The presence of a union could not make it close a store as it did in Canada, where it closed the store in Jonquiere that had organized and won a union. (4) In Texas, the meat cutters in Jacksonville had formed a union. Wal-Mart closed several hundred meat departments, and brought in packaged meat. They claimed it was not profitable to have anything but packaged meat, actually "firing" 540 members of the UFCW. (5)

In England they couldn't close a distribution center. If the depots were closed, the stores had no food. English workers moved "300,000 tons per day of ambient, fresh, chilled, and frozen produce from 20 distribution depots to 300 Asda Wal-Mart stores around the country." The union, the GMB, won on the grounds that Wal-Mart "was found guilty of offering financial inducements to the staff in return for surrendering their union rights," and Wal-Mart was fined 2,500 pounds for each member, in compensation. (6) The courts had a law, which they always enforced—and Asda was breaking the British labor laws. Yet, Asda would break any labor laws it could, if it would help do away with the GMB. And it was staffed with angry men; not a single woman drove a truck or lifted a bag of potatoes. Asda distributed to its managers "The Manager's Toolbox to Remaining Union Free." Embodied in it was what the GMB union called the "chip-away strategy" mentioned above. It is one of the most insidious books of tactics that a company has ever produced, and that a union has ever seen. It is "confidential" and only available to managers. To managers it says that Wal-Mart is "strongly opposed to third-party representation. We are not anti–union; we are pro-associate," or "It is our position every associate can speak for himself without having to pay his/her hard-earned money to a union." Or things like, "Open communication is the key to stopping a union organizing attempt before it ever gets started." In the U.S. Wal-Mart's management personnel hammered away at a variety of themes: that "the unions only wanted workers' dues; that they cannot guarantee better wages and benefits; that they want to put Wal-Mart out of business; and that they foment walkouts in which the strikers can lose their jobs." (7) They were faced with attacks from moderate British politicians. The company has been fighting back from its war room in Bentonville. (8) When the facts got to court, the British lawmakers, who decided to sue Asda, were shocked at all the devious moves that Asda made. In fact, the strategies that worked in America, where there was no union and no national admiration for trade unions, didn't succeed in England. Wal-Mart had displayed the worst sort of Americanism, and was viewed as thoroughly backed by Bentonville. Asda looked like an imitation of a company in England. After employing a whole grab-bag of American managers who Bentonville thought could do a better job, Asda finally put an Englishman in charge— Anthony Bond. After many years he was given the position of CEO in the spring of 2005. He had to be better than an American and a lot "nicer."

But the English CEO did not do much better than the American. He followed orders that came straight from Bentonville. Bentonville, in the person of F. Lee Scott, the chairman of Wal-Mart, and Wal-Mart refused to believe that Asda workers were any different than American workers. It believed that they were just as quiescent as Americans. Then when Bentonville refused to let them bargain collectively, Asda faced the wrath of the union, the GMB.

The action started in the early part of 2006, when Lee Scott said that the workers would not get their yearly bonus. The 300 pounds that was given to most workers at Christmas time was a big boost to their low salaries, and it came at the time of year when they needed it most. They would not get their yearly bonus because that year they did not make the profit goals which Asda imposed, and they suddenly lost a chunk of their yearly salary. Of those who "earned" it, Asda only paid the bonus to three out of five workers. The previous year they paid nine out of ten workers their bonus. The retailer was accused of channeling those saved bonuses into Wal-Mart's purse, which was just what it was doing. (9)

In addition, Asda workers got raises to just 5 pence above the British minimum wage. According to what Asda told them, they were supposed to get 7.75 pounds for working Saturdays, and 10.27 pounds for working Sundays, but Asda's actual wage for those times was only 5.44 pounds for working the "unsocial hours." While the truckers were angry at not getting their bonuses, Asda simply imposed pay rates and conditions. So, the GMB vowed to have a demonstration with placards reading "Stop Asda pocketing the bonus difference." (10) While the wages of the other supermarkets—Tesco, Sainsbury, Morrison's, and Safeway—were all somewhat higher than Asda's, they were not much higher because all supermarkets keep wages low. Asda was effectively trying to keep wages even lower than its competitors.

Tesco also has a union, but not a very active one. Jude Brimble, a GMB director, said "Asda/Wal-Mart is looking for these increased profit levels while paying their staff the National Minimum Wage." (11) Asda had "282 stores and 22 depots all in all, and 25,000 workers." Nine of the depots were organized, and thirteen were not. Despite the fact that the depots are supposed to be automated, with automated belts taking merchandise from the inbound trucks where they entered the depot, to where they come out for delivery, those boxes, just as in the U.S., must be moved by hand. This amounted to about 9 to 95 pounds a minute [between 4 to 44 kilos]. The weight of the boxes was between 5 and 20 kilos—[or 11 and 44 pounds]. Per day, the weight they had to lift was calculated at equivalent to about five automobiles." Asda also wanted to eliminate the single-man loading for jobs that involve heavy lifting, and have two men do it.

Eddie Gaudie, a GMB organizer responsible for the Asda distribution workers, also said: ". . . work experts who have measured what the worker can physically move in a day. GMB is seeking to apply a safety screen to this figure under the Manual Handling Regulations 1992— the work study team has recommended that the work study experts limit the work by 30 percent to 50 percent to remove the danger of personal injury to the warehouse worker." Workers are also subject to hearing loss when wearing RFID equipment. The GMB wanted to test the workers "in case the workers lose their hearing in the future." The workers put it this way "Asking someone to shift 1,400 boxes a day is equivalent to asking someone to work out in a gym for eight hours a day, every working day. It is equivalent to asking their staff to work themselves to death". (12)

But Wal-Mart wanted to run the depots like a sweatshop, as it did in China. For example, there were no hearing tests and no "safety screens." In the depots, the workers were now being scheduled to lift a total of 1,400 instead of 1,100 boxes a day, a little over one-fourth more weight than before. The extra loads caused a public relations disaster, which was just what Asda wished to avoid.

At the same time, in Germany, Robert Greenwald previewed his American movie, "The High Cost of Low Price," a film which is highly critical of Wal-Mart in America. The bad news crossed the English Channel when Greenwald said that, "Wal-Mart is the poster child for the worst in corporate behavior." Asda was also condemned by the British War on Want.

Some of the other tactics Asda used were especially brutal, or especially stupid, as the case may be. First, Tony Blair's former deputy secretary, Tim Allen, became the owner of Portland PR, a consulting firm. In 2004 and 2005, Asda paid Portland PR to develop some "literature against collective bargaining" to convince the GMB members not to vote for the union. Fortunately for the workers, a government tribunal took a dim view of Portland's writings, which were "hostile to trade unions and highly disparaging of the process of collective bargaining." (13)

The literature was used to induce their distribution workers in Washington, Tyne and Wear to vote "no" in union elections. The workers were furious that they did not get their bonus, and that they had to lift more weight. They were angry because the company "had more money for wages than ever before, yet it refused to pay all of them their bonuses." The profit at Asda was 770 million pounds for 2005, a substantial sum.

In January 2005, management offered a 10-percent "pay rise" to 340 GMB members if they would give up their right to collective bargaining and their union rights. It was as if all hell broke loose. "Asda was found guilty of trying to bribe its way to a union-free company." (14) There were 340 workers at the depot at Washington, Tyne and Wear who Asda tried to deprive of their wage rise. The workers refused to give up their union rights and Asda refused to give them their pay raise. The Employment Tribunal in Newcastle on Tyne, hearing of this, penalized Asda to the tune of 850,000 pounds only one month later, in February. Since they still haven't given it to the workers it is subject to interest, but Wal-Mart has appealed it, and it has been increasing by 268 pounds a day.

Asda tried the same thing at its Lutterworth and Sunderland depots, this time without naming the consultant. It was trying to pick off one depot at a time. Asda management was taking its cues from Wal-Mart's "human resource personnel." And again, Asda defended itself by saying it was a company in which "colleagues" were "free to talk with management about any problems they have on the job, through the open-door policy."

The key to understanding Wal-Mart's policy toward labor is the codicil in Wal-Mart's handbook, in America. It says, "We are not against unions. They may be right for some companies, but there is simply no need for a third party between our associates and our managers."

David Smith, Asda's People Director, spoke to the press in England. He said, "[the GMB] has openly said to us that [it] is a large organization that is desperately seeking to increase its dues" just as it tells the unsuspecting people in America. (15) Asda workers didn't want a strike, they couldn't afford it. They just wanted to stop Asda in its tracks.

Yet, by March of 2006, the GMB was already planning a five-day walkout on June 30, 2006. It was to last for five days, until July 4, 2006. (16) The union felt five days was enough to wring out the pride of Asda. In June of 2006, the GMB called a strike or walkout. It was approved by a three to one majority, or 74 percent in favor of the walkout, despite the fact that only half of the workers were represented by the union. They had 20 depots, with 25,000 workers; and 115,000 workers in the stores also went on strike. Asda threatened to fire strikebreakers, but the union wrote to each and every agency that could provide "scabs," telling them it was illegal to work in England, when a union was on strike. (17)

The strike, however, was averted through a last-minute deal. The deal came in the morning, shortly before Asda management was to go to high court to try to block the strike, after long talks between the two parties. The GMB consciously picked the time in June, the time of the World Cup, the time that is supposed to be "the busiest time of the year." The strike would also have coincided with an important event for Englishmen—if the protest had gone ahead. "The anticipated sale of 100,000 bottles of beer, from Friday afternoon to Sunday morning before the English match," could have put Asda at a disadvantage. It was a time for Englishmen to drink lots of beer and celebrate being Englishmen. Asda would have lost a great deal of money when the truckers threatened to disrupt getting the beer to the stores. (18)

The strikers were the drivers, and the warehouse pickers and loaders. One newspaper said: "There appears to be a real clash of cultures between the way workers do business in Britain and the way Wal-Mart does business. It is significant that the strike dates set by the shop stewards cover Independence Day, because GMB members wanted independence from the anti-trade union tactics of Wal-Mart worldwide." The paper also wrote: "The union is calling for proper national bargaining structures between the company and the GMB, covering pay conditions and union facilities in all 20 distribution depots." (19,22) It "was widely condemned" by all those sympathetic to unions, as it showed its desire to "reduce wages and increase productivity." (20)

The meeting that was held between George Kenny, Acting Secretary of the GMB, and Andrew Bond, CEO of Asda/Wal-Mart, supposedly ended the struggle between the two adversaries and their constituents. But it never ended what Wal-Mart saw as the basic struggle to end the union. (21) In a little piece of the union bulletin the company said that, "the 11th April deal did not mean any extension to collective bargaining in the distribution depots." (23) Wal-Mart was not going to submit to any union, regardless of what the government said.

The Denouement

As early as June 13th, Asda tried again to put a monkey wrench into the strike settlement. Just six days after the would-be strike date, shop stewards again accused Asda of bullying tactics, "including putting CDs in drivers' cabs, urging them to vote against the strike and (on June 12, 2006) by "writing to their families in their homes warning them against strike action again." Asda may have used all the wrong tactics. Perhaps they would have worked in the United States, but they didn't work in the U.K. Nevertheless, Asda may have been the first and only company in Britain to be prosecuted for union busting.

Before the strike Asda, on the surface, had a seemingly friendly management policy, which was backed by the Work Foundation and encouraged by the New Conservative Party, presumably designed to enhance the work and family lives of their employees. Employees had the right to watch World Cup Games at their local depot—with free snacks and drinks supplied by Asda. They could also take unpaid leave or a holiday. Staff could take an unpaid half-day leave to take their children to school, or have five days to go to a fertility clinic. But, one didn't get paid for these "leaves," and one had to make up the time working.

The GMB did not favor this policy. One union member who has been with the company since 1989 says, "It looks good on paper but when you come to ask for say paternity leave, it's not so easy—there is a bullying attitude". (24) Or, Wal-Mart might have pulled one of its stalling tactics, and delayed an agreement until the GMB was exhausted. Despite theoretically getting a collective bargaining agreement, the workers don't trust the company. They felt that Asda, when push came to shove, would not engage in collective bargaining at all.

After the Strike

For example, when the GMB signed the agreement with Asda, it had to make payments to the people harmed by race and disability discrimination; it had to give 750 pounds to each of 37 GMB members for racial discrimination, and make a public apology for it.

But when the smoke cleared, from their happy response the Asda workers appeared to have gotten what they wanted. According to the English labor laws, they got their due—a union with collective bargaining rights for all the workers in the depots. But in actuality the workers got very little. Although at Christmas time they were promised a 250 pound bonus. But, they never received a penny of it. Asda was on the telephone with Wal-Mart officials at the highest level when Wal-Mart said "yes" to the bargaining agreement. It was a "yes," but what kind of finality did it have? (25) Jeff Goswell, a GMB official in the southeast of England, said: "Members are convinced that the deal that Andy Bond signed with Paul Kenny, the president of the union, has been suppressed by Wal-Mart." It's anybody's guess!

They felt that Asda might ultimately balk at the need for collective bargaining. It was feared that Asda might pull one of its stalling tactics, and delay an agreement until the GMB was exhausted. Despite the image of having won the strike and gotten what they wanted, the workers don't trust the company. (26)

In the Interim

They were right! Although as of 2011 they got an offer for a slight raise in pay from Asda, since 2006 the workers have been furious with the company. They have gotten no raise since 2006, and there are many complaints about the 2 percent pay raise that Wal-Mart offered to give them in April 2011. Their response to this was "a massive rejection" of Wal-Mart's offer, when 99.24 percent of the workers said "no" to this offer. (27) Gary Smith, the National Secretary of the GMB, in his report to them said about these negotiations in 2011, "I am afraid that more patience from us all will be needed." Pay, however, is the greatest issue of them all.

When Wal-Mart cedes something, it makes sure to take away something that was desirable to the workers, as well. In March 2007, a little less than a year after Wal-Mart signed the agreement with the union (which the government forced Wal-Mart to do), the workers in the GMB decided they ought to get what Wal-Mart had promised them in the new contract—higher pay. Wal-Mart agreed, but only if the staff would agree to give up "valuable perks" such as "being able to work bank holidays and instead get double time and a day off." (28) They would not accept it.

The 2 percent they offered was for the stores as well, for the workers in the stores were finally incorporated in the settlement. The 2 percent they offered was so poor that in July 2011, without any raise at all, the GMB came out with a survey stating what the workers in the stores wanted from their jobs at Asda. Although the most important thing they wanted was higher pay, they also wanted to be treated like human beings.

What was most significant to them was that they wanted more time with their families. Asda takes no heed of this, because it has decided that they will come to work whenever it is convenient for Asda. And, indeed, the survey responses showed that Asda's requirements were for the stores' staff to work entirely when it suited the company." (29)

The most common type of issue is one that can best be described as "problems with management." The workers say the managers can't "deal with people." They "bully and intimidate" and "ignore company policy." They "make up rules" as they go along. Asda managers "show little or no respect to colleagues." They "show favoritism" toward some, and discriminate against others. They are intransigent and won't listen. (30) As to the conditions of work, they ignore health and safety issues. They have "inadequate staffing levels" and they send workers home early, and without pay, to save wage costs. These and many more issues are similar to the ones Wal-Mart has in its supermarkets in the United States.

With the Tories in power in England, the working class is taking a beating because the workers at Wal-Mart are so frightened of being fired when they try to act to support their union. But the Trades Union Congress (like the AFL-CIO in the U.S.) is fighting against the way the (Tory) government, and Wal-Mart, have interpreted and set the rules.

In 2006, when Wal-Mart and Asda reached an agreement "covering full union recognition," Wal-Mart claimed "that the deal was to set up a national negotiating committee for all the depots, but it did not go so far as to set up collective bargaining with them." (31)

A second thing was the two-year law the government had passed:

"The government claims that this move will increase jobs, but there's simply no evidence to back this up. At the moment there are three million people who have been at their job more than one year, but less than two. Thanks to this government, they are no longer protected from being sacked unfairly. This new law, which the Tories have passed, is "nothing short of a charter for rogue employers." (32)

The Trades Union Congress is seeking improved protection from such a law. According to a resolution adopted at the meeting this year, is a Parliamentary bill in for "improved protection for workers taking part in industrial action."

This bill led to a new agreement being signed in which:

". . . covering one thousand of their members employed in transport and warehouse operations in many depots in England Wales and Scotland, was the first of its kind anywhere in the world involving the United States-owned company." (33) Wal-Mart finally got its union!

Evidently, Wal-Mart came to England with the same kind of "formula for business"—the same type of anti-union "tricks" that it had used in the United States. Wal-Mart attempted to defeat the men in the GMB depots, as it tried to defeat all the unions.

The British worker comes from a very different culture than the workers in the U.S., and, finally, when the Tories came to power, the British demonstrated that they had a much stronger labor movement than the Americans. The Trade Union Congress wasn't going to allow its workers, the British workers, to be treated like sweatshop workers. But Wal-Mart thought they could do the same thing in the northern English countryside, as they could in the southern United States.

In 2010 Asda bought Netto, with 193 supermarkets, from AP Moeller-Maersk. The Wal-Mart unit said it aims to convert the Netto stores, low-price supermarkets, into its smaller-format supermarkets, by the middle of 2011. We will have to see what happens. (34) Now that the GMB has the right to recruit Netto workers into the GMB, will Asda start playing its game all over again? (35)

But all the negotiations may leave the workers at Asda just as frustrated in the future. For Asda always has a reason to demur. In the last analysis Wal-Mart may have gotten a union, but that did not change Wal-Mart.

Footnotes

1. Andy Rowell, "Welcome to Wal-Mart: Wal-Mart's Inexhaustible March to Conquer the World," Multinational Monitor, October 2003.
2. Nikki Brownlie, Department for Business Innovation and Skills, Trade Union Membership, 2011.
3. War on Want, "Asda Wal-Mart: Cutting Costs at Any Cost," Corporate Watch, October 19, 2005.
4. Katherine Griffiths, "Wal-Mart Crushes Union by Closing Store," May 11, 2005.
5. Al Norman, "Wal-Mart's 'Meat War' With Union Sizzles On," Huffington Post, March 16, 2008.
6. Anita Awbi, "Wal-Mart UK Staff to Strike Over Working Conditions," Food and Drink, June 27, 2006.
7. "The Manager's Toolbox," Wal-Mart Stores, 1991.
8. Richard Adams, "Wal-Mart May Be Just Too American to Succeed Globally," The Guardian (UK), August 26, 2006.
9. "Asda Staff in Pay Ballot Dispute over Bonus Payments," and "Lack of Bargaining Rights," Jan 30, 2006. (union newspaper)
10. Anita Awbi, Asda—"Wal-Mart Guilty of Anti-Trade Union Activity," Food and Drink in Europe, February 14, 2006.
11. Interview with Jude Brimble, May 17, 2007.
12. Abeceder: Independent Minds, Unique Solutions, no date.
13. David Hencke, "Asda under Threat of Prosecution for Union Busting," The Guardian (UK), June 12, 2006.
14. "ASDA Found Guilty of Anti Trade Union Activity," GMB Press Release, February 13, 2006.
15. Mike Berry, "Asda HR Chief Slams 'Cynical' Union Tactics," GMB Website, March 14, 2006.
16. Jonathan Birchall and Andrew Taylor, "UK: Wal-Mart Faces Asda Workers' Strike," The Financial Times, June 22, 2006.
17. See the Conduct of Employment Agencies and Employment Business Regulations 2003, which came into force in April 2004.
18. Gavin Haycock, "Asda Agreement with the Union Avoids Depot Strike," Reuters, Jun 29, 2006.

19. Anita Awbi, "Wal-Mart UK Staff to Strike Over Working Conditions," Food and Drink, (June 27, 2006); and Anita Awbi, "Diplomacy Diverts Wal-Mart Asda Strike," Food and Drink, (April 14, 2006).

20. Gerry Bates, "Anti-union, Stingy, Deceitful, Anti-worker," Workers' Liberty (June 24, 2006).

21. David Hencke, "Asda Under Threat of Prosecution for Union Busting," Ameriprise Financial, The Guardian (UK), June 12, 2006. Op. cit.

22. "Wal-Mart's Asda Depot Workers to Hold 5-Day Strike," Reuters, 2006.

23. GMB and Asda Members (union bulletin) November 21, 2006.

24. David Hencke, "Good Shop, Bad Shop," The Guardian (UK), June 30, 2006.

25. Barrie Clement, Labor Editor, "Wal-Mart Accused of Vetoing Asda Union Recognition Deal," The Independent, April, 2006.

26. Personal Interview with Jude Brimble, February 17, 2007.

27. Report of GMB Asda Members—Survey 2011.

28. Interview with Jude Brimble, February 17, 2007. (op. cit.)

29. Report of GMB Asda Members—Survey 2011. (op.cit.)

30. Ibid.

31. United Kingdom, 2007 Annual Survey of Violations of Trade Union Rights, ITUC, 2007.

32. GMB@Asda Newsletter, "We All Lost Out on March 13, 2012."

33. "Asda Signs Historic Deal On Workers' Pay and Conditions After 14 Months of Talks with GMB Union ," The Daily Record , June 12, 2012.

34. "Wal-Mart's Asda Buys Netto in U.K for 1.13 Billion Pounds," Bloomberg News, May 27, 2010.

35. Regional Update, All the News from GMB, Netto Gains, no date.

4

Why Did Wal-Mart
Fail in Germany?

In the late 1980s, Wal-Mart was already the "biggest supermarket in the world." When it entered Germany in 1997, and England in 1998 ("the heart of the old world"), it had hopes of becoming the dominant player in the international market. Germany was the third biggest retail market in the world, after the U.S. and Japan; and Wal-Mart, with its hubris, believed it could make an ambitious international drive to take over supermarkets all over Europe. Having stores in the two richest countries in Europe (England and Germany), Wal-Mart planned for the German stores to be so lucrative that they would contribute a third of Wal-Mart's total profits—by 2005. Wal-Mart would have an imperial presence in Europe. Wal-Mart, in Bentonville, had plans of owning supermarkets and hypermarkets throughout Europe, all the way from Denmark to Russia. These plans were never accomplished.

At the same time, the Western European retail market was frenzied, as it worried where Wal-Mart would strike next. "Wal-Mart is all they can talk about . . . at conferences, over coffee, the likes of Carrefour and Ahold are obsessed about what [Wal-Mart] will do next." "Fear of a European invasion by the world's largest retailer, which had acquired a foothold in Germany and was already wreaking havoc," Before Wal-Mart had even gotten established, by this time it was having an effect. Many predicted a wave of mergers within Europe. (1) In France, Lee Scott, the chairman of Wal-Mart, boldly announced plans that Wal-Mart wanted to buy stores "in every European country." Supermarket executives of Europe were "wondering where Wal-Mart will go next."(2) With its extremely low prices, the word was Wal-Mart would buy up much of its competitors' chains.

It was rumored in the press that Wal-Mart was preparing to buy the heftiest retailer in France, Carrefour. But Carrefour quickly merged with Promodes; the two would have combined sales of $94 billion. "The French supermarket group Carrefour said yesterday it [was] acquiring rival Promodes in a deal that will create the world's second largest retailer in Europe." (3) And Tengelmann, in Germany, formed an alliance with Edeka. The combined retailers were much too big for Wal-Mart to take on. (4)

Wal-Mart then turned its attention to Metro, the second biggest German supermarket chain. " . . . Metro, which in Germany alone operated 246 Real Hypermarkets, about 500 Extra supermarkets, 81 cash-and-carry outlets called Metro or Makro, and 220 consumer electronics stores under the Media Market or Saturn names. With stores in 20 countries that produce annual sales of roughly $42 billion, Metro had 217,000 workers in 21 countries . . ." While Metro was only one-fourth the size of Wal-Mart, it was the largest in Germany and Wal-Mart was ready to gobble it up. (5) There were also questions about its buying Tengelmann, Kaufland, and Anuga.

But it had to settle for Interspar and Wertkauf. (6) And that is why Wal-Mart finally had to sell its 95 German stores to Metro, and leave that country with its tail between its legs, and with a loss of over $1 billion after only 8 1/2 years.

Ultimately, Wal-Mart didn't, or couldn't, buy the stores, or as many stores as it wanted. In fact, Wal-Mart entered the German market by buying only 21 stores of the Wertkauf chain, for $1.04 billion dollars. One year later it bought 74 stores of the Interspar chain, (owned by the French Intermarche Group) for 560 million euros. It was not a productive purchase.

The New York Times said Wal-Mart would, nevertheless, build 50 stores in three years. (7) But "labor, real estate, taxes, and transportation are comparative bargains in the United States." (8) In America, it could set down a supermarket pretty much anywhere it wanted. On the other hand, in Germany, supermarkets were far from cheap, and labor was very expensive. And with the 14 competing retailers, Wal-Mart was only allowed by the government to open 20-25 new supermarkets a year in Germany. It was pure fantasy to think it could conquer the world.

Yet a spokesman for Wal-Mart said, not auspiciously, "The move is part of Wal-Mart's goal of doubling its German market share in hypermarkets to 20 percent in the next three years." Jurgen Elfers, the President of Metro, said, "Obsessed with the idea of large hypermarkets, Wal-Mart expected to be profitable 'within a few years.'" or at least it boldly said so. (9)

Three years later Wal-Mart found itself with only 91 stores, and 1.3 percent of sales. It had bought the stores "without really examining what it was buying." While the 21 Wertkauf stores were adequate, the 74 Interspar stores were not.

The Interspar stores it had bought were scattered throughout Germany, and on the outskirts of the cities. The German magazine Wirtschaftswoche, had said of them, "Stores are described as dirty and poorly kept, cartons and pallets are lying around, vegetables are not fresh. Expediters have to wait for hours to load goods at the central warehouse. The largest German competitors, many of them with much more modern and well-kept stores, have successfully answered the challenge of "everyday low prices." Wal-Mart had bought what was available, and dreamed they would grow. "By acquiring the outlets of a second-tier retailer, Wal-Mart wound up with a hodgepodge of stores, geographically dispersed and often in poor locations." (10)

Lidl and Aldi

What Wal-Mart didn't count on was that Germany's retail food market had been in the doldrums. By 2002, only a decade later, German households spent only 30 percent instead of 40 percent on food. They suffered from overcapacity in food, and in supermarkets. Prices in supermarkets were very low.

Into this market came Wal-Mart, eager to bombard the country with its famous "everyday low prices" (EDLP). But Wal-Mart soon found out that Lidl and Aldi had "no frills—cheap supermarkets." They already had prices which were even lower than Wal-Mart. They were like Wal-Mart hard discounters with small stores. With a market share of 40 percent, they were ready to snuff out their rivals. Lidl had 5,600 stores and 80,000 employees in Germany alone. Aldi, had had 4,000 stores, and Germans preferred to go shopping at the small stores. (11) Wal-Mart's were also too distant from most of the population—in the far-off suburbs. Finally, McKinsey published a report saying that:

"The success of hard discounters Aldi and Lidl changed traditional retailing and supermarkets more fundamentally than had been thought until now . . . The discounter's business model is based on extreme simplicity, efficiency, and speed. Thus, Aldi and Lidl are visibly changing the behavior of the Germans." (12)

Lidl, if not Aldi, was also a difficult employer to work for. In fact Ver.di, the union to which all service workers belong—a group of three million workers—says of it, "Lidl in Germany must be something of the worst that European retailing has ever seen in the way of systematic violations of workers' and trade union rights . . . Lidl seems to take 'Walmartization' of its employer policies to new heights." (13)

Since about the end of World War II, the Germans have been strongly unionized; it is an important part of their culture, and an important part of their workplace experience. They deal with the unions in every aspect of their relations with management. They have works councils; the Chairs of the works councils are elected from their ranks, and represent the workers to the company. In most German workplaces which have over ten workers a Chair of the works council is elected by the workers. A worker represents his or her firm and sits on the Board of Directors. They must "sign off" on everything management does, "from hiring and firing, to the position of desks in an office." (14)

But Lidl and Aldi don't permit unions in their stores, and in Germany that's a violation of the spirit of the country. Ver.di has written a book about Lidl, attesting to the ways it violates workers' rights—and most of its workers are women. The Black Book on Lidl, the "Schwarzbuch," with a reference to company founder Dieter Schwarz, was written in 2006. "Schwarz" in German, means "black"; thus, the "Black Book." The book argues that Lidl " . . . has failed to adapt to trade unions, social dialogue, and collective agreements" and, much like Wal-Mart, even has closed stores rather than accept unionization. "Trade unions have not been able to force the company to behave, with the result that an atmosphere of fear and intimidation can freely reign." (15) But, just like Wal-Mart in America, the German customers, rather than the employees, love it and shop there.

When Wal-Mart was the leading supermarket in the United States, its German stores were ranked at the bottom of the German retail market. As early as 2001, its "future expansion in Europe has been slowed dramatically." Indeed, Wal-Mart only managed to survive as long as it did through the beneficence of the parent company in Bentonville. Already, in 2001, the Financial Times Deutschland estimated that the company had accumulated over $250 million in losses for the past year. (16) Wal-Mart, at the time, was the only foreign-owned supermarket in Germany, and it did manage to open two hypermarkets in the next three years.

"Every-Day Low Prices"

The corporation also challenged the State in Germany. As early as 2000, Wal-Mart cut its prices below wholesale price levels. Aldi and Lidl, in response to Wal-Mart, cut their own prices by up to 25 percent, leading to a price war that ended up in court. The court found that, against the law, all three of them had cut their prices too low on milk, butter, flour, and cooking oil. Nevertheless, Wal-Mart firmly refused to raise its prices even when the court determined that the low prices were illegal. Then Wal-Mart took its case to the state court in Dusseldorf for an appeal, and it won.

Incensed at Wal-Mart's behavior, the Federal Cartel Office took Wal-Mart to the Supreme Court, which finally ruled in 2002 that "selling products below wholesale prices hurt competition by creating an unfair environment for smaller and mid-sized stores," confirming its illegality. The case was ultimately settled by a final ruling. Wal-Mart was forced to raise its prices. (17)

However, while the case was before the Supreme Court, Wal-Mart announced another round of price cuts. It sent a circular to German homes (which had never been done in Germany before), to announce there would be price cuts on "300 products, both food and non-food, at its 95 supermarkets."

The Unions

Ver.di and Wal-Mart faced each other over the union. Wal-Mart refused to sign the company–management agreements, (which are voluntary), and even refused to have the union enter its store. As a result, the shop stewards who, in the absence of union rules had to obey management found themselves facing the prospect of reprisals. Although they couldn't be fired (according to German law), they were nevertheless coerced to work after hours, and not paid for their time. (18) In this way, the kind of wage abuse that Wal-Mart practiced in some of its stores in the U.S., was carried over into Germany.

After a series of strikes by its workers, and warnings from Ver.di, Wal-Mart consistently refused to enter into, or to negotiate, its own deal with Ver.di. Ver.di had met with the executive in charge of Wal-Mart in Germany, and he had refused to budge. It was said that Wal-Mart had threatened to fire the workers who insisted on meeting with the works councils. "Apparently afraid of their own staff, Wal-Mart had strictly forbidden the works councils of the previously separate companies, Interspar and Wertkauf, to meet together."

At one point, Ver.di wrote a letter to the Arkansas headquarters demanding the company either join the German employers' association or sign a collective wage agreement. Wal-Mart did neither. It ignored the letter. Ulrich Dalibor, the head of the German union, said, "I don't think they won't sign. I think they can't because Wal-Mart U.S. won't let them." (19) Yet, finally Ver.di forced Wal-Mart to "apply" all the union's "collective agreement provisions." And then Wal-Mart put leaflets on its bulletin boards "complaining that the "bad trade union" had forced them to respect collective agreement for worker's' wages and working conditions." One worker said of this, "Bentonville didn't want to have anything to do with unions. They thought we were communists." (20)

Ver.di said it was anxious to see Wal-Mart's profits and losses, to open its books, so it could judge how to treat their rivals. Wal-Mart claimed it "was organized as a limited partnership under laws that permitted it not to disclose earnings and other financial data." Wal-Mart even appealed to the German Supreme Court against a ruling that would force it to open its accounts. (21)

"Flirting" at Work

Then, in 2005, Wal-Mart made another faux pas. The giant retailer attempted to impose a code of conduct on employees, complete with a secret informant hot line. Workers were under threat of job loss if they failed to report co-workers' suspected code violations. (22)

And what was Wal-Mart's "code of conduct"? The code "forbids intimate relationships" among employees. No flirting, off-color sexual jokes, or even relationships between the workers are to occur in the workplace. This was de rigueur in the U.S. The most egregious flaw in it was that all employees were required "to inform on each other if they suspected violations." This code was exactly what was adhered to, and enforced, in the Wal-Mart stores in the United States, and presumably still is today.

Ver.di argued that Wal-Mart was implementing this "ethics" code without consulting them. German Wal-Mart headquarters claimed that they had "informed" the worker-management councils about it "when the ethical guidelines were distributed." (23) Then Ver.di told

Wal-Mart that the "ethical guidelines" had to be approved by works councils, they could not simply be "told" about it. Of course, the informer "hotline" was never "approved" by the staff, because it reminded many Germans of the "dark and distant past of fascist and communist rule, of which this was an essential part." (24) Also, the workers could not see that there were "ethical guidelines" involved at all. They had not voted on the code and Wal-Mart had not asked them to do so.

Inevitably, the Germans and Wal-Mart went to court over this almost trivial issue as well. The court "gutted Wal-Mart's code of conduct, and upheld the right of workers to flirt on the job." But much more important, the law says, "An informer hotline is a violation against the German constitution." And the fact that the company refused to consult with the works councils before imposing the doctrine also was seen as illegal. (25)

"Friendliness" One More Defect

Once more, the Americans also brought with them their "smiling" policy—straight from America; more explicitly from the South. It has permeated all the stores. However, in Germany customers perceived the pervasive smile as "phony," as a sign of deception. "Germans and most Europeans view friendliness as a prelude to an unwanted sales pitch. And when clerks followed orders to smile at shoppers, male customers took it as a come-on."

There was also a "ten-foot rule,"—or a "three-meter rule." Sales "associates" were supposed to say, "May I help you?" at a distance of three meters or less. This rule was taken as a sign of intrusiveness by the Germans. Customers felt they had their space violated. They certainly thought the "greeter" was even more insidious. "I hate when someone walks next to me carrying my stuff," says Matthias Queck, who is a student in Frankfurt. It's like he's my slave. My next thought is, "Do I have to tip him now or what?" The Germans look down on "friendliness," since it is perceived as "hypocrisy or currying favor. They want to sell me something, that's why they are so friendly." (26)

And then there was the bagging. When the customers checked out their purchases there was, as in every supermarket in the U. S., someone to pack their bags. But German supermarket patrons wanted no one to touch their purchases. No other German supermarket had a bagger. "Helpfulness" should not be intrusive.

The Failure of Wal-Mart—In Germany

Wal-Mart knew it was over when the competition "snatched up" a number of store chains that were selling right under Wal-Mart's nose. Although it tried to buy more stores from its German competitors, the sellers were not "playing ball." At that point Wal-Mart knew it had to abandon its plans in Germany, and leave. "I think Wal-Mart is talking to privately-owned chains every couple of months about buying branches, but the word is that no one is willing to sell." (27)

Meanwhile, the German stores weren't making more than 1 percent profit on sales at most stores. In America each year, Wal-Mart made about 8 percent profit; business was good there.

Towards the end of its stay in Germany, the huge giant had little choice—it was losing money, and lots of money, for each year it was there. Bentonville saw only a flood of German red ink.

Wal-Mart had spent money refurbishing its stores and engaging in massive advertising; it even advertised on television, which other stores wouldn't hear of. And it got no tax-breaks in Germany like those it got in the United States. Faced with regulations unlike those it had ever seen before, the only thing it could do was to lower its prices. For if Wal-Mart were to succeed in Germany, it would have to buy more stores. It would then be able to purchase more cheaply from distributors. But that was not to be.

The Failure

It was ironic that Wal-Mart sold its German stores to Metro. When its assets were totaled in Germany, it seems it lost over a billion dollars. Lee Scott said as early as 2000 that "the foray into Germany had been a "failure." For each year for all the time it was there, it lost money. Wal-Mart had generated great hostility. It wanted to bring "American culture" to Germany with its big American hypermarkets and its Wal-Mart cheer, as well as making big profits. In reality, the "associates" (they were called that in Germany, too) hurried off to the bathroom whenever it was time to do the Wal-Mart cheer.

Only later, when Wal-Mart left Germany, did it acknowledge that it had made mistakes. And, needless to say, Germany as well as Ver.di was only too glad to agree.

Footnotes

1. "Who's Afraid of Wal-Mart?" Financial Times (London), May 5, 1999.
2. Teena Lyons, "Wal-Mart to Storm Europe," The Mail on Sunday, June 20, 1999.
3. Susannah Patton, "Merger Mania Hits Europe: Fear of Wal-Mart Prompts Businesses to Seek Partners," The Ottawa Citizen, August 31, 1999.
4. John Schmid, "In Germany, Wal-Mart Touches Off a Price War," The International Herald Tribune, November 11, 1998.
5. "Wal-Mart Stores in German Press Insists that Wal-Mart is Discussing a Take-Over," UNI Commerce, July 19, 2000; "Operations Evolve to Offset Doldrums in Deutschland," DSN Retailing Today, June 2000.
6. "Facing Up to the Threat of Wal-Mart," Retail Week, September 24, 1999.
7. Lauren Mills, "Merger to Create French Retail Giant: Carrefour, Promodes to Unite: Move Expected to Make it Harder for Wal-Mart to Find Route Into France," National Post (Canada), August 30, 1999.
8. Julian Hunt, "Wal-Mart Eyes Three German Operators," October 16, 1999.
9. Wal-Mart, Chain Store Age Executive with Shopping Center Age, September 2000. "Discounters Seen as Opportunity for Wal-Mart," Food and Drink, (Europe), November 11, 2005.
10. "European Commerce Workers Don't Want to be Low-Paid Cheerleaders, Unions Say," UNI Commerce, March 7, 2000.
11. "Why Did Wal-Mart Fail in Germany (so far)?" Andreas Knorr and Andreas Arndt, Department of Business Studies and Economics, Institute of World Economics and International Management, Bremen, Germany.
12. The Schwarz Group (Lidl) March 1, 2004.
13. "Employer Rules Over Workers by Intimidation and Fear," UNI Commerce, March 22, 2006.

14. "Wal-Mart Throws in the Towel in Germany as Social Dumping Did Not Work," UNI Commerce, July 28, 2005.
15. The Schwarz Group (Lidl) March 1, 2004.
16. "Wal-Mart Concept Fails in Germany," Deutsche Welle (DW-World.De), February 11, 2001.
17. "Wal-Mart Sells Milk and Butter Below Cost Hurts Competition: German Court, Associated Press, November 12, 2002.
18. "Wal-Mart Throws in the Towel in Germany as Social Dumping Did Not Work," UNI Commerce, July 28, 2000. (Op. cit.)
19. "Wal-Mart Throws in the Towel in Germany as Social Dumping Did Not Work," UNI Commerce, July 28, 2000. (Ibid.)
20. Mark Landler and Michael Barbaro,,"Germany: Wal-Mart Finds That Its Formula Doesn't Work." The New York Times, August 1, 2000. Progressive Grocer. Com. April 4, 2003.
21. Progressive Grocer. Com. April 4, 2003. (Ibid.)
22. "Wal-Mart Imposes KGB-Style Informant System on German Employees," Wake-Up Wal-Mart.com, March 18, 2005.
23. "Wal-Mart Violates German Labor Laws," Workers Independent, May 12, 2005.
24. "Wal-Mart Cannot Seem to Get it Right in Germany—Informer Hotline was Closed by German Court Order," UNI Commerce, December 7, 2005; "Wal-Mart Faces Criticism on Ethics Code," Associated Press Forbes Magazine, March 16, 2005; "Wal-Mart Violates German Labor Laws," Workers Independent News, May 12, 2005. (Ibid.)
25. "Customer Service Translates Differently in Germany," The Denver Business Journal, January 25, 2002.
26. "Wal-Mart Runs into Culture Shock in Germany," Knight Ridder/Tribune Business News, December 27, 2001.
27. Harald Schultz, "This is Not America. Why Wal-Mart Left Germany," The Atlantic Times, A Monthly Newspaper from Germany, September 2006.

5

Mexico—The Jewel in the Crown

❧

"I really don't see what is to prevent us from owning all of Mexico and running it to suit ourselves."
—William Randolph Hearst

Wal-Mart de Mexico, or Walmex as it is called, is the largest supermarket chain in Mexico. Except for the United States, Mexico is the biggest Wal-Mart chain in the world today, and it is growing bigger every day. At the end of 2011, it had 2,041 retail outlets and 24 distribution centers. As of December 2011 there were supermarkets under the names of Wal-Mart, Suburbia, VIPS, Bodega Aurrera, Mi Bodega Aurrera, Superama, Bodega Aurrera Express, Suburbia, Farmacia Wal-Mart, and two restaurants—El Porton and Ragazzi—in 348 cities. It had 209,000 employees. (1) Some 40 percent of Mexicans are employed by U.S. companies and American companies employed 50 to 60 percent of the retail sector in 2009. (2) The latest news is that Wal-Mart will build 252 new stores in Mexico in 2009, and plans to add 300 stores in 2010. And it will employ 14,500 more workers. (3) In fact, the idea that "nobody can beat Wal-Mart" is not that it has grown by adding more shoppers, but by adding more stores. (4) It also is the happy owner of a national bank in Mexico, thanks to NAFTA. The Banco Adelante de Mexico is

Wal-Mart's bank, of which it says it will open 1,500 banking units all over Mexico. (5)

It was largely NAFTA, the North American Free Trade Act, which enabled Wal-Mart to penetrate Mexico. In 1991, when NAFTA was under discussion in Congress, Wal-Mart bought a 6 percent share of Cifra, a large Mexican chain of stores. In 1997, after NAFTA was passed, Wal-Mart then went ahead and purchased a 51 percent and controlling share. Cifra operated the strongest and largest supermarket chain in the country, and Wal-Mart rapidly added Supercenters and Sam's Clubs to Cifra's existing market. As Kenneth Bensinger of The Christian Science Monitor said, "Indeed, since a consolidation in 1997, Wal-Mart de Mexico, or Walmex . . . has steadily gobbled up everything in its path." (6)

Mexico had already signed the World Trade Organization's General Agreement on Tariffs and Trade (GATT) as early as 1987. As one journalist said, "It is "NAFTA and the WTO [which has] paved the way for Wal-Mart to become the world's largest corporation." And "there is no debate over the dramatic changes in Wal-Mart's operations, following the passage of NAFTA in 1994." (7) In 2007, "fourteen years of incremental decreases had wiped out 90 percent of all protectionist barriers." (8)

Wal-Mart is truly a major power in Mexico, and throughout the world. Its other off-shore establishments account for one-quarter of Wal-Mart's international sales, and Mexico is the second most successful retail store chain in all of Wal-Mart's far-flung empire.

Wal-Mart in Mexico is like a game of Monopoly. The executives do not have to think about if, or where, to build stores. They decide on the most lucrative place they can be located, and then Wal-Mart officials bribed the gatekeepers. This kind of bribery had been going on for almost seven years, since 2005, until the U.S. got wind of it. And. Wal-Mart knew all about it. Wal-Mart, put its highest ethical ideals against its relentless desire for growth, and built more stores. (9) It was as if you would add "houses" to your "property" in Monopoly. Why did they do it? They did it because they had $24 million to spend, that's what they spent on bribes—and, of course, Mexico was an easy place to bribe officials.

Walmex in Mexico is very different from Wal-Mart in any other place. In England, for example, Asda has struggled a long time for control of its markets, but it hasn't gotten where it wants to be, at the number one spot in the U.K., because it can't build or buy additional supermarkets. And this has led to an impasse in some cases.

But Wal-Mart has come to virtually "own" Mexico's retail sector. Most importantly, it has come to dominate South America. During these years it would open stores in Argentina, Brazil, Costa Rica, El Salvador, Guatemala, Nicaragua, Chile, and Puerto Rico—although it already had large holdings in Latin America; particularly Brazil, Chile, Argentina and, of course, in Central America.

Sinergia

In 2004 Mexico approved Sinergia. It was a marketing cooperative in which the native Mexican supermarkets wanted to participate along with Wal-Mart. In that year it was formed as a marketing cooperative in an attempt to give Soriana, Gigante, and Comercial Mexicana an opportunity to give the three indigenous Mexican chains an opportunity to share with Wal-Mart access to its suppliers in Mexico. But in August 2011 it failed, because Wal-Mart refused to give the three other store chains access to its vast overseas supply chain from which it got 97 percent of its produce.

Wal-Mart was much larger than the others. It had reached 1,364 stores while Soriana had only 508 stores. The imports were responsible for destroying 200,000 jobs, including 130,000 manufacturing jobs. (10) And, for the whole of the Walmex empire in Mexico, its profits were a total of three times those of the three competitors (Gigante, Soriana, and Comercial Mexicana). In fact, Carrefour, a key global rival of Wal-Mart, pulled out in 2005 after failing to gain a share of an increasingly competitive market dominated by Wal-Mart. (11)

Just as it is putting people out of work, Walmex is also putting smaller stores in Mexico out of business, just as it did in the United

States. Walmex sells at low prices and is making its products a "bargain." "By seizing upon the new opportunities offered by 'free trade' and exploiting its massive buying power and distribution network, Wal-Mart, Middle America's most popular merchant, is replicating its U.S. success." (12) Consider the example of Act II Popcorn! Sam's Club was buying Act II Popcorn, which is made in the U.S. A small Mexican shopkeeper, Carlos Huerta, would go into Sam's Club and buy $6,000 worth of popcorn, and then resell it in his shop. Before NAFTA he used to get it from a distributor in Mexico "for only a few cents more than U.S. stores."

Wal-Mart stores now can deliver the popcorn to its Mexican Sam's Club outlets for only a few pennies more than to U.S. stores, undercutting the product's Mexican distributor, and undercutting Mr. Huerta. Mr. Huerta and the distributor have lost a lot of business. "Now, thanks to NAFTA, Wal-Mart can buy Act II directly from U.S.-based ConAgra foods, which manufactures the product, and even slaps on a Spanish-language label at Wal-Mart's behest."(13) However, a lot of people go directly to Sam's Club, now rather than to Mr. Huerta for popcorn.

Wal-Mart has put out of business "an estimated 28,800 small-to-medium-sized businesses" as "Wal-Mart has undercut small, local shoe, candy, and toy manufacturers and other small retailers." (14)

In the developing world, in countries like Mexico most of the traditional producers of food are small farmers. They have been badly hurt by NAFTA. For example, U.S. corn growers were only paying 18 cents of the value of their exports of corn to Mexico, because the American government had provided them not only with "free trade" but also with massive subsidies. Tortillas, a food that all Mexicans eat, cost 9 pesos a kilo, too much for the typical Mexican. As the Mexicans say, "Without Corn, There is No Country—And Also Without Beans." (15)

In Mexico, most of the farmers in the south are corn farmers. When the United States lowered its price for corn and subsidized it, it came flooding into Mexico at prices way below what the farmers could produce it for. The farmers in Mexico couldn't produce it cheaply enough to compete with the price of American corn. These farmers could not sell their corn, which is the lifeblood of Mexico. Therefore, Mexico's small food producers, have been excluded from the new system of food retailing, and have lost their farms.

It is hardly surprising that the farmers are becoming impoverished, and tend to migrate to the cities in the north of Mexico in the hope of finding some type of work, or fearfully cross the border to the United States. But now it is more dangerous; it is illegal. The only things that have helped the Mexicans to fend off poverty and keep some of the Mexicans in Mexico have been three factors—remittances from the United States, migration to the U. S., or, at the very least, political protest. (16)

In the center and south of the country, where the bulk of the agricultural population is located, the rural communities have become unstable and impoverished. There has been a decline in subsistence agriculture, widespread rural poverty, and food insecurity. "We cannot compete against this monster, this monster the United States," said one farmer, Enrique Barrera Perez, who is 44 and works about five acres in Yucutan. "It's not worth the trouble to plant. We don't have the subsidies. We don't have the machinery." (17) No one will lend to farmers because they have no collateral, especially those in poverty with their small acreages.

There has been impoverishment followed by a new dependence on remittances. The displaced Mexican farmers, with the old laws, and even the ones who feared being displaced, were not averse to protests. In 2006 "demonstrators stormed a Wal-Mart on the outskirts of Mexico City." Then 250 protesters chanted "Out! Out!" in front of Wal-Mart's corporate headquarters, where they blocked aisles in the adjacent store for about 30 minutes before leaving. (18) In response to this strike Wal-Mart issued a very ambiguous statement. It agreed to grant some of the workers' demands and it signed a new labor contract. Camacho said, "Whether collective bargaining will result from this contract is anybody's guess."

Remittances from the United States are sometimes what hold the people in Mexico. "The rate of remittance growth slowed to just 1 percent in 2007, far less than the average annual increase of 19 percent from 2003 through 2006," because the U.S. housing slump squeezed the construction industry. Mexicans make up 20 percent, or 2.9 million workers in the construction industry in the United States, down from 3.3 percent last year. (19)

Remittances to families are the second biggest source of income in Mexico. Their decline was the largest since the Banco de Mexico started counting in 1995. What is more disturbing is that remittances pay for 90 percent of consumption. That is, in part, what ties the U.S. to Mexico.

Remittances from those who have gone to the United States make up 2.8 percent of the Mexican GDP, an amount only slightly less than oil revenues. (20) But small holders have no lobbying power that might influence the government.

Mexicans have a love/hate relationship with the United States. Mexicans are always anxious to immigrate to America; they come here as to the "promised land." But some of those who remain in Mexico dislike the "Americanization" or "the globalization" of Mexico, given its impoverization of small farmers.

Supermarkets for the Poor—and Some for the Rich

When the recession hit, the Mexicans got poorer and poorer. To cater to their needs, in Mexico Wal-Mart has built and opened 132 stores, including 113 Bodegas Aurrera, the vast majority of which are to cater to the poor. Wal-Mart also noted that more of the Mexican shoppers in their supermarkets than ever before "are spending less each time and buying necessities rather than discretionary items." (21) Its sales rose in the Bodegas Aurrera stores more than twice as much as in the other stores it owns. It rose 11.9 percent at the Bodega Aurrera, while its other stores rose only 4.7 percent.

Bodega Express is offering "smaller, cheaper products and allowed the stores to tap into demand for single boxes of cereal, milk and Tortillas [for] Mexicans who buy meal-to meal." At the same time, Wal-Mart had, by contrast, built only ten Wal-Mart stores for people who can buy more, and purchase for a longer time. In Mexico, a full 73 percent of the 270 stores Wal-Mart opening that year were be Bodega Express units. (22) President and Chief Executive of Walmex, Eduardo Solarzano had said, "Purchasing power has been diminished. We're trying to adapt as much and as fast as we can." (23) They were trying to build stores as fast as they can. And Wal-Mart hurried to build more of these stores with the crisis.

Wal-Mart also has Suburbia department stores for the mid-brow, and its Superama supermarkets for the "luxury" items such as imported teas along with everyday produce. Thus Walmex can target the whole Mexican population, a feat which no other supermarket chain can do.

In 2010, Mexico opened 300 stores and invested $971 million. Part of this was for the 20 percent of the population who are middle-class or rich. Retailers are building malls "across the country" for the well-to-do. Wal-Mart has spent at least $1.5 billion thus far, and is currently building a shopping center that costs $43 million. When it opens, it will have "a multiplex cinema, a children's play area, an outdoor food court, a chapel, some 100 small stores, and an outdoor theatre for live entertainment," instead of the usual Mexican plaza with a simple fountain in the middle." It is designed to be a town center. Wal-Mart, after all, "has the second highest market capitalization of any company on Mexico's stock exchange." (24)

When "Wal-Mart builds a store, there is nothing you can do except protest." Wal-Mart wanted to build a store near a historical monument or site that has ancient significance in Mexico, in Merida Yucatan, Tchamacalso Puebla. It has been besieged and stalled by activists and demonstrations. (25)

In an interview with the Financial Times, Wal-Mart CEO Lee Scott said the company was looking at acquisition opportunities all over the world, "in countries like Hungary, Poland, and Russia." (26)

Wages and Women's Wages—In Wal-Mart, Mexico

One can make some inferences about their wages. One journalist said:

A Wal-Mart de Mexico cashier making the starting pay of $7.45 per day would have to work eight hours to be able to buy a loaf of bread, a gallon of milk, and toilet paper. Security guards start at even less—$6.63 per day. (27)

Accordingly, a Mexican woman worker (nearly 80 percent of those who work for Walmex are women) can earn approximately $1,937 a year. Or, according to Chris Tilly, a woman who works in the Sonora Walmex earns $1,133 a year; while one working in a store in some rural states, where the wages are lower, earns only $1,068 a year. (28) Thus, depending on location, the pay varies greatly, from about $1,000 to about $2,000 at the maximum, a significant difference from the point of view of Mexican women workers, and certainly a much greater variation than for women who work in a U.S. Wal-Mart. Women who work in the U.S. earn about $8.50 an hour, or approximately $17,580 year. That difference in absolute wages between the US and Mexico is, in part, what makes Wal-Mart so wealthy. Wal-Mart workers in Mexico earn almost ten times less than what Wal-Mart workers earn in the USA. Hardly a good wage! And prices are not often that much more in the United States. For example:

The Mexican product prices used in the purchase calculations above come from Minneapolis-based Resource Center of the Americas, a non-profit organization that promotes human rights. The organization gathered the prices of ordinary items such as bread, toilet paper, milk, and deodorant in Nuevo Laredo, Mexico and found the costs were about the same as prices in Minneapolis. Eggs, beef, potatoes, and cornflakes were more expensive in Mexico. (29)

According to Chris Tilly "A Mexican earns $2,496, on average, in national compensation in retail." A supermarket worker's wage then is even less than in other retail stores. Furthermore, women's retail jobs account for nearly one job in five in Mexico. And, if the level of pay in large national Mexican chains is equal to Walmex's pay, the actual entry-level pay in Mexico for supermarket workers is only 30 cents per hour more than that for workers in market stands. (30)

Tilly and Alvarez also report that "Mexican law requires employers to provide paid vacation . . . and medical coverage for full-time work-ers. Wal-Mart in the U.S. gives its workers a paid vacation, but the "medical coverage" is poor. But in Mexico, the laws governing health care and vacations are widely broken. And the turnover rate for retail workers is high. It's not surprising then that 30 percent of supermarket workers left the staff of Walmex "in the third trimester of 2004; imply-ing an annual turnover rate of 120 percent."

The Volunteer Program

Furthermore, an additional 19,000 youngsters between the ages of 14 and 16 work after school in hundreds of Wal-Mart stores, mostly as grocery baggers, throughout Mexico—and none of them receives a red cent in wages or fringe benefits" . . . Thus there are "thousands of Walmex baggers working for tips only, no salary." (31)

The "volunteer" program, as it is called, is for teenagers 14 to 16, and their only compensation is also "tips." There are 19,000 youths who work for no pay at Wal-Mart. But the Mexican law expressly for-bids any "associate" from working without compensation. The young-sters are happy to do it even though none of them are paid anything; mostly as grocery baggers only for tips. In fact, there is a long queue for these "jobs. Wal-Mart was criticized for this when the Federal District Labor Secretary Benito Miron Lince spoke out, saying, "In economic terms, Wal-Mart does have the capability to pay the minimum wage [of less than $5 a day], and this represents an injustice." Mexican Labor Under-Secretary Patricia Espinosa Torres says, "If you ask me, I don't think these kids should be working, but there are cultural and social circumstances (in Mexico) rooted in poverty and scarcity." (32)

The company's headquarters in the United States says that the gro-cery baggers cannot be considered workers. Nevertheless, the baggers are providing a service that benefits the company by serving the cus-tomer better. Wal-Mart learned how to pay baggers nothing in Mexico, simply because it was done that way in Mexico. (33) It was done no-where else.

Keeping Unions Out

Inevitably, Walmex "suffered its first strike ever in the week of November 2007, when 300 workers from two stores and a restaurant walked out for a day in a dispute over pay and conditions." Jaime Carnacho, a top official from a grass-roots workers' movement (Revolutionary Confederation of Workers and Peasants, or CROC), was one of the people who went on strike. He said, "The Wal-Mart workers had complained about bad treatment from managers that they were not being paid overtime or given benefit packages similar to those awarded by other Walmex stores in the country." (34)

Workers typically strike or protest when they haven't any recourse, as in China. There are thousands of strikes in China by employees, because the workers are powerless against their employers. There is no one to adjudicate their grievances, because The All China Federation of Trade Unions (ACFTU,) only intervenes to help them when it serves the purpose of the state to do so. Mexicans often face the same problem. Walmex is unionized, but the accepted trade unions never intervene on the workers' behalf.

There is "universal coverage" of all Walmex workers. However, the workers' pay union dues, while they get no health insurance or anything else, and they demand little of the employer. The existence of a union serves to keep more militant and other "unions" out of the factory or other business concern. The existing unions "do little more than codify existing labor law," and company executives remarked that "the unions had minimal impact on their operations and policies. In most companies, workers were unaware that they were even covered by a union contract." (35) The Wal-Mart workers in Mexico have a "sweetheart contract," which is just as good as having no contract at all.

Wal-Mart, of course, has in reality an anti-union policy, which it has in all countries. Wal-Mart claims they have created a large number of jobs—over 160,000 jobs, to be sure. But the official minimum wage was higher than the wage Wal-Mart paid. It was at least 18 percent lower than the actual [minimum] wage in Mexico.

Recently, there has been a move to change this labor law (which is not in reality followed) to something that would put the workers in jeopardy. The government, the PRI, and a group of leading industrialists want to change the labor law to reflect their interests. The Mexican Labor Law is derived from the 1920s. It was a hard and fast labor law. As it says in Article 123 of the Mexican Constitution, "Workers have the right to jobs and permanent status once they're hired. If they're laid off they have the right to severance pay. They have the right to housing, health care, and training. In a legal strike, they can string flags against the doors of a factory or workplace, and even the owner can't enter until the dispute is settled." (36)

Changing the labor law would mean the right to eliminate all the "good" laws. It would mean eliminating the minimum wage: the wages would be set by the bosses; companies could contract out work; and workers would find it difficult to go on strike. Ultimately, it would increase both poverty and political submission. The industrialists themselves say the PRI reform will lead to a "paradise of firings." This law would only benefit the country's oligarchs, the men who have been on the political offensive for years. (37) And Wal-Mart is part of the oligarchy.

Instead of a decent union practice, Mexico now has "protection contracts"—and Wal-Mart alone has 200 of them in its stores in Mexico City. They are "collective agreements between the government and an enterprise known as a 'ghost' union." They needn't be published or made available or covered by the union or workers covered by the agreement. Workers have no knowledge of being represented by a contract. When workers have tried to request a copy of the contract they are immediately fired.

It is virtually impossible to replace a ghost union. Workers who try are frequently subjected to reprisals, intimidation, threats, violence, or blacklisting and firing. The "ghost" unions belong to corporate lawyers with whom the government has signed contracts with before an employee is hired. These contracts strip workers of their rights. Then the lawyer goes on to take the fees for the corporations of 1 to 3.5 percent from the workers' wages.

One of the most important methods of control are "protection contracts" rather than real collective bargaining agreements, Officials sign agreements with factory owners, who pay 'dues' for workers who often have no idea that the union organizes any independent effort to raise wages or improve conditions. The company and official union claim a contract is already in place. If workers try to protest, they're forced into a process before 'tripartite' labor boards dominated by business owners, politicians dependent on them, and the official unions. (38)

Banking

Wal-Mart attempted to establish a bank in the United States, called an "industrial loan corporation." Congress, both Democrats and Republicans—and especially the small bankers—vehemently opposed it. The small banks, like the small retail stores, feared that a monster like Wal-Mart would put them out of business. Wal-Mart realized its application for an industrial bank would be a death blow to the small banks if approved. Yet, Wal-Mart was all set to gobble them up. But, as it said, its bank was not really a bank, it was really an "industrial loan corporation." The "bank" was only to process credit card transactions. It had no desire to get into the business of retail banking.

Small banks in the U.S., as well as larger ones, have joined Wal-Mart's usual detractors, unions, small merchants, and community activists who challenged the bank in Congress, in special hearings. The Senate Finance Committee, due to the overwhelming opposition, issued a delay of a year before deciding whether the proposal of Wal-Mart's industrial bank was legal or illegal. At the point when Wal-Mart realized the bank proposal was not to be, it withdrew its banking application from Congress for an "industrial loan corporation." Several months later, it opened a bank in Mexico. Needless to say, the bank was warmly received.

This bank, Wal-Mart de Adelante as it is called, is targeted towards low-income Mexicans just as Wal-Mart targets its stores in the United States. The goal is "Low cost so we can be low-priced, low commission, low interest." It will not compete with foreign banks like Citibank and Spain's BBVA and Santander, which have banking primarily for the rich. It is unlikely to fail, because Wal-Mart's clients "have deposited more money than they have borrowed," and it is "likely to become a significant boost for sales as it hands out more credit to customers." (39)

Wal-Mart pays its "associates" with a bank card that employees can only use to withdraw their salaries at the store's ATM machines. They can use any money that is left over, with this electronic card—but only for purchasing products at Wal-Mart.

In September 2008, the Mexican Court ruled that electronic cards usable only in Wal-Mart stores were unconstitutional and exploitative like 19th century wage schemes in which rural workers were only allowed to shop at the "company store," at outrageously high prices—a practice which kept them in a state of debt. However, the ruling only applied to the worker who brought the lawsuit. (40)

The U.S.-owned Banamex, the Canadian–owned Scotia Bank, the United Kingdom's HSBC, the Spanish-owned Bancomer and Santander, and Bank of America, Prudential, Wal-Mart, and J.P. Morgan have entered the financial services market of Mexico.

Eighty percent of Mexicans, were "unbanked," i.e., did not even have a bank account as of 2009. There were then 44 million low-income unbanked Mexicans, who earned between $2,000 and $8,000 per year. These people have been excluded from any kind of financial services, and there are only eight banks for every 100,000 people. After Wal-Mart has set the stage, other supermarket owners like Chedraui, Coppel, and Famsa are planning to open banks as well. The Wal-Mart de Mexico's Banco Adelante in the next five years is expected to have 900 "credit stores." It will have many outlets, like its supermarkets, to make it accessible and beat out the competition. In 2011, Wal-Mart's bank has 1,356 banking outlets.

While the older foreign banks served only the elite, the hope was that the Wal-Mart bank would charge less, and induce the foreign banks (the famous seven) to also charge less for all their services. Yet, Wal-Mart de Adelante charges a 75 percent rate of interest for each personal loan—for a refrigerator or a business debt. (41)

This rate of interest is a bit less than the foreign banks charge, but not much. With no legal limits on interest levels and little government oversight, for-profit banks in Mexico impose annual interest rates on poor borrowers that typically range from 50 percent to 120 percent. "The worldwide average is 31 percent among non-profit micro-lending institutions, unlike the 22 percent to 29 percent that Americans pay if they have bad credit ratings." (42)

The Credit Card Scam

The foreign banks still have extraordinarily high "fees and interest rates." Now, all the banks are purveyors of credit cards. "Nowadays, not only Wal-Mart but Citigroup's Banamex, Santander, HSBC, and other foreign–based outfits" offer credit cards. (43)

In 2008, the recession interfered with Wal-Mart's development plans for banking in Mexico. More recently, in 2010 Wal-Mart planned to double its number of Banco Adelante banks, planning to open more than 160 new branches throughout the country.

Banco Wal-Mart will "focus on the lower-income market and undercut rivals." It will be easy to use by the poor. "It will be located just outside store entrances. It will have a teller window and cubicles where three or four employees can sign up new customers for credit cards and checking accounts."(44)

Fewer than half of Mexicans now have checking or savings accounts. It will serve as a "source of credit," so the poor can go shopping at Wal-Mart. If this is what Wal-Mart initially had in mind for the United States, no wonder the other stores and small banks were opposed to it.

The Wal-Mart bank, Wal-Mart de Adelante, operates like Banco Azteca, the one which is a model for Wal-Mart. A Supercenter just west of Mexico City sold a Whirlpool refrigerator for $1,100—with 104 weekly payments. The interest more than doubles the cost to $2,295, at an annual percentage rate of 86 percent over these two years. (45) But the population has faith in Wal-Mart as a "symbol of multinational power." The hope is still that Wal-Mart will "make banking in Mexico more competitive" and "force down interest rates and fees." The Banco

Wal-Mart Adelante started "modestly" with a stake of $25 million. (46) Banking is another way for Wal-Mart to leverage its income outside the U.S., and they are very great profits indeed. (47)

Between the stores and the banks Wal-Mart had two great sources of profit in Mexico. It was planning to increase the size and the reach of both. Although it doesn't break down the source of it profits, we can guess the best part of the company's profits come from Mexico. Walmex has dominated food sales in Mexico. As of January 2008, Walmex had about 30 percent of all Mexican food sales and approximately 6 percent of all retail sales in that country. (48) As the number one retailer, with its stores and banks that span the country, it also has a great deal of power. Wal-Mart is on its way to "colonize" Mexico, and now is reaching out to all of Latin America.

Job Losses

After 1997, we observe a faster increase in Wal-Mart's imports in real terms compared with competitors. If we look at the imports-to-purchases ratio, we see that all the enterprises have been significantly increasing the share of imports in their purchases,, but also that Wal-Mart has shown a much more dramatic evolution: from 20 percent to more than 55 percent in 2002 and 2003. (49) Wal-Mart's pursuit of low prices significantly affected the total levels of imports into Mexico. These findings echo similar conclusions by the Economic Policy Institute, which analyzed Wal-Mart's effects on imports and jobs in the U.S. It concluded that Wal-Mart's imports alone were responsible for destroying 200,000 jobs—including 130,000 manufacturing jobs—between 2001 and 2006. Wal-Mart's massive bargaining power and its import practices would also lead to increased job losses, just as the Economic Policy Institute found.

La Ventosa

Mexico has "scams" for everything. Although, Mexico needs the power, Mexico has built a wind farm that will supply the electricity only to Wal-Mart stores. In 2009, Mexico launched La Ventosa, or

Windy, the world's largest wind farm project. "Critics argue that foreign companies build the turbines, rent the land, run the project, and
produce the power for companies like the U.S.-owned retailer, Wal-
Mart." Costing $550 million . . . the project hasn't been welcomed
by local residents, who say they see few benefits and aren't being paid
enough for the use of their land," and "around 7 percent of the people
have no electricity at all." (50)

But what the people do not know is that the 14 percent of aid to
the United Kingdom has been taken from the World Bank, and used to
fund La Ventosa, although "agriculture, particularly corn plantations,
is the essence of our region and will be completely displaced by the
wind farm projects." (51) In the euphoria of growth, it was often said,
"Wal-Mart is changing the landscape of Mexico." Wal-Mart is so flush
with cash that "Walmex also plans to set up its own electricity plants
and infrastructure next to its facilities," to offset that which Wal-Mart
lacks and needs. (52) Wal-Mart's massive bargaining power, and its
import practices, are demonstrated in its report "Power to the People."
The report details how money taken from the U.K. aid budget has
been used by the World Bank to finance wind farms by the Mexican
State of Oaxaca without the consent of the indigenous peoples who
owned the land. The project cost $860 million and produced enough
electricity to power 160,000 homes, but is instead being sold at a discount to Wal-Mart. The project is 99 percent controlled by the French
electricity giant EDF. The La Mata and La Ventosa wind park is in part
funded by the World Bank's Clean Technology Fund which receives 14
percent of its money—or 385 million pounds—from the U.K. overseas budget. The fund's objectives include poverty reduction but the
wind park has done nothing to increase energy access among the seven
percent of Oaxaca's population who have no electricity. (53) "It will
supply renewable power to establishments owned by the subsidiaries
of Wal-Mart." (54)

The World Development Movement's policy officer, Murray
Worthy, said that developing countries need financing to help them
go from a high-carbon economy to a low-carbon economy. But the La

Mata and La Ventosa Wind Park shows how dangerous it is to throw money at multinational companies like EDF and Wal-Mart. Of course, they don't help the people of Mexico who haven't any electricity at all.

It was built because the Mexican government could take advantage of "loopholes." As of recent days, concern with NAFTA and the WTO has taken a back seat to concern with the drug trade and the senseless violence that has ensued. But there has been little action to rescind NAFTA and put the farmers back in business. Too busy with the drug traffickers, President Calderon has said "his government was making strides against corruption" but the massive drug trade and the violence that has touched Mexico and parts of Central America, and even the United States, is continuing. They say that thousands of people have died so far. Gruesome gangland-style murders and targeted assassinations of law enforcement officers have claimed headlines in what Mexicans now refer to as war. Unfortunately, the would-be Mexican migrants are having increasing difficulty getting to the United States, much as the ones who had gotten here many years ago.

One might say that Mexico is almost becoming a colony of the United States. Its workers are getting poorer: they have no labor rights and there are no real unions. There are no banks except for the rich, and they charge more than 75 percent interest, at the lowest levels. Through NAFTA it has come into the country, built its supermarkets and banks, and profited from it. And Mexico was so poor it has given rise to drug lords and gangsters, and that has made it even poorer.

Footnotes

1. Wikipedia, Mexico, December 2011.
2. Chris Tilly and Jose Luis Alvarez Galvan, Lousy Jobs, Invisible Unions: The Mexican Retail Sector in the Age of Globalization, International Labor and Working Class History, No. 70, Fall 2006, pp. 61-85.
3. Sam Taliaferro, "Wal-Mart Set to Open 300 Mega Stores in Latin America," Latino Business Review, June 24, 2010.
4. Chris Tilly, "Wal-Mart Goes South: Sizing Up the Chain's Mexican Success Story," in Wal-Mart World, edited Stanley D. Brunn, 2006.
5. Karen Talley, "Wal-Mart to Expand Its Financial Services," The Wall Street Journal, 2009.
6. Kenneth Bensinger, "Like the U.S., Mexico Feels Wal-Mart Era," The Christian Science Monitor, March 15, 2005.
7. Marla Dickerson, "Retailers in Mexico Offer Discounts to Fight Inflation," Los Angeles Times, January 28, 2008.
8. John Ross, "Zero Hours, NAFTA and Mexico's Agrarian Apocalypse," Counterpunch, January 15, 2008.
9. David Barstow, "Vast Mexican Bribery Case Hushed Up by Wal-Mart After Top-Level Struggle," The New York Times, April 21, 2012.
10. "Wal-Mart Effect on Mexico Shows the True Price of Bargains," Bloomberg News, August 2, 2011,
11. John Lyons, "In Mexico. Wal-Mart is Defying Its Critics," The Wall Street Journal, March 5, 2007.
12. Chris Tilly, "Wal-Mart and Its Workers: Not the Same All Over the World," Connecticut Law Review, Volume 39, Number 4, May 2007.
13. David Luhnow, "Lower Tariffs, Retail Muscle Translate Into Big Sales for Wal-Mart in Mexico," The Wall Street Journal, August 31, 2001.
14. Another America is Possible: The Impact of NAFTA on the U.S. Latino Community and Lessons for Future Trade Agreements, A Joint Report from Labor Council of Latin American Advancement and Public Citizens Trade Watch, August 2004.

15. John Ross, "NAFTA and Mexico's Agrarian Apocalypse," Synthesis/Regeneration 47, Fall 2008.
16. Nathalie Gravel, "New Mexican Smallholders Adrift: The Urgent Need for a New Social Contract in Rural Mexico, Journal of Latin American Geography 6.2 (2007) 77-98.
17. James C. McKinley, "Mexican Farmers Protest End of Corn-Import Taxes," The New York Times, February 1, 2008.
18. Kathleen Miller, "Protesters Storm Wal-Mart in Mexico City," Associated Press (Baltimore Sun), November 14, 2006; Michael Thomas Derham, "Here Comes Wal-Mart," Latin Finance, September 1, 2006.
19. M. Angelos Villaroel, Specialist in International Trade and Finance, "US.-Mexico Relations: Trends, Issues and Implications," Congressional Research Service, April 3, 2009.
20. Elizabeth Malkin, "Money Sent Home by Mexican Workers in U.S. Falls Sharply," The New York Times, June 1, 2009.
21. "Hispanics' Hard Times Hit Wal-Mart," The Wall Street Journal, August 29, 2007.
22. Emily Schmall, "Wal-Mart Bodegas Lift Profit in Mexico," Bloomberg News, October 6, 2009.
23. Ibid.
24. Elizabeth Malkin, "Ole! Shopping Malls Sprint to Mexico," The New York Times, March 2, 2006.
25. John Ross, Counterpunch,"Wal-Mart Invades Mexico," March 17, 2005.
26. Brenon Daly, "Wal-Mart Looks Beyond the US, The Daily Deal, June 30, 2005."
27. Lynda Edwards, "Wal-Mart Pay Strife Crosses Borders," Arkansas Democrat-Gazette, August 3, 2006.
28. Chris Tilly, "Wal-Mart Goes South: Sizing Up the Chain's Mexican Success Story," in Wal-Mart World, edited by Stanley D. Brunn. 2006.
29. Ibid.
30. Chris Tilly, and Jose Luis Alvarez Galvan, "Lousy Jobs, Invisible

Unions: The Mexican Retail Sector in the Age of Globalization, International Labor and Working Class History," No. 70, Fall 2006, pp. 61-85.

31. Chris Tilly, and Jose Luis Alvarez Galvan, "Lousy Jobs, Invisible Unions: The Mexican Retail Sector in the Age of Globalization, International Labor and Working Class History," No. 70, Fall 2006, pp. 61-85.

32. "Pay the Kids," Wal-Mart Watch, (2005).

33. Joseph Contreras, "Mexico: Thousands of Unpaid Teens Bag Groceries for Wal-Mart," Newsweek, August 1, 2007.

34. "Workers Strike at Three Units of Mexico's Walmex," Reuters, February 7, 2008.

35. Chris Tilly, "Wal-Mart and Its Workers: Not the Same All Over the World," Connecticut Law Review, Volume 39, Number 4, May 2007.

36. Constitution of Mexico, Organization of American States. Also, see David Bacon, Labor Law Reform—A Key Battle for Mexican Unions Today, The Institute for Cross Border Social Change, June 6, 2011, for a full outline of this law reform.

37. "Walmex Issues Positive Steps on CSR Reporting But Falls Short on Labor Rights Issues," Maquila Solidarity Network, March 14, 2011; David Bacon, Labor Law Reform—A Key Battle for Mexican Unions Today, Truthout, June 6, 2011.

38. Chris Tilly, "Wal-Mart and Its Workers: Not the Same All Over the World," Connecticut Law Review, Volume 39, Number 4, May 2007.

39. Karen Talley, "Wal-Mart to Expand Its Financial Services," The Wall Street Journal, 2009.

40. Kent Peterson, "Mexico's Other Crisis: Foreign Banks," CorpWatch, May 15, 2009.

41. Carolyn Whelan, "Wal-Mart Gets its Bank—in Mexico," Fortune Magazine, January 29, 2008.

42. Noel Randewich, "Wal-Mart Rides Mexican Retail Banking Wave," Reuters, November 17, 2006.

43. Kent Paterson, "From Wage Slavery to Debt Slavery," America's Program, June 15, 2009.

44. Noel Randewich, "Wal-Mart's Mexico Bank Aims at First-Time Savers, Commodities and Future News, June 18, 2010.

45. "Wal-Mart Banks on the 'Unbanked'," Business Week, December 13, 2007; Keith Epstein and Geri Smith, "The Ugly Side of Microlending," Business Week, December 13, 2007.

46. Elizabeth Malkin, "Wal-Mart Will Offer Retail Banking in Mexico, an Underserved Market," The New York Times, November 24, 2006.

47. Tricia Juhn, "Wal-Mart: Mexico's New Bank," Latin Business Chronicle, July 23, 2007.

48. "Wal-Mart de Mexico: A Growing Behemoth from the South," Seeking Alpha, January 2, 2008.

49. Bloomberg News, "Wal-Mart Effect on Mexico Shows the True Picture of Bargains," August 2, 2011.

50. The Associated Press, "Mexico Turns Toward Alternative Energy," New York Daily News, January 23, 2009.

51. Maximilian Clarke, "UK Foreign Aid Spent on Powering Wal-Mart in Mexico," Fresh Business Thinking, February 2, 2012.

52. "Wal-Mart Invests $987 Million in Mexican Operation," Food International, February 14, 2006.

53. "UK Climate Aid Fund Electricity for Wal-Mart in Mexico," December 2, 2011.

54. "Wal-Mart Will Be Supplied with Wind Energy," Eolic Energy News, December 10, 2009.

6

Wal-Mart Captures South America

❦

BRAZIL

Everyone is Unionized

Brazil used to be a "poor country" but, over the past 15 years or so, it has become more affluent. Wal-Mart arrived in Brazil in 1995, and is currently present in 18 states, has more than Brazil has 534 stores, and counts more than 219,000 employees. (1) Wal-Mart is planning to spend $632 million to open new stores there.

Brazil itself grew 49 percent in income as a whole. This has reached the poorest part of the population, the lowest 10 percent. (2) Brazil missed the worldwide recession, and GDP grew about 5 percent "above the average of most dynamic economies" in 2009. And "the continued growth of its GDP now has the highest buying power in its history." This growth has led, some would say, "to a booming middle class." (3)

However, Brazil is one of the countries where Wal-Mart is being scrutinized for "foul play." For, during 2012, Mexico has been the scene of the bribery scandal. The "damage from its corruption scandal has left a mark on all of the company's operations in the region" (4), and the rest of the world believes that all of South America, particularly Brazil, may be implicated in the fraud. The New York Time has written that "Brazil… it is still suffering from the effects of the scandal." It writes, "The damage to its reputation from the corruption scandal left a mark on all of the company's operations in the region." (5) At the end of last year (November, 2012) the allegations of corrupt practices seems to have " extended beyond Mexico to China, India and Brazil, some of the retailers most important international markets. (6) Some have said that Wal-Mart ought to investigate all of the countries where it has stores.

In 2002, the new President, Inacio Lula da Silva was elected. He fostered a new interest in unions. In Brazil, for the unions, there was a different scenario. The Brazilians had a good government, as far as the workers are concerned, unlike in Mexico where unionism was at the very lowest and corruption was at its height. The newly elected regime of the President was elected because he headed a union. He was formerly the head of a union, the Central Unica dos Trabalhadores (CUT). In Brazil the unions have taken a special place. In addition to "Lula" being elected, "nine ministers, and another 56 high-level officials who were from the executive branch, also came from union ranks."(7)

Indeed, everyone who works for a wage or salary is de facto in a union. All working people must pay union dues, "guild taxes", whether they belong to unions or not. Everyone must pay a day's wages, once a year. One pays for one day of work. With a fee from every person, the union doesn't need to have many workers to be highly represented. Many unions have only a membership of 10 percent. A few can talk for the many, even though many of the union members disagree. (8) There is disagreement with this policy, but it is written into the Constitution. So, whether they want to be or not, everybody who works is de facto a member of a union. Company–specific unions are not permitted. A national union for each sector is what is called for. This has caused many problems for Wal-Mart.

Among the many undesirable consequences, such "state unionism" assures the subordination of workers to the state. All grievances in the workplace must be adjudicated by the state. Some see it as similar to Peronism in that respect.

Workers in Brazil were formerly concentrated in unions in heavy industry, mining, metal manufacturing services, the public sector, and agriculture. But the industrial sector has been transformed towards one that is heavy in services. Now women are working as well. Due to the globalization of the world economies, Brazil turned more to the service sector. The meaning of "work" changed, as did the role performed by unions. (9)

This transformation, brought about due to the growth of globalization and the need for greater productivity, was inevitable. With the ascendancy of Lula to the presidency of Brazil, in the 2002, two-thirds of the Brazilian people knew nothing about the link with international markets. That means that two–thirds of the people in Brazil, primarily those who lived in rural areas, knew nothing about the vast change in the world. Only with Lula, in 2002, did this consciousness awaken.

However, transformation of the economy did not make the society richer, nor did the unions. It was the trade and investment with China and others that, in part, helped the economy flourish. Chinese companies began to invest in commodities to fuel their country's economic development. Brazil could export to them oil, soybeans, iron ore, beef and, of course, automobiles—all things that China needed. In fact, Chinese companies have already invested $25 billion in Brazil. As of 2009, reciprocally, $82 million had been invested in Brazil, and it continues to export to China.(10) There was also a vast change in the way the economy was run.

Lula wanted austerity. The austerity for the people was transformed into savings from trade and investment, and money was "saved" for industrialization, to assure the boom kept going. Now the Brazilians want to benefit from the growth in the economy. In fact, recently Brazilian unions are having a plethora of strikes. Brazilians want to live better; they want to shop, and they want to shop in Wal-Mart, a large new bargain basement, which they have never done before.

When Wal-Mart entered Brazil in 1995, Brazil was a relatively poor country. But Wal-Mart had a strategy of entering, not industrialized countries, but countries that were "on the way up." The BRIC countries, Brazil, Russia, India, and China, Wal-Mart entered them all.

Wal-Mart made some mistakes in Brazil. The chief of Wal-Mart, who only spoke English, had meetings with suppliers who only spoke Spanish. Wal-Mart sold golf clubs when the Brazilians played soccer. In 2001, Wal-Mart had 20 supermarkets there. They were small supermarkets called "Toda Dia." Wal-Mart had high hopes that the stores would succeed. In 2001 it opened a distribution center, large enough to serve 100 stores.

Toda Dia planned to sell its fruits and vegetables at prices five percent lower than neighboring stores, trying immediately to get a "leg up" on the other neighboring stores. Wal-Mart was able to build these stores in three months, because of their simple construction. They are supermarkets for low-income people, and they "look and feel like a warehouse. They have no air-conditioning, and they have concrete floors". (11) They were very successful and people thronged to Toda Dia.

Wal-Mart had a way of dealing with "poor people." Wal-Mart had a way of making their environment feel "rich" even though the people were poor. "A produce section styled after a fruit stand is piled with fresh oranges. A huge display hawks the black turtle beans and salted pork ears needed to cook a feijoadora, a traditional Brazilian stew. "This format is very close to the people," says store manager, Francisco Dias. (12) It helps them feel rich by supplying a super abundance of all of their needs.

In every Toda Dia outlet there is a "Wal-Mart-funded community center." It has within it "a gynecologist's office, an Internet café, and a bank offering microloans," at an interest rate of 75 percent. (13) As is natural for Wal-Mart, it soon started lowering its prices, and the manager of the store was "locked in a heated price war with five neighborhood rivals."

Only two years later, on March 1, 2003, Wal-Mart bought 118 Bompreco stores from Ahold.(14) It was on its way to being the largest supermarket in Brazil. And so, from 20 stores in 2001 to 495 only a decade later, Wal-Mart was soon competing neck and neck with Carrefour. It was also was competing with Pao de Azucar, the upper stratum of Brazilian supermarkets. It had planned to invest close to $1.2 billion dollars to open 110 new stores. Though it was outspending Carrefour, the investment amounted to less than 10 percent of its budget. Carrefour is spending 20 percent of its budget to compete with Wal-Mart. (15) Until 2001 that was the largest investment Wal-Mart had ever made outside the U.S.

Wal-Mart had spent the intervening years buying up small supermarkets. It already owned BIG, Wal-Mart, and Hiper Bom Preco, which are "big-box" stores. And like always, it owns a large number of stores—Nacional, Marcadorama, Bom Preco, Toda Dia, Maxxi, and Sam's Club. In 2011, Wal-Mart received an offer to merge its stores with Pao de Azucar, the high-priced supermarket in Brazil. (16) And only two years after that, Wal-Mart made an offer to merge with Carrefour. Wal-Mart has already invested $3.8 billion in Brazil in the past five years, and had more than 450 stores in Brazil, under nine retail brands. (17) In Brazil, Wal-Mart is third in sales, behind the world's second largest retailer, Carrefour, while Pao de Azucar is first.

Yet, as the universal unionization is also lodged mostly in the "service sector," all of the supermarkets are organized, whether they want to be or not. Again in 2010, there was a burst of strikes—even the police and firefighters struck, for they wanted a raise in their salaries. As a result of the strike bank workers got a 9 percent increase in their salaries and increased profit sharing. (18) In Brazil workers profit from the fact that all the workers are organized—if the unions win their fight.

The Unions and Wal-Mart

It was obligatory for Wal-Mart to have a union. It was not happy about it, but it was not about to jeopardize such a massive growth by leaving Brazil. Unionism is accepted, although unwillingly. Wal-Mart was forced to join the National Confederation of Workers of Commerce and Services (CONTRACS), which is the union responsible for all the supermarket workers of the country, and other working groups.

It accepted this, along with it the hope that it might soon merge with its favorite competitor, Carrefour. Unfortunately, it never made that merger. So Wal-Mart remained only third in market share. (19)

When working at Wal-Mart, the workers had a stressful work environment and an extra-long workday. It was reported that two cashiers fainted in the store because of work overload and lack of ventilation. As a result of this, Wal-Mart was forced to sign a Conduct Adjustment Agreement, which required that Wal-Mart agree to reduce its hours.

Wal-Mart was not so successful with the next grievance. In Brazil, at one point in the year every profit-making business is required to give a portion of its profits to its workers. Naturally, in 2009 Wal-Mart "said" it didn't make any profits, so there was ostensibly nothing to give.

But finally, after a considerable amount of pressure from its "associates," Wal-Mart gave 150 reals to its workers as an "advance." Unfortunately, the money could only be spent in Wal-Mart stores.

It used the same deception which it had used successfully in Mexico. Be that as it may, the workers did not accept this as a long-term strategy. However, CONTRACS was still urging Wal-Mart to give some portion of its profits to the workers the next year in 2010. The year passed and Wal-Mart was talking about giving part of the profit back to the unions. They did nothing for the workers. In addition to this, there is a distressing lack of sensitivity to the cultural needs of Wal-Mart's workers. It refuses to close the stores in Supermercado Toda Dia on special holidays that are sacred to the Brazilians.

On Friday, January 25, 2013 the workers in Supermercado Todo Dia had their first strike. The Strike was against everything they had been fighting for over a period of years. They have been fighting against low wages, "which they say are not enough to make ends meet." (20) "Workers are obliged to work overtime, offered no compensation, no pay increase, and most worryingly, they also lack protective health and safety equipment." (21) Some workers have quit because they can't take the psychological pressure of excessive workload.

ARGENTINA

Michael Bergdahl, former Director of Human Resources at Wal-Mart, wrote, "With the self-aggrandizing attitude of Wal-Mart executives, Wal-Mart, is taking advantage of its strong performance in Brazil and Mexico, has now undertaken the massive task of conquering the rest of Latin America." (22) Wal-Mart opened its stores in Argentina in 1995 and it has been its most disappointing venture in the Western Hemisphere. The Argentinean economy is troubled. "Argentina's presidency seems to be a revolving door and inflation is spiraling upward." (23) This was part of the process of becoming "neo-liberal," as it adopted the International Monetary Fund program. It went from a national economy to one where all the national corporations were privatized and sold to international investors. The national airline, the banks, and even the national postal service were privatized. Yet, its dependence on foreign capital was pervasive. And unemployment soared to 17 percent. Then Argentina simply collapsed. Wal-Mart closed its stores because "sales ground to a halt during the political unrest." (24) Wal-Mart hit Argentina in the years before the country faltered. But Wal-Mart sold food and a variety of household goods—things that all families and individuals need absolutely. Wal-Mart maintained 11 stores there, in the hopes that the economic factors would soon turn around.

The year 1995 was the year of the big push in South America,—the year it entered Brazil as well. But, like with Brazil, it didn't do its homework when it entered Argentina. It brought with it American footballs, when the national game was soccer; and leaf blowers, which couldn't be used since there are no trees; and cordless tools, which South Americans do not use. And the manager did not even speak Spanish. The meat that was sold featured American cuts such as T-bone steaks, rather than "the rib strips and tail rumps" that Argentines prefer. The cosmetic counters had bright red lipsticks and the jewelry counters sold emeralds, sapphires, and diamonds—while Argentine women like a softer look. (25)

After this slight cultural faux pas, Wal-Mart managed to turn itself around. It "re-examined the Argentine culture." Wal-Mart was only too willing to do this in order to change its ways in terms of how it catered to the market—but not the way it treated its workers.

In Argentina, its stores have used aggressive tactics against labor unions and Wal-Mart is not well liked by the workers. When Wal-Mart consistently fired union activists in 2007, it drew the attention of lawmakers. The leaders of Wal-Mart were ignorant of the ways Peronism had treated the workers in the past. Not only did they once have Peronism, but Wal-Mart used these same tactics.

Past Incidents

In 2007 Wal-Mart was called to appear in Buenos Aires before the Argentine Chamber of Deputies (which is like the United States Congress), to answer charges of anti-union activity, and to respond to criticism of its hiring of a retired military official as Wal-Mart's Head of Security, who was officially linked to detention centers,. When the detention centers were still operating in Argentina, Wal-Mart "hired the same ex-military officers who served during the nation's bloody 1976-1983 military junta." (26) Some of them were involved in the disappearance of 256 former military personnel and members of the military government. Some had been accused of human-rights crimes, and still others had served in the country's 375 detention centers.

Alfredo Oscar Saint John "served during the nation's bloody military junta in cities where clandestine detention centers operated." Apparently innocent of these crimes, he was hired to head Wal-Mart's Security Department. The workers resented this because Argentina has a vivid memory of that war. They remembered it as something like the way the Jews regard the Holocaust. Their children were "los Desperaceidos." They disappeared, and parents soon learned that that their children had been murdered by the Argentinean military.

Former military personnel from 375 detention centers were made to torture and make some 30,000 people forcefully disappear. Alfredo Oscar Saint John was a military man who served not only in Tucuman, "a military detention camp," but several military detention centers.

From these places they terrorized the sugar workers. "They terrorized entire villages to make sure that no workers complained of the slave-like working conditions in the sugarcane fields."

These members of the military government have been accused of human rights crimes. In all, 256 await trial. In rejoinder an executive of Wal-Mart said, "We have not had any formal notification from the judicial system that Saint John is connected to any crime." But as all the people know, military officers have long-term impunity.

At the 2007 National Congress hearing, after Wal-Mart had been told by the Chamber that they had better not fire anyone, Gustavo Cordoba, one of the workers who had been fired from one of the non-union Wal-Mart supermarkets—not once, but twice—told the National Congress that "he had received phone calls from anonymous callers who threatened him that if he did not stop organizing he would be physically assaulted." A union activist said at the hearing, "After all our reports and accusations, Wal-Mart fears to fire anyone [which they had been doing before the hearing]. (26) But the company continues to hold meetings with workers, telling them they are 'associates,' telling them that Wal-Mart is the best place to work in the world," just as it does in the United States.

In the Interim

In 2011, again Wal-Mart was back in court to answer to some similar charges. They said that a union had only 31 "union delegates" (or union members); that this Wal-Mart store was open for 11 years and still did not have a union. (27) They were made to re-hire the two Wal-Mart workers that had been dismissed for being union activists.

Since that time there have been other examples of anti-union-ism. "Even in Argentina, where collective bargaining is mandatory, Wal-Mart resists the efforts of FAECY'S," says the UNI Commerce Affiliate there. Wal-Mart has openly challenged union formation in Argentina, and workers have successfully fought back collectively to preserve their rights. In 2007 Wal-Mart recently had suspended a union delegate in a store in Constituyentes, and workers at that store re-elected the delegate on June 1. It sent a message to Wal-Mart "that anti-union behavior toward democratically elected delegates will not be tolerated." (28)

When the town opened a new store four years ago in Rio Cuarto, the workers and management met to discuss whether the store would remain open on Good Friday. Stores have always been closed on that day, because Good Friday is a very important national holiday in Argentina, a Catholic country. When Wal-Mart insisted it would remain open, the union responded with a picket line. The store was kept closed. (29) In Argentina Wal-Mart always fights over holidays— Virgin's Day, Women's Day, Children's Day, Father's Day, Commercial Workers' Day, Mother's Day, and Good Friday—these are all holidays in Argentina. But Wal-Mart won't recognize them, even when they are a major part of the traditions. Wal-Mart wants its stores open all the time. In that respect, Wal-Mart in Brazil is like the American stores.

Wal-Mart hired over 250 people to take care of the expected sales in Rio Cuarto. When sales fell below expectations, slowly but surely they began to fire these new employees. Wal-Mart had the idea of keeping only 120 workers. But the union, once again faced with a massive picket line, kept as many as 200 workers.

It seems that Wal-Mart even made them work overtime—without pay—often using the same forms of "wage abuse" that it does in the United States. Workers in nations such as Argentina have been able to win minimal union representation in their country—but not without withstanding intense opposition from Wal-Mart's management.

Wal-Mart even used punitive measures to assure that the stores prohibited workers from taking "bathroom breaks." For example, in one case a cashier, 19 years old, was stopped from going to the bathroom—after she asked for permission. She waited for 30 minutes, and she was menstruating. When she had stained her pants and her dress, a supervisor came to accompany her to the bathroom. She was humiliated.

There was one store in the Wal-Mart repertoire of stores that did not have a union, "because the company openly challenged the formation of a union." During the meeting shop stewards and union leaders identified the issues they felt were important at Wal-Mart, about the increase of temporary workers, the increase of additional assignments, and Wal-Mart's lack of respect for the traditional holidays. All Wal-Mart could say to this was that "the 15 stores operating provide customers with the lowest prices possible." (30)

And there was trouble with its supply chain. Sofia Sassera, who testified on behalf of South Africa in its decision on whether to let Wal-Mart merge with Massmart, said that Argentina "uses a trade agreement between China and Brazil." It imports goods from Asia. Then, protected from tariffs, it imports the merchandise from Brazil which goes into Argentina. She says, "Local apparel makers watched as shirts, jeans, and underwear poured in from Chinese factories into Argentina.

Even when Argentineans used local producers, the suppliers were victims of constant pressure to sell their products at lower prices. Sasserra cited one situation when Wal-Mart offered to sell air-conditioners. She said that the retailer (Wal-Mart) demanded that the supplier "donate" some free merchandise. "The first notification the supplier had about this was when Wal-Mart sent them a check for less money than they were expecting." The last troubling thing is that Wal-Mart Argentina began firing its unionized workers and hiring new workers from sub-contract agencies. (31)

On May 22, 2012 in Lujan, Argentina, they finally launched a national Argentine Wal-Mart Workers Network. They were FAECY's, the national union which represents Argentina; UNI Americas, which represents Uni International; and the UFCW, the union representing workers in U.S. supermarkets. FAECY's is helping to fund the Wal-Marts in South America, Brazil, Argentina, and Chile, to form an organization like "Our Wal-Mart".

This is where the company openly challenged the formation of the union. However, in Lujan, Wal-Mart workers, their local commerce union, and FAECY's (the Argentinean union) all stuck together and collectively fought to install the union in the store by electing shop stewards." UNI says, "The union is thriving in the Lujan store." (32)

CHILE

Wal-Mart's conflict with Chile became apparent in 2006 when Charles Fishman wrote his book, The Wal-Mart Effect. He wrote it three years before Wal-Mart actually entered Chile, or even looked at a D&S store, (which it was later to buy.) Wal-Mart was exporting salmon to its stores. A great delicacy, Wal-Mart was—and presumably still is—exporting salmon to its stores, and charging only $4.84 cents a pound (2006 prices). Sixty-five percent of the salmon is exported to the United States, and one-third of the salmon catch is purchased by Wal-Mart. It has transformed the economy of southern Chile. (33)

In the south of Chile, thousands of the subsistence farmers and fishermen have become low-paid factory salmon-processing workers. And the artificially grown salmon have polluted the harbor with "their excess food and feces settling into the ocean floor." Wal-Mart does not own the fisheries, but Wal-Mart, with its tremendous finances and terrible power, is not doing anything about the problem. Then Wal-Mart made an offer to buy D&S, a Chilean supermarket chain. (34) It would give Wal-Mart a foothold in Chile. It would be twice the size of Mexican Cifra, which it purchased in 1997. Once accomplished, four years after the U.S./Chile Free Trade Agreement was passed in 2004, it allowed U.S. exporters to win back the trade share they had lost from Chile, from the European Union, Mexico, and Canada. (35)

The first thing it did was to announce that it would no longer buy from Cuba any rum that was so much a part of Chilean life, thereby antagonizing many shoppers. Besides not buying the rum from Cuba, another one of Wal-Mart's insensitivity to workers) Wal-Mart's D&S announced "it would stop selling more than 40 products from countries subject to U.S. embargo or blockade." (36)

The real coup is that, only three years after Wal-Mart bought D&S, it now controls about one-third, or 34 percent, of Chile's supermarket industry. (37) It operates more than 180 supermarkets, hypermarkets and convenience stores, ten shopping centers, and 85 financial service branches, and it has about 34,500 "associates." Wal-Mart also purchased Econo supermarkets and Acuenta discount stores—as part of the deal. As a result it now claims about a third of Chile's supermarket sales. This purchase is part of the biggest deal done by Wal-Mart in Latin America. The whole market is only worth some $10 billion a year, and that to Wal-Mart, with global sales of $405 billion, is "peanuts." Yet, between 1991 and 1995 15,777 small shops went out of business, mainly in Santiago, a city of 4 million, representing 21-22 percent of small general food, meat and fish shops, 25 percent of deli/ meat and fish shops and dairy shops and 17 percent of produce shops. Chile's food and retail sector has continued the process of consolidation to the point of negatively impacting free competition. (38) Wal-Mart now has hundreds of stores in Brazil, Argentina, Mexico, and Central America and, of course, in Canada. It is fulfilling Wal-Mart's "international strategy," by expanding its empire in the Americas.

But Wal-Mart is known for having one of the worst trade union records in the world. Only a week after the purchase of D&S was announced on December 30, 2008, Cristian Cuevas, the leader of the D & S union, said "they would take action if Wal-Mart stores fail to respect current labor conditions after it buys the company." (39) Afterwards, he accompanied 5,000 D&S employees in a televised media conference. Cuevas, the union leader, said "Wal-Mart has refused to negotiate with the union which actually represents the workers there." He said, "Wal-Mart bargained with another group which Wal-Mart created and co-opted. This "union" has engaged in anti-union activities." Wal-Mart was one of only four companies to receive such a reprimand. (40)

In response to these violations, the Chilean government, in August 2012, finally announced that it was banning government contracts with the whole chain of D&S stores for two years, because of the company's repeated violations of workers' rights. But in Chile Wal-Mart doesn't adhere to union policies in any way. In Chile, though Wal-Mart was denied contracts with the Chilean government, Wal-Mart has no contracts with the Chilean government—so that will hardly be a "punishment." Wal-Mart was fined some $4,000 dollars. Four thousand dollars was so little, that it hardly hurt Wal-Mart at all. Wal-Mart responded cheerily that Wal-Mart "works with unions in the markets in which it operates." But:

"Wal-Mart often violates the collective contracts that it has signed with unions in Chile, and commits violations of labor laws." Chile's D&S actually increased [its violations] after Wal-Mart's acquisitions, from 58 in 2007 to 72 in 2009 and 123 in the first six months alone of 2011. Between January 2009 and June 2011, the Chilean Department of Labor sanctioned Wal-Mart Chile a total of 84 times, 50 of which took place in 2011, for violations including those related to compensation, scheduling, hygiene, and security and contracts." (41) Chilean workers fear that they will have to go on strike because of this. (42)

Chile's supermarkets have consolidated the food sector, negatively impacting free competition. "In December 2011, government competition authorities announced an investigation of Chile's highly concentrated grocery sector, where Wal-Mart is the largest player, for possible price collusion of basic products including meat and detergents. (43)

And, of course, according to the U.S. Department of Commerce, "Upon entry into force of the U.S./Chile Free Trade Agreement in 2004, 80 percent of U.S. consumer and industrial goods exports to Chile became duty free." (44)

The Credit Cards

In signing the deal for D&S, Wal-Mart also got a great host of other benefits. In buying D&S, Wal-Mart took over its credit card business. (45) D&S had had a $2 million customer base and 85 Presto Financial Service branches as of 2008. The credit cards were very lucrative. There was a 10.7 percent increase in the average outstanding account from 2007 to 2008. The rise was attributable to the higher use of the card by customers, another source of profit for Wal-Mart.

The Presto credit cards are a way to make Chile's citizens pay for credit through the nose. Presto credit cards can be issued to anyone and used at the Lider supermarkets to pay for food and other purchases. The interest rate limit on these cards was 22 percent and it had risen to 70 percent by 2011. These cards were supported by transnational banks such as the U.K.'s HSBC and Itau-Unibanco. There are also no limits on the level of interest rates in Chile, and no way for an individual to be able to file for personal bankruptcy. And the terms and levels of the interest rates are adjusted without any notice to the customer.

When one's credit expands and gets too large, there is DICON, an unrated credit scoring business. If you are listed on DICON, you're in trouble. You cannot get a loan—or rent an apartment, buy a car, subscribe to Internet or cable—you cannot even get a job. You cannot apply to college or see a doctor for a non-emergency visit. It is often called "a debtor's prison without walls." (46) Fanny Fuentes, a holder of one of Lider's credit cards, is struggling to pay off a large debt she incurred on her credit card. She owes $2,000 dollars on her credit card, which is one-fifth of her yearly salary of $10,000—quite a debt. An economist from the University of Chile, Esteban Puentes, says she doesn't know how much she is paying in interest. According to Lider it is all legal.

No one in Chile is angry about the debt situation. People manage their finances by borrowing on their credit cards, because no one has much money. People buy on credit, and pay a high amount of interest. That's what keeps the stores open.

But there was some "progress" on this in July 2011. El Mercurio, a newspaper, reported that DICON had "decided" that "they would delete from the DICON system the accounts of certain credit card holders whose debt had been reported to DICON." But it was only those whose debts had been settled with Lider, and still had their names on DICON'S list. Wal-Mart had been sued by SERNAC, which is a consumer advocacy group. However, on February 17, 2010, a new law was passed saying that no one on Dicon's list could be discriminated against with reference to work, to education, or to health services. (47)

Potentially, the worst thing that Wal-Mart can do is to keep the workers "in a constant fear of dismissal as a means to prevent them from exercising their rights." If a worker decides to raise his or her voice against the arbitrary discipline, that worker is fired—or directed to speak to his or her supervisor, in what Wal-Mart calls their "open-door policy." Most feel that work is not valued, and their skills are not recognized. Wal-Mart has also reduced the workforce, as it does everywhere, but demands more work from the fewer workers who are left. (48)

GlobalPost said of Chile, "Alarms are already ringing, as Supermarket Lider workers fear that Wal-Mart may dismantle their unions or revoke their benefits. Small retailers, meanwhile, are nervous about being squeezed out of business." (49) Supply chain intermediaries, like wholesalers, supplier companies and other middlemen, will feel immediate effects of the entry of multinational retailers.

Wal-Mart now has stores in Chile, but "it does not have a presence in Peru, a country that, with its 9.8 GDP growth last year and low supermarket penetration, offers interesting opportunities . . . ." (50) The next market it will try to conquer is Peru's. "It has developed its first site for Acuenta [in Peru] . . . and is reported to be in advanced talks for the acquisition of a number of other locations . . . " Once the U.S./Peru FTA goes through, Wal-Mart is planning to extend its supply chain there; and from there to build an empire in South America. Finally, in 2013, Wal-Mart entered Peru. (51) But the most important objection as to how the company operates was testimony given by a lawyer for a union in Chile. Attorney Claudio Alvarez at the Competition Commission in South Africa testified as to why they should let Wal-Mart into that country. He said, "There is a dangerous union strategy" on the part of Wal-Mart. In the long term, "Wal-Mart has the goal of debilitating worker organization" through its ploy called "the open-door policy." This requirement is to insist that an "associate" makes sure he or she talks to his immediate supervisor about some problem he is facing, one on one. This avoids the "intervention of unions to represent workers' problems" because it causes "individual complaints to prevail over collective complaints. This strategy is typical of corporations that undervalue the role of unions."

"Wal-Mart was using the same open-door policy" it had in the United States and, as I have said, there is not one single store in the U.S. that has a union. Obviously it works! For in the United States, a country with 1.3 million people working for Wal-Mart, there is not a single union. America's Wal-Mart workers have tried many times to unionize, but Wal-Mart has continued to deflect their organizing efforts.

On the other hand, in Chile where there are several unions and a history of strong labor unions, this simply cannot be done so easily. After the protests about this, the Labor Department in Chile declared illegal various clauses of the framework agreement in its January15, 2009 judgment (N, 1214/ 004), and welcomed bargaining proposals from the variety of other unions that represented (Lider) workers. But we must not ignore the power of Wal-Mart. When the "open-door" program and others were initiated at Lider, they provoked union in-fighting, which in turn allowed Lider to figure out which workers were the most sympathetic to management. Inevitably, the one with which Wal-Mart chose to deal had a paternalistic relationship with (Lider). Therefore, Wal-Mart eventually created a "company union" to wage a fight with the regular union. And then Wal-Mart played its anti-union tricks. There were frequent anti-union practices such as precarious ar-bitrary dismissals, among others.

Claudio Alvarez ended his testimony with the statement in South Africa:

"I am of the opinion that it is absolutely necessary that govern-ment agencies, unions, suppliers, and consumers maintain permanent vigilance over the behavior and actions of this company, because of what has occurred in Chile. I believe that Wal-Mart is formulating a strategy to neutralize unions in Chile to the detriment of thousands of workers."

Footnotes

1. Brazil Fact Sheet, January12, 2012.
2. Tony D'Altorio, "Profit from Brazil's Success with the Wal-Mart of Brazil," Daily Markets, December 17, 2009.
3. Jose Alface, "Brazil Offers Samba of Confidence to Investor," International Business Times, July 9, 2009.
4. Graziele Dalbo, "Why Wal-Mart Can't Beat the Competition in Brazil," Worldcrunch, October 22, 2012.
5. "Why Wal-Mart Can't Beat the Competition in Brazil," By Graciela Dalbo, WorldCrunch, 2003
6. "Wal-Mart Inquiry Reflects Alarm on Corruption," by Stephanie Clifford and David Barstow, New York Times, November 15, 2012
7. "The Crisis of Unionism Latin America?—Aspects of the Brazilian Experience", by Iram Jacome Rodriques.
8. Mario Osava, "Brazil an Exception to Trade Union Crisis," IPS News, March 12, 2003.
9. Mario Osava, "Brazil: Weakened Trade Unions Look to Lula for Help," Corporate Watch, March 12, 2003.
10. Solana Pyne, "China's Brazilian Shopping Spree," The Global Post, November 22, 2010.
11. Miriam Jordan, "Wal-Mart Gets More Aggressive in Campaign to Dominate Brazil," The Wall Street Journal, May 25, 2001.
12. Miguel Bustillo, "After Early Errors, Wal-Mart Thinks Locally to Act Globally," Work, August 14, 2009.
13. Ibid.
14. Kerry A. Dolan, "Latin America: Bumps in Brazil," Forbes Magazine, April 24, 2004.
15. Chris Burritt, Joao Oliviera and Ladka Bauerover, "The Three-Way Fight for Brazilian Shoppers," Business Week, March 25, 2010.
16. Daniel Gatti, Wal-Mart Watch, "Wal-Mart's Brazilian Boom," translated from the Spanish by NACLA, July 17,2009.
17. Shubh Datta, "Wal-Mart Pins Hopes on Brazil's Mighty Potential," The Motley Fool, May 10, 2011.
18. Graziele Dalbo, "Why Wal-Mart Can't Meet the Competition in Brazil," Worldcrunch, September 10, 2012.

19. UNI Global Union," Respecting the Local Culture" United Food and Commercial Workers, n.d.

20. UNI Global Union, "Brazil: First Ever Strike Against Wal-Mart," Upside Down World, July 16, 2013

21. Knowledge@Wharton,Wal-Mart Next Conquest: Latin America, Latin Business Chronicle March 27, 2009.

22. Argentina Wal-Mart: The Global Retailer, October 15, 2012.

23. Roger Cohen, "Argentine Economy Reborn but Still Ailing," The New York Times, February 6, 1998.

24. Clifford Krauss, "Selling to Argentina," The New York Times, December 5,1999.

25. Marie Trigona, "Wal-Mart Faces Accusations of Anti-union Practices in Argentina," Americas Program Policy, November 19, 2007.

26. Al Norman, "Buenos Aires Wal-Mart Charged with Anti-Union Persecution," Huffington Post, July 23, 2007.

27. UNI Global Union, "Wal-Mart's Global Strategy: Undercutting Worker's Rights," October 2012.

28. UNI, Wal-Mart, Americas Alliance, circa. 2012.

29. UNI, Americas Alliance In Argentina, 2012.

30. "Competition Authority: A Foreign Investment Policy Tool?" Times Live, October 19, 2011; Report Issued by the Ministers of Economic Development; Trade and Industry; Agriculture, Forestry and Fisheries (South Africa).

31. UNI International, Argentina.

32. Charles Fishman, The Wal-Mart Effect: How the World's Most Powerful Company Really Works—And How It's Transforming the American Economy, Penguin Press, 2006.

33. "Wal-Mart Bids for Chilean Supermarket Chain," The New York Times, December 20, 2008.

34. US-Chile Free Trade Agreement, How Can US Companies Benefit?, U.S. Commercial Service, Chile, FTA.

35. Pascale Bonnefoy, "Wal-Mart's Entry Into Chile Market Threatens Cuban Rum," Huffington Post, January 22, 2009.

36. Ashley Lutz, "Wal-Mart Took Over Chile in Only Three Years and Other Countries Are Terrified," Business Insider, September 24, 2012.

37. Carolina Bank Munoz, Organizations, Occupation and Work, A Section of the American Sociological Association, November 15, 2011.

38. Data Received from the Direccion de Trabajo, Chile 2011.

39. Chilean Unions Fight Back, Bulletin of the UNI Alliance Americas Alliance Wal-Mart, n.d.

40. UNI Global Union, Wal-Mart's Global Strategy: Undercutting Worker's Rights, October 2012.

41. Ashley Lutz, "Wal-Mart Took over Chile in Only Three Years and Other Countries Are Terrified," Business Insider, September 24, 2012.

42. Jorge Porter, "Wal-Mart Tender Offer Ends Battle for D&S-Presto," Business Chile Magazine, March 1, 2009.

43. Rodrigo Pizarro, The Free Trade Agreement Between the USA and Chile: An Instrument of Commercial Interests, Paper No. 02/2006, Ideas Working Paper Series, 2006.

44. A Corrupt Credit Business Model Travels to Chile and Brazil, Organizacion de Consumidores Y Usuarios de Chile, July 24, 2011.

45. Chile Cumple, Nueva Ley DICON, May 9, 2012.

46. Randall Woods, "Chile Consumer Watchdog Files Suit Against Wal-Mart DF, Unit Says," Bloomberg News, July 19, 2011.

47. UNI Americas Alliance-Chile (no date).

48. Pascale Bonnefoy, "Wal-Mart's Entry Into Chile Market Threatens Cuban Rum," Global Post, January 22, 2009.

49. Julian Dowling, "Wal-Mart in Chile: Low Prices, High Expectations," Business Chile, March 1, 2009.

50. Ibid.

51. Omar Mariluz, Reuters Exclusive: Wal-Mart to Start Work on Opening in Peru, July 1, 2013.

7

Central America

The Washington Post reported yesterday that the U.S. Government is suspending training for new Peace Corps volunteers in Guatemala and El Salvador while they "reassess security concerns." The volunteers currently in place will remain and Peace Corps officials will see that they are all safe and accounted for . . . The Times article stated, however, that Peace Corps Journals, an online portal for blogs by Peace Corps volunteers, has an entry referring to a volunteer who was shot in the leg during an armed robbery on a bus. "Peace Corps Pulling Out of El Salvador, Guatemala, and Honduras," December 22, 2010.

Wal-Mart is now not only the largest chain of supermarkets in the world but, with over 552 supermarkets, it is also one of the biggest chains in Central America. In the free trade agreement between the United States and five countries in Central America (Costa Rica, Guatemala, Honduras, Nicaragua, and El Salvador), the Dominican Republic, and, of course, the American protectorate, Puerto Rico, which it considers a "foreign" country although it is really a part of the United States, it has managed to incorporate all of them.

In 2004 President George Bush revealed that the Central America Free Trade Agreement (CAFTA) was on the drawing board. It seems odd that the United States wanted to form a free trade agreement with all of these countries, because Central America is a morass of poor and troubled lands. The countries of Honduras, Guatemala, and Nicaragua are the poorest, while Honduras, Guatemala, and Nicaragua had bloody civil wars which occurred from about the 1960s to the 1990s. Guatemalan's fought each other from 1960 to1996, for almost 36 years. They fought until 200,000 people were dead and 45,000 "disappeared." In El Salvador, the leftist guerillas struggled with government security forces from the 1980s to the 1990s, and left 75,000 dead, while 7,000 disappeared. And Nicaragua battled Somoza until 50,000 were left dead. Then, in 1998 there was a hurricane in Honduras and Nicaragua and two earthquakes in El Salvador, which led to 9,000 more deaths. (1) This was followed by deep and long-lasting poverty which has lasted until this day.

But the Bush administration nevertheless lobbied for CAFTA. In the House of Representatives, Congressmen said their constituents were against it 30 to 1. There were articles from Business Week, The Washington Times, Financial Times, and The Congress Daily, which also alluded to this. (2)

President Bush at that time was accused of threatening and bribing members of Congress in order to get the measure passed. He was successful. It, indeed, did pass the Senate and the House of Representatives, by the narrowest of margins, with heavy campaigning and threats from President Bush, while there was also heavy opposition to the administration from both parties, interest groups, unions, and citizens nationwide.

CAFTA, Bush had promised, would increase the investment in the agricultural sector, and would create new sources of employment for Central Americans. That is certainly not what happened. CAFTA, as it is known, is "much feared in Central America." They said of it "CAFTA equals misery," which is printed on the roadsides in graffiti. CAFTA was clearly an imposition on Central America. "It would be difficult to find another multilateral negotiation with less balance of power," said Carlos Pacheco of the Center for International Studies in Managua, Nicaragua. "Our mainly agricultural economy is going to be destroyed by the big transnational agribusinesses from the United States." (3)

The Daily News in New York City ran the headline, "Murder Rates in Central America Highest in the World, UN Study Shows." It was reported by the United Nations that there were 6,200 killings in Honduras and 4,000 in El Salvador, respectively.(4) And the murders are directed towards all those who are in trade unions. In Guatemala, "in 2010 ten trade unionists were murdered; sixteen trade unionists were assassinated in 2009, and nine in 2008." Among those who were campesino leaders, the figure is much higher. "Seventy-five percent of union leaders were threatened prior to their assassinations, and 98 percent were assassinated within a few weeks of advocating for worker rights."(5)

In Guatemala, most of the fertile agricultural land is in dispute. First there are the small farmers, some of whom are the descendants of the tribal people—those who lived and worked on it before the Spanish came. What is left of them are the "campesinos" who work the land on small acreages, growing subsistence crops. Then there are "the plantation elite, the landed elite, the gentry," who grow food and other products to export. Roughly 2 percent of the population owns 70 percent of all the productive farmland, so there is an intense struggle over the lands.

Much of the food for export is produced by the plantation owners. The government protects the landed elite, because these people produce all the food that is grown for export, which is Guatemala's major source of income. The 2 percent of the people, the "gentry," protect their own land with private armed guards because the land is so valuable. There is a "war" between the indigenous people and the "gentry," and the gentry, the "plantation elite," inevitably win.

After 2006, the year that CAFTA was passed, the number of small- and medium-sized farmers and cooperatives, who grew mainly rice, corn, beans, and a few other vegetables, and raised cattle, decreased by 28 percent. Now in Central America all the countries have at least a 50-percent poverty rate, and the crime rate has increased. Violence followed directly from the passage of CAFTA.

The same multinational exporters and importers, the producers of food for export like Wal-Mart, are the ones who are driving up the price of food, making it harder, if not impossible, for all the poor farmers from Central America, to compete with U.S. exports.

Nicholas Kristof wrote in the New York Times, "The U.S., Europe, and Japan spend $350 billion each year on agricultural subsidies (seven times as much as global aid to poor countries), and this money creates a glut that lowers commodity prices and erodes the living standard of the world's poorest people" (6)

The "rich" countries like the U.S. subsidize their farmers, and the farmers in the poor countries must buy the cheap, imported food. It is so expensive for them that the poor countries cannot afford to buy the food produced in their own countries. Mark Malloch Brown, the head of the United Nations Development Program, estimates that the total aid from the "rich" countries costs poor countries about $50 billion a year in lost agricultural exports. This is the total of the rich countries' aid to poor countries. "But we take with our left hand every cent we give with our right." (7)

Porfirio is a farmer who produces beans to eat and to sell. He is told that the best he can do is to switch his farm to produce sesame. He cannot get a decent price for his beans under CAFTA, because the cheapest ones are imported from America. His crop will be dependant on the market. And, if it fails, he cannot eat sesame.

If CAFTA were an ideal agreement, it would encourage these farmers to enhance their food production, and not encourage the exporting and importing of food. CAFTA would be a policy that promotes land reform which, as we will see, it doesn't. Instead, it "arranges" vast plantations for landowners who produce bananas, sugar, and coffee to export. And they import as well, from other Central American countries, rice, beans, and corn, which are just what the small farmer produces—and lives on.

Should many of the small farmers in Guatemala, Honduras, and El Salvador fail—and many of them will—the 5.5 million farmers will be put at risk. What will they do? They can give up their land and move to the cities of Central America, or move north to Mexico. Immigration to the U.S., alas, is prohibited now. These poor farmers and workers are small agricultural producers, and they are worried. (8)

In Central America all the countries have at least a 50-percent poverty rate. The price of food has risen for the rural populations, and so has the poverty rate. It soared 140 percent from 1995 to 2007. The CAFTA-DR countries import 75 percent of the total consumer food products. Central America has always been seen as a vital place for American producers, as well as those from Japan and Europe, to export their food. Now, with all the "free trade" agreements between Central American countries and the U.S., it is simpler than ever. The United States has free trade treaties with Canada, Mexico, Central America, and the Dominican Republic. It has treaties pending with Colombia, Panama, and Peru. (9)

CAFTA is very similar to NAFTA in what it provides and, just like NAFTA, in what it doesn't provide. There are three things that are egregiously wrong with this trade agreement. First are the poverty programs; second, the labor rights law; and the last and final one is the way it passed the United States Congress. Then there are the drugs and the drug war, both of which are resultant from and have a large bearing on the shape of violence in Latin America.

Wal-Mart's Role

The supermarket diffusion started sometime in the early 1990s and signaled a profound take-off of supermarkets, which grew "meteorically." (10) They started to grow at the very time when Wal-Mart started to go "offshore." When the United States passed its free trade agreement with Central America in 2005, Wal-Mart was invited to become a member of Central American Retail Holding Company (CARHCO), in which they bought a 33 1/3 percent interest. (11)

In 2005 Wal-Mart had two partners—the Paiz family, the major shareholders of La Fragua; and Corporation de Supermercados Unidos. Wal-Mart bought CARHCO in one blow—a total of 362 supermarkets. But CARHCO still "has three operative companies": La Fragua, founded by the Paiz family, which operates 209 stores in Guatemala,

Honduras, and El Salvador; the Corporation de Supermercados Unidos; and the third operator, CSU, which operated 154 stores in Nicaragua and Costa Rica. In 2009 Wal-Mart bought 51 percent of CARHCO, as of today it has a controlling share. All around, everybody involved in the CARHCO deal is very well off.

Wal-Mart owned 363 supermarkets in Central America at the time of the purchase; as a result of the takeover it now has 552. Wal-Mart has opened at least one new store in each of the five countries every year. And sometimes it has opened more than that. (12)

Today, Costa Rica has 182 supermarkets; it has the most super-markets—and it is the richest country in Central America. Guatemala has 176, and El Salvador has 78, Honduras 55, and Nicaragua only 61, for a total of 552. Since it bought into CARHCO, Wal-Mart has had a growth of 52 percent in six years. Wal-Mart then expanded its share of the supermarket to 51 percent in September 2005. Significant investments were planned over the next few years. (This was, of course, before the alleged Mexican "Bribery scandal.)

Wal-Mart Centroamerica SA is the number one leader of all the supermarkets in Central America and it has "an aggressive expansion strategy." It is opening large modern stores in the region. Supermarkets only have a 4.9 percent share in food, a small proportion of all the food that is eaten. Nevertheless, Wal-Mart has 56.6 percent of all the food delivered to its supermarkets, and it has many supermarkets—Paiz, Hiper Paiz, Dispensa Familiar, Maxi Bodegas, and ClubCo. (13) Wal-Mart is growing so fast in Central America that it has imported over one-half the food in its supermarkets, worth $350 million dollars in 2009. Wal-Mart says it will build additional stores in Central America and Mexico. It boasts that the Mexican and Central American division of the retail giant plans to invest almost $1.5 billion in the six countries under their jurisdiction in 2012, adding over 400 stores to the chain from 2012 to 2015.(14)

Before CAFTA was enacted, Central America was promised two things: 1) CAFTA would help diversify its agricultural economy by al-lowing agriculture and nontraditional goods from the North American market; and 2) increased investment in agriculture would create new sources of employment.

There is a great deal of difference between the people who are in favor of CAFTA and those who are opposed to it. Those who are in favor of CAFTA argue that food should be produced for international export and import. Those against it believe that food should be produced mainly for people to eat.

Guatemala, for example, has the largest number of people. Fifty percent of the people in Guatemala are in the agricultural sector. They are stubbornly poor. Guatemala's poor farmers have poor children who are engaged in child labor: about one in six children, who work at selling goods on the street, clean houses, or work in small factories. (15)

Guatemala also lacks trade union rights. It is a country that has suffered a wave of assassinations. For example:

"Ten trade unionists were assassinated, and there were violations of every kind in municipalities, enterprises, and maquilas . . . .The Ministry of Labor and Social Welfare, far from fostering labor rights, is the obedient servant of the national and transnational employers. When there are decisions by the labor courts in favor of the workers, they are not applied." (16)

In this environment of poverty and crime, why did Wal-Mart locate here? It is interesting to note that Wal-Mart has no unions in Central America, which is very comfortable for Wal-Mart. The drug traffickers have not (yet) begun to attack Wal-Mart. For Wal-Mart is part of the "national and transnational employers."

In part, the growing concern about crime is a consequence of the growth of the drug trade. There has been an infiltration of the Mexican drug cartels from Mexico into Guatemala. "Cool highlands are an ideal climate for poppy cultivation." Weapons, lenient gun laws, and a long history of arms smuggling . . . and "an impoverished, underemployed population is a ready source of recruits." (17) But it is poverty, and the lack of unions, which has drawn Wal-Mart to Central America. Wal-Mart will grow its supermarkets without any anxieties about unions appearing.

The Food Machine

Nicaragua is one of the poorest countries of Central America. While Wal-Mart imports most of its food, it does buy some of its food from the poor and small farmers in Nicaragua, but not a great deal. We are told that Wal-Mart in Central America has an agricultural project to attract small farmers to sell fruits and vegetables to Wal-Mart. Wal-Mart:

". . . supports the improvement of the livelihoods of local communities through an alliance with Hortifruti Guatemala and the Norman Borlaug Institute for International Agriculture of the Texas A and M University System through the AGTEC Project. The purpose of the partnership is to provide capacity building to growers of the Tierra Fertil program in a variety of topics, including good agricultural practices and manufacturing." (18)

At first it says the program "benefit(s)" 3,894 families by providing 9,000 jobs. Then we learn more about exactly what it does. The program is for three years only, and it is funded by $1.1 million from USAID, $500,000 from Mercy Corps, and $600,000 from Wal-Mart and:

"Through this project approximately 4,800 beneficiaries, including small farmers, students, teachers, and technicians, have received practical and theoretical training on a variety of agricultural topics. About 600 small farmers have been supported through the facilitation and negotiation of new local, regional, and international markets, as well as through improved access to microcredit." (19)

It actually aids a total of 600 small farmers' families, not 900 as was originally stated, to grow vegetables to sell to supermarkets. But for those who choose to grow and sell to Wal-Mart, they must be grown exactly the way Wal-Mart wants to sell them. The vegetables must have plenty of water, preferably by irrigation. This is because "Wal-Mart follows a tightly guarded manual of product-specific quality standards, codifying required attributes such as variety, size, coloration, cleanliness, damage, and weight." However, USAID will furnish the rain fed farmers with loans to purchase irrigation systems. USAID has programs like this one all over the world. The farmers who get irrigation systems and other kinds of agricultural technology, are the ones who can sell to Wal-Mart at a stable price.

Six hundred families isn't much of a project to solve the problems of a nation of 14 million people, half of whom are poor. And USAID picks up the largest portion of the bill for its funding; $1.1 million, the largest of any of the three funders. It is a "gift" from the U.S. taxpayers. And Wal-Mart gets the benefit of it—the lion's share of the deal—it benefits from the inexpensive fruits and vegetables that the farmers sell them.

In 2009 a group called Mercy Corps, "a global relief organization," teamed up with Wal-Mart to help farmers grow fruits and vegetables in Guatemala, as well as Nicaragua. The folks at Mercy Corps are perhaps wondering how this will play out. Some are anxious for it to work out well, and hope that it will make the farmers richer. Others are wondering how Mercy Corps' relationship with Wal-Mart will hurt the growers. Some see the "Guatemala scheme" as a self-serving ploy to make the growers dependent on the company, which they predict will ratchet down purchase prices, stranding the farmers.

While acknowledging that Mercy Corps has the best intentions in helping the farmers, Wal-Mart Watch was fearful of what this project could do. It states that Wal-Mart will use such a relationship to pressure farmers to continually reduce prices. Still others see it in Guatemala as a situation reminiscent of United Fruit Company's "monopolistic run." (20)

And Wal-Mart writes in answer to this statement: "Wal-Mart is committed to the future of Central America, and we are proud to be part of efforts to promote economic growth and improve the quality of life in the region."(21)

In reality, most of the small farmers of Nicaragua don't grow fruits and vegetables. Seventy-six percent of (small) landholding farmers grow basic grains including maize, beans, and sorghum, which Wal-Mart doesn't buy. And, in all the countries of Central America, the horticultural producers are the ones that constitute a tiny share of small- and medium-sized farmers. In Nicaragua, they grow 21.4 percent of toma-toes, 1.23 percent green peppers, and 0.25 percent cabbage." (22)

And Wal-Mart only uses, on average, 70 percent of the produce that the farmers supply, and discards 30 percent, which it says does not come up to its standards. The farmers sell the rest of the harvest on the open market. "Wal-Mart culls out, or buys," only the best of the farm-ers' harvest, and only specific fruits and vegetables. Then "Wal-Mart uses buyers to source products in rural areas, rather than relying on farmers to manage transport." Wal-Mart's procurement division picks up production from supplier farmers in the farmer's field or commu-nity. (23) This function has an impact on the price it pays the farmers for their crops.

There are two supermarket chains in Nicaragua. One is La Colonia, a family-owned national chain, which has operated in this country since the 1960s—it has ten stores. Then there is Wal-Mart Central America. Operating since 2006, it already has 52 outlets. Both super-markets participate in the program.

Wal-Mart doesn't merely purchase the domestic produce from small- and medium-sized farmers; it first makes them undergo a "com-petitive round" with the "A Hand to Grow" program. The "Business Round" is a competition in which the farmers who are vying against one another bring their food products to Wal-Mart for consumer test-ing. (24)

Those suppliers who comply with the requirements will have the opportunity of commercializing their products in Wal-Mart's store. Once accepted, their products will be sold at "designated product stores" for an initial "testing" period of time—90 days. Those prod-ucts well regarded by consumers will be incorporated into the regular inventory.

As of June 25, 2009, "Through this project, 45 producers have joined Wal-Mart's network of suppliers." (25) So far, 30 percent of agricultural products sold by Wal-Mart are from local producers. Wal-Mart's goal is to get 40 percent. As we can see from an advertisement in the local papers, Wal-Mart's goal is to get as many new products as they can—not to open the doors to the country's agricultural produc-ers. They only have 45 producers so far, and the project is judged in terms of whether the consumers buy it and like it.

At the same time, Wal-Mart has purchased Hortifruti, which is a large food importer in Central America, to run its supply chain. Actually, Wal-Mart doesn't fill its stores with the fruits and vegetables of small farmers because it has "very high standards." It chooses its fruits and vegetables from the big growers. The big growers have the wherewithal to provide the technology that supermarkets want—to provide the insecticides, the fungicides, and the post-harvest technol-ogy that is needed to grow large red-ripened tomatoes and other fruits and vegetables, which farmers produce very little of.. And very few of the smaller farmers have this equipment. Very few of the small farmers grow them to the "perfect standards" of Wal-Mart. Wal-Mart gets the bulk of its produce from imports, or from Hortifruti.

But all the supermarkets are worried about Wal-Mart. The to-mato producers were shocked when they found themselves competing with Costa Rican tomatoes, via the procurement system of Hortifruti. Because of the recent purchase of Hortifruti, a regional distributor had the same CARHCO–specific standards as Wal-Mart. When the farm-ers realized that Wal-Mart and Hortifruti were one, and it sells to other supermarkets, they were very angry.

But Dr. Thomas Reardon, an agronomist and an expert from the University of Michigan, says that Wal-Mart:

". . . tend(s) to emphasize the marketing of (fresh fruits and veg-etables) of high quality as a way of competing with traditional markets, and this quality tends to be defined mainly in terms of appearance (i.e., spotless, uniform fruits and vegetables in terms of size, shape, and color, firmness, ripeness, etc.). Those quality standards, when applied locally in the export market, create an incentive for an increase in the use of insecticides, fungicides, and other production and post-harvest technologies that can harm people."(26)

Aside from the small farmers being cut out, they may be actually harming the consumers.

The larger farmers and Wal-Mart, for sure, are prospering, despite the potentially harmful effects on the consumers. In 2008 all the other supermarket owners, of which there are 16, started a group called Supermercados de Centroamericas y Panama, or SUCAP, as it is called. Its members include 16 supermarket owners, and together it has 281 stores in Central America, barely enough to compete with the 552 of Wal-Mart. SUCAP will buy in bulk all the products that the supermarkets have in common but, most of all, it will try to "fight regional competition" led by Wal-Mart." As might be expected Wal-Mart is the strongest performer of the leading hypermarkets, supermarkets, and discounters in South and Central America " (27)

Wal-Mart has developed a program to teach small-holders how to produce the glossy fruits and vegetables desirable to Wal-Mart. By 2015, "Wal-Mart is 'committed' to selling $1 billion worth of food supplied by one million small- and medium-sized farmers" and "providing training to one million, farmers," including 50 percent of women. Wal-Mart wants to increase its customer base. As it makes up for its win in Dukes vs. Wal-Mart, has won the nationwide class-action discrimination suit, in the United States, against women. So it is not very interested in women's rights even though it says it is in favor of "women's rights. But in Central America "Women are always raped, beaten, killed. Always humiliated." (28)

But Wal-Mart, like it does almost everywhere, gets the lowest price—on everything. The Alliance Project in Nicaragua shares its purchasing with another domestic supermarket chain, La Colonia, which has 52 supermarkets to Wal-Mart's 552. That is about ten times more supermarkets. The authors of this study "find that the mean prices paid to suppliers of Wal-Mart supermarkets are significantly lower than the traditional market. But La Colonia pays a higher market price than Wal-Mart. Wal-Mart pays less for its fruit and vegetables than La Colonia. The price (as a percent of the Wal-Mart price) is between 34 and 54 cents. Again, the 30 percent of the produce that Wal-Mart does not buy is sold in the local markets of Nicaragua.

The farmers may be accepting a lower price from Wal-Mart, but at least they are getting paid something for their produce, while getting paid a price that the market bears for the other 30 percent. The market price may be higher or lower—it fluctuates. So it may be that farmers who accept the Wal-Mart price "are paying too much for this implicit insurance against price variation," particularly those who do not have irrigation systems. That may be why the farmers are switching to La Colonia. (29)

Conclusion

Wal-Mart is a bold operator. It goes wherever the market is, even if it is in a region like Central America, with its land wars, its crime and its murders, that have plagued the region with wars for 30 years. There were no other supermarkets competing for a place with Wal-Mart, aside from the small La Colonia, when President Bush created the regional free trade agreement—with no demand for human rights standards, and no significant labor laws.

But the partnership, between USAID and Wal-Mart developed in 2008, was a partnership for only three years. Since then it has not been continued. That partnership has been replaced with one between USAID and a German firm, Hanns R.Neumann Stiftung, a not-for-profit fund in Hamburg, Germany, which is a coffee trading company. (30) Hopefully, the Guatemalan people will do better with a "not for profit" fund, and no mention is even made of Wal-Mart.

Footnotes

1. Diego Cevallos, Anti-Poverty Programs Abound, But Poverty Deepens, Institute for Policy Studies, September 17, 2005.

2. Mariah Wojdacz, "CAFTA: How it Passed, and What it Means for America," Legal Zoom, 2005.

3. Tom Ricker, "Re-colonizing Central America: Competition or Massacre? Central American Farmers or Dismal Prospects under CAFTA," The Multinational Monitor, Volume 25, Number 4, April 2004.

4. The Daily News Staff, "Murder Rates in Central America, Highest in the World," The Daily News, October 7, 2011.

5. Guatemalan Labor, Indigenous, and Campesino Movement Report, U.S, Labor Education in the Americas Project (LEAP), April 23, 2008.

6. Nicholas D. Kristof, "Farm Subsidies that Kill," The New York Times, July 5, 2002.

7. Ibid.

8. Deborah James, "Food Security, Farming, and the WTO and CAFTA," Global Exchange, 2011.

9. See Kevin Hagen, "Taking Advantage of Free Trade Agreements in Order to Export," Yahoo.com, January 30, 2008.

10. Julio de Berdegue, Fernando Balsevich, Luis Flores, and Thomas Reardon, "Central American Supermarkets' Private Standards of Procurement of Fresh Fruits and Vegetables," Food Policy, Volume 30, Issue 3, July 2005.

11. "Wal-Mart Announces Central American Investment," Wal-Mart, September 20, 2004.

12. Central America Market Profile, Food Export Association of the Midwest, USA, no date.

13. "More Wal-Marts in Central America," CentralAmericaData, February 22, 2012.

14. Cesar Augusto Sancion, Promises and Failures of DR-CAFTA in El Salvador, the Stop CAFTA Coalition, circa 2008.

15. Lucy Wang, "Guatemala: The Odd Couple," Global Envision, September 2, 2008.

16. "Annual Survey of Violations of Trade Union Rights," ITUC CSI, IGB, 2012 http://survey.ituc-csi.org/Guatemala.html.

17. International Crisis Group, Guatemala: Drug Trafficking and Violence, Latin American Report, No, 39, October 11, 2011.

18. "AGTEC Project Partners with Wal-Mart to Provide Training to Small Farmers," by AGTEC Partners, Vince Partida, August 16, 2012.

19. Hope Michelson, Thomas Reardon and Francisco Perez, Small Farmers and Big Retail: Trade-offs of Supplying Supermarkets in Nicaragua, Department of Agricultural, Food, and Resource Economics, Michigan State University, Staff Paper 2010-02, April 2010.

20. "Wal-Mart Responds to Wal-Mart's Alliance with Mercy Corps and USAID in Guatemala," March 6, 2008.

21. Wal-Mart, Central America, 2011.

22. Julio de Berdegue, Fernando Balsevich, Luis Flores, and Thomas Reardon, "Central American Supermarkets' Private Standards of Procurement of Fresh Fruits and Vegetables," Food Policy, Volume 30, Issue 3, July 2005.

23. Hope Michelson, Thomas Reardon and Francisco Perez, "Small Farmers and Big Retail: Trade-offs of Supplying Supermarkets in Nicaragua," American Journal of Agricultural Economics, Volume 94, Issue 5, 2012.

24. "Hortifruti Expands Its Network of Salvadoran Suppliers," La Prensagraphica, June 19, 2009.

25. "Wal-Mart Continues Round of Negotiations," Wal-Mart Central America, September 4, 2008.

26. Julio de Berdegue, Fernando Balsevich, Luis Flores, and Thomas Reardon, Central American Supermarkets' Private Standards of Procurement of Fresh Fruits and Vegetables," Food Policy, Volume 30, Issue 3, July 2005. Op. Cit. ???

27. "Supermarkets Form Regional Alliance to Boost Efficiency," Central American Data, May16, 2008.

28. Paula Todd, "Central American Women at War," Maclean's Magazine, February 12, 2012; Vanessa Kritzer, "What the Company

Did to Us: Rape and Displacement in Guatemala." Latin American Working Group December 13, 2011.

29. Hope Michelson, Thomas Reardon and Francisco Perez, "Small Farmers and Big Retail: Trade-offs of Supplying Supermarkets in Nicaragua," American Journal of Agricultural Economics, Volume 94, Issue 5, 2012.

30. USAID and Mercy Corps Expand the Impact of Alliance to Help Guatemalan Farmers Earn More, Improve Nutrition, Mercy Corps, 2012.

8

Wal-Mart in China

❧

Between 1990 and 1995 the growth rate in China was 11 percent per year. Wal-Mart, and the entire world, was dazzled by the fact that China had grown so fast. The Wal-Mart engines were propelled by economic liberalization and a large pent-up demand for consumer goods. So Wal-Mart entered China in 1996 a little wary of this move. They arrived knowing little of the culture or traditions of Chinese society.

Wal-Mart entered China in the southern Chinese city of Shenzhen, in Guangdong Province right near the Hong Kong border—in a region which is the heart of the export–processing zone. In that city the factories were hard at work, with migrant workers making everything from firecrackers to shoes to electronics, for the American market. This region is where the heart of the migrant population is employed, where the young women work 14 hours a day and live 10 to a room, while they send money to their families back in the provinces.

This is where Wal-Mart located its first supermarket. Then, over the years, Wal-Mart spread out all over the country, even building stores in Beijing. Today it has 370 stores, and plans to open 100 more in the next three years, depending on what the "climate" is. (1)

During the now 17 years it has been there, eye-opening things have happened to Wal-Mart. First, Wal-Mart, which had no truck for unions, learned (or, perhaps, it knew) that there was a massive union in China. It has about 134 million trade union members. China was undergoing a wide learning experience while, at the same time, there was a resurgence of its unions and union organizing.

The reawakening of the unions was due to the new capitalist investment in China after the state-owned enterprises, (SOEs) were disbanded. At that point, the Communist Party, through the All-Chinese Federation of Trade Unions (the ACFTU), planned to reinvigorate the new industrial structure with a union in every factory with more than 25 employees.

The ACFTU was a traditional union bureaucracy, a state union. It is an arm of government; the chairman of the ACFTU sits on the board of the Politburo. The union is part of the national government, and from the national government it takes its orders. It was, and is, still illegal and severely punishable to advocate, or form, an alternative union to the ACFTU.

During the days of the SOEs, it would visit the sick, and give gifts during the time of the major holidays. But, nevertheless, its typical behavior was to side with management. For the Communist system was one in which there was supposed to be "harmony." This was a union which did little to reform the workplace, or arbitrate a disagreement between workers and management. There was no collective bargaining.

At the beginning it took its cue from management. To organize a union, an ACFTU official usually had a talk with the management of the firm. Management would agree that a union was necessary, and agree to join. Then the ACFTU appeared in the workplace, and a committee formed by management would proceed to collect the 2 percent for every worker that worked in the shop or factory. That was the union. Most of the year the workers in the plants ignored the ACFTU, and the ACFTU ignored the workers.

Yet by 2012 the Chinese have learned to work with the ACFTU, in part because the migrant workers are terribly dissatisfied. Migrants are by far the most exploited in the province of Guangdong, as well as in other parts of the nation.

Wal-Mart "Joins" the Union

In 2006 the ACFTU demanded that all foreign national corporations have a union at their shops and workplaces in China, and that the "foreign nationals" be the first to be organized. They declared that China would have 80 percent of the workers organized by the ACFTU "by the end of 2007," only seven months away. Wal-Mart was the first on their list.

What did Wal-Mart have to do, be a member of the union? To join a union in China was perhaps the easiest and the most non-threatening thing they could do. Management had to "sign a contract with the ACFTU" in the usual way, and to pay the 2 percent of the salary of each person it employed, per year. The "fee," paid to the government was a pittance to Wal-Mart, and there was no collective bargaining. Nor was there anything else that a traditional union had to do. Unions had no means to drive up wages, or take control of workers situations in the plant.

But organizing Wal-Mart was a very difficult thing to do. For Wal-Mart was ideologically opposed to unions of any kind, and was absolutely loathe to treat workers fairly. No one believed that Wal-Mart would accept a union, especially in China. But Wal-Mart did accept the union.

Perhaps Wal-Mart had the notion that the union could be controlled. Perhaps after talking with the bureaucrats of ACFTU, they realized that it was harmless. Because, in the end it allowed the union, not only in one store, but in all of the 60 stores which it had then, and it signed a voluntary agreement to do so. It now has all the stores in "union shops."

Wal-Mart had been in China since 1996, but it was ten years later when it joined, in 2006. But, it wasn't until 2003 that the ACFTU made a strong push for all foreign-owned enterprises to join. At first, Wal-Mart claimed it had a special dispensation not to join the union. As it refused, Wal-Mart said in its usual disconcerting way that it wasn't resisting trade unions in China, but said:

"Currently there are no unions in Wal-Mart China because associates have not requested that one be formed. Should associates request the formation of a union, Wal-Mart China would respect their wishes and honor its obligation under China's Trade Union Law, and no Wal-Mart worker had expressed an interest in forming a union."

It openly said the above, trying to avert any controversy. But in reality it actually believed:

"Staying union-free is a full-time commitment. The commitment to stay union–free must exist at all levels of management—from the Chairperson of the Board down to the front-line manager . . . . The time involved is 365 days per year."(2)

It all started with Wang Ling, who was the local organizer of foreign-owned companies for the ACFTU. He said he had learned "that Wal-Mart had warned workers against speaking with trade union officials during working hours." (3) But the piece de resistance came when "the local union in Nanjing, China said that the ACFTU was never even granted a meeting with the store manager to have a discussion about organizing Wal-Mart." He went not once, but 26 times in two years. It turned out to be a humiliating experience, "and was repeated many times in different Wal-Mart stores in other cities." (4) Wal-Mart even faced criticism from the National People's Congress.

Such was typical practice for Wal-Mart. But for the Chinese government, it was demeaning; an insult to them. As a result, the ACFTU threatened to take Wal-Mart to court for violating China's labor law, a decidedly unpleasant experience in China, where Wal-Mart didn't know the laws and few Wal-Mart officials even knew how to speak Chinese. And the union called Wal-Mart's bluff, after pressing the company to have discussions for two years.

When Wal-Mart would still not budge, the ACFTU then tried something new; it tried organizing from the "bottom up," the way American unions and all other countries in the West do it. In China, there is a different approach. The union organizer goes to the "top." He talks to the top management and asks that they join. That was the traditional way for a firm to get unionized.

Instead, at this point, when Wal-Mart did not want to join under any circumstances, the people mobilized from below. They went to the "grass roots," since Wal-Mart was so recalcitrant to join. The ACFTU would bypass company managers and go straight to employees.

The workers, at least 30 of them, got together in a building right next to Wal-Mart, and created an ACFTU chapter. When Wal-Mart discovered its workers had formed a trade union seemingly "right under its nose," Wal-Mart's "anti-union activities went into high gear." Wal-Mart then called a meeting in which it was announced "that those who joined the union would not have their contracts renewed," a dire threat, a typical threat of Wal-Mart. It tried to discredit the union by "accusing it of trying to bribe employees to join." Wal-Mart said "that the workers did not join voluntarily" and then spouted a number of baseless threats.

Finally Wal-Mart called for a meeting with the ACFTU. It wanted a "face-to-face" meeting with "active communication." It wanted a "win-win" situation with the ACFTU, with, of course, no one from the press being allowed to participate. (5) The workers at Wal-Mart in the union, from the store in Nanjing, were tired of the situation. For two years they had tried to unionize, and out of this came no response. Finally there was a response. The government said that Wal-Mart, faced with organization, had to give in. It had to give all its workers a pay raise with fringe benefits. To some, that was a good reason to have a union, since Wal-Mart didn't even want to pay the 2 percent union dues for its workers. (6)

Gao Haitou

Gao Haitou was a 29-year-old employee of the Wal-Mart in Nanjing. He had been working tirelessly for two years, to set up a local branch of the ACFTU. "With the guidance and support of local trade unions, 30 workers at Wal-Mart's Jingjiang store filed an application to the Quanzhou Trade Union Council, asking to join and form a trade union." (7) Gao Haitou and his co-workers could not meet at Wal-Mart. Instead they had to meet in secret, at the Jingjiang District trade union. Not ten feet away from the store, the union met secretly to plan what they should do, much as unions do all over the world. In the summer of 2006, when they had been organizing for two years, they found the requisite 25 members to establish a trade union. They elected the members of the committee and the Chairperson of the union. Then they presented themselves to Wal-Mart, with a fait accompli. More than threatening the wages, it was making a threat to Wal-Mart's raison d'etre. Wal-Mart didn't want to give up the control of its stores to a union.

Ultimately, the ACFTU and Gao Haitou won. It became clear that the ill-will of the Chinese ACFTU and the Communist Party would affect Wal-Mart, making it unlikely for it to prosper in China. Obviously, that was the last thing Wal-Mart wanted. As a result, Wal-Mart gave in to the union. Then, surprise of surprises! On August 9, 2006, Wal-Mart announced that all of its stores would set up labor unions; it would support labor organizations in all of its 60 stores. By fiat, all of its 60, stores at that point were organized. Wal-Mart had decided to live with the ACFTU, and it worked out a modus vivendi to do so. Or, as Marc Blecher has said:

"More strongly, it reinforces the state's capacity to monitor and stabilize state labor politics. In part, this will involve preemption: a reinvigorated ACFTU can provide the state with the means to keep major foreign employers like Wal-Mart from engaging in practices that would infuriate workers . . . ." (8)

In the United Kingdom and in Germany, and in India as well—unlike the United States—Wal-Mart had finally been made by the courts to acquiesce to the unions. Wal-Mart did not want another showdown with a union—especially not in China.

In addition, by comparison, French retailer Carrefour already had 240 supermarkets, and was unionized in China. Wal-Mart did not want to start a battle with Carrefour, its arch rival in China, with the ACTFU at its back. The news that Wal-Mart had established a union in China shocked the world, especially that Wal-Mart would have to bargain with the union.

At first, Wal-Mart presented the union bargaining committee with a contract, having settled on a wage increase of 9 percent the first year and 9 percent the next. Wal-Mart expected it to be accepted, as always.

But, Gao Haitou pointed out it was much too low. What's more, this wage increase "did not even come into effect until next year." (It was reported as 9 percent by this Wal-Mart store, and 9 percent by the newspapers.) Gao then made it clear that these wages fell far "short of inflation rates of 30 percent for food in 2007 and 2008, and also fell short of the average 18 percent increase in national urban wages," which was the wage increase he argued for.

He was right; in 2006 the average monthly wage was about 1,800 yuan. But, of course, Wal-Mart was not going to budge. Then the struggle began between Wal-Mart and the union, the struggle over who would win the argument over wage increases—the executives of Wal-Mart or the "grass-roots" union. First, without making an announcement, Wal-Mart replaced Gao with someone from its management as the head of the union. Gao was told "someone from the high levels of company management would be included on the union committee." Yet, according to the Trade Union Law, "the union committee is to be determined through an election of the workers." Then, as a diversion, Wal-Mart proposed a "steering committee" to incorporate three of the stores in the Nanching area into a larger committee of the union body. The director of the committee was to be Nanching Wal-Mart's deputy manager, an idea that was supported by Nanching's ACFTU.

"The ACFTU typically acquiesces to changing the union representative to management. This is how it is traditionally done in China. The trade union and management appoint someone from management to be the union head."

So Gao Haitou sent an urgent message to the ACFTU's Grass-Roots Works Department. They replied by an "urgent notification" saying he was well within his rights. The two branches of the ACFTU were at odds: Nanching's ACFTU and the Grass-Roots Works Department, a strange dilemma. But after the Grass-Roots Works Department supported Gao Haitou, he victoriously maintained his place as president of the union.

The second issue that disturbed the unions was the "administrative benefits" given to the workers. Wal-Mart wanted to deny the type of holiday benefits that Wal-Mart had traditionally given to employees, including some "50 RMB worth of moon cake, 50 RMB worth of cooking oil, and a 150 RMB Chinese New Year bonus." Not surprisingly, the previous year "Wal-Mart firmly reject[ed] these 'unreasonable requests.'" That which was formerly paid by the company, in turn, would be taken out of the union budget—from the 2 percent the company was to pay for each worker. ACFTU officials from Shenzhen came to Nanching to "investigate the matter." That year, the issue of the "administrative benefits" was never resolved.

Wal-Mart, already having lost two battles with a skinny 26 year old, was frantic. But China's Trade Union Law stipulates that "grassroots unions" are independent entities, but they are subordinate to the upper levels of the ACFTU. In reality the upper levels of the ACFTU are subordinate to the government. And that was the final verdict of the government.

Wal-Mart and the government called the shots here. The government always pegs the wages of its store employees to slightly more than the minimum wage. What is more, the "the negotiations lasted only five hours, suggesting it was a largely pro-forma exercise." But Gao Haitou and his colleagues pressed on. When Gao pushed them to amend the contract, Wal-Mart was decidedly not going to give in to the workers, even if it had to lie. Wal-Mart simply bypassed Gao Haitou. Wal-Mart said that the draft contract was the one Wal-Mart and the ACFTU had already agreed upon. All a worker had to do was to sign it!

A reporter covering this story called the ACFTU Grass-Roots Works Department office. The reporter was told a different story— that the "specific content of the contract needs to be determined by the enterprise and employees." At that point the chairperson, Gao Haitou, implied that Wal-Mart had lied, and said overtly that "this type of negotiation was a forced agreement." Ultimately, Wal-Mart found another union chairperson to sign it; a different chair at another store. This was highly illegal, but it passed, and the workers were held to a 9 percent raise. Gao Haitou simply resigned at this miscarriage of justice;

he could nothing more. The union never interfered with running the stores, just as Wal-Mart wished. But at least the workers got a 9 percent increase. (9)

The Chinese Women Workers at Wal-Mart Stores

This approach works well in China in the Wal-Mart supermarkets. In many Wal-Mart supermarkets they can pay their staff, who are most of the time almost all women, just pennies a day. And that's what they do in some Wal-Mart stores.

The women who work in the unionized Buji store in Shenzhen are clerks and cashiers. They largely come from surrounding villages, where they go home every night. They do not live in dormitories, and some are married. They live in their village, "where domination by men is rife, since young rural women are considered more pliant and less aware of their rights than their male counterparts." (10) The minimum wage in each village or city each year is decided upon for a 40-hour week, by economic planners.

While some workers in factories or men on construction crews do not get paid at all, workers at Wal-Mart always get paid, and paid on time. But they are "unskilled," and particularly for that reason AND because they are women, they get especially poor wages. Workers, or "associates" as they are called, were paid 900 yuan per month ($1.00 = 8 yuan). For a retail worker that is not necessarily a bad wage.

Wal-Mart has a very "good" system for manipulating its wage structure. It is very much in Wal-Mart's style and its interest to pay the women's wages at the Buji store in Shenzhen. "Wal-Mart, by allocating some 40 percent as a subsidy," and 15 percent as a housing allowance, in total, pays the women less than it should. Wal-Mart pays the women a "basic wage," which is lower than the "monthly wage" (or the "standard wage"). If the "basic wage" is 15 percent below the "monthly wage," as it was in 2008—550 yuan instead of 700 yuan—Wal-Mart was legally permitted to deduct that 15 percent because it was a subsidy for the housing allowance, which most of the women don't use. That is considered a "fringe benefit." After that, Wal-Mart deducts "some

40 percent as subsidy." The "subsidy" is also a "fringe benefit." It helps "Wal-Mart to avoid paying its full contribution to its social security premium." The Wal-Mart workers are cheated out of the wages they should be paid, by having their wages cut like this. Instead of getting 8,400 yuan a year, they get R5240 a year, or 720 yuan a month, instead of 450—a big disadvantage.

Year after year, they will get less and less of a wage increase when it is calculated like this. After a number of years, they will find themselves way behind.

"This also helps Wal-Mart to avoid paying in full an employer's contribution to its employees' social security premium, which is calculated as a percentage of the worker's wage. That means Wal-Mart gets away with only paying about half the social security premium." (10)

This procedure is exactly like the wage rates Wal-Mart likes and wants—and it is not legal, even though it is "unionized." But the Buji store in Shenzhen sets the base wage far below the minimum wage. Instead of having to make them "work off the clock" to diminish what they pay as they did in the United States, Wal-Mart has found a way, in China, for women to work legally, and to pay them almost nothing.

And on top of that, Wal-Mart has in one of its Shenzhen stores, a large percentage of part-time and "casual" workers. Again, in the Buji store, there are 440 out of 600 workers, almost all of whom "receive lower pay and no subsidies." As in America, Wal-Mart turned to a system where workers could be called up to work any time of the day, whenever Wal-Mart needed them. But as part-time workers they received no housing subsidies because they didn't live in dormitories, and did not get bonuses either.

To become full-time workers, they need to have been working for a year. Yet many don't want to take the "test" that is given to become a full-time worker. Because the Shenzhen workers live in the village, they are only earning some extra money for their families. Actually, only "some of them were given a chance to sit for an exam for promotion to full-time status." Taking the test was a sign that one wants to go further in Wal-Mart, and few do.

In Kunming Province, in 2007, part-time or "casual" workers in Wal-Mart are also paid 600 yuan a month. This is the same wage as in Shenzhen. But the managers do not schedule the part-time workers for a 40-hour week; they schedule them often for a 30-hour week "and, when customer volume is low," the managers "generally require" them to end their shifts early, and they don't get their full pay. They earn even less than the workers in Shenzhen, about the same as Wal-Mart in Shenzhen, about 500 yuan per month. That is about the same wage as the workers in Shenzhen get.

Wal-Mart always has different rules or systems for determining workers' pay, always to Wal-Mart's advantage, so it is always the lowest. Even though Wal-Mart has a "union" in all of its stores and in some of its factories, unions are not designed to help workers flourish. In six branches of the Wal-Mart union, in the stores that were studied by Anita Chan, there was no union activity at all. In fact, most unions with women in them don't have real unions, or not effective unions. "If there were any activities at all they were an outing, a sports event, and an annual celebration of festivals, with a distribution of festive gifts." (11) The female workers don't expect anything more. They have gotten nothing from the union in the past, even in the "state-owned enterprises." And so they do not expect the unions to struggle on their behalf. What do they do in the stores in Kunming ?

"Employees reorganized clothing bins and swept the floor. But most present were the staff who hovered at every stack of shampoo or home appliance display, handing out samples, yelling out prices, and demonstrating the fabulous capabilities of vacuum cleaners." (12)

In Wal-Mart stores in China there are too many saleswomen because the Chinese have so many people willing to work. So it is not hard to find someone to "sweep the floor, or help customers." In contrast, in the United States you will find a dearth of saleswomen. They are all rushed, and there is no one to help you. Wal-Mart in the U.S. economizes on its labor as a way of driving its total costs. In China, it must satisfy the government and show it is providing jobs.

Working in Wal-Mart's Factories

This is not true in the multiplicity of Wal-Mart's factories. Certainly there are few "sweatshops" in the retail stores, where consumers come to shop, but in the factories Wal-Mart cares nothing about sweatshop conditions, and there is no one to stop the owners and managers of factories—not the union, not the government. It is a blessing for the migrant workers to have any job at all.

There are at least 6,000 factories that contract to Wal-Mart. The Hantai factory is one of them. Hantai makes shoes for Wal-Mart. At Hantai, there are 2,000 workers—all women—and most of the workers are between the ages of 18 and 24. They are young women, very similar to the workforce at Foxconn.

How does Wal-Mart treat the women who work in the Hantai plant? As it does for the Mietai factory, a non-Wal-Mart plant which makes computers for Hewlett-Packard, Dell, Lenovo, Microsoft, or IBM? Does it pledge to follow the labor laws, pay their salaries on time, and give them compensation when they are laid off? Or, do these factories flout the New Labor Contract Law, just as the other factories do?

The women workers are given contracts for one year. The New Labor Contract Law, a law passed in 2008, is something like the Fair Labor Standards Act passed in the U.S. in 1938. According to this law, it is now incumbent on employers in China to give each worker a contract, stipulating the conditions of employment: wages, hours, and what the employer can and cannot do.

However, the law is not enforced. Workers must agree to write in "I will work accordingly to employer's arrangement and adjustment," a clause that negates the Labor Contract and makes the workers, the employees, almost slaves to the company. The employer then has carte blanche to make them work as hard and as fast as it wants them to. The law says they must be paid by the 7th of each month, but they are asked to forego this by writing, "I agree to extend the wage distribution date to the 12th of each month." They are not allowed to quit during "the busy period," and they must also write in, "During the busy period, I agree to let my employer arrange overtime accordingly." Thus the employer easily abrogates the rules that protect the workers. Actually, there is no employment contract at all at Hantai. Effectively, at the Hantai factory the employer can hold workers responsible for anything it wants to, anything that will allow it to get the work out on time.

The workers also formally commit themselves to an eight-hour-a-day working week, a reasonable amount of time. But on top of that they are given fully five hours of unpaid overtime a day. Workers must agree to complete this extra five hours, or they are not to be given any paid overtime for that month. They cannot make a living on their pay without paid overtime. That would substantially decrease the worker's income, so the women never refuse the overtime. And they work 13 hours a day.

And the living conditions are the same. Unless one is married, one has to live in the dormitory and pay the rental fee. Ten to twelve women share a room, where they sleep on metal bunk beds. Bathrooms are too few and dirty to boot. If they arrive at work late, the supervisor may withhold overtime work for one week, or use physical punishment. One thing has changed though! The security guards do not attack the workers like before—in the workshop, canteen, and even in the dormitory. The women do not get "workers' compensation" or health insurance, except that which they have to pay for themselves. The food they get in the workers' cafeteria, for which they pay 180 RMB, is poor and not nourishing, and sometimes tastes rancid.

There is also a union at Hantai, but there is no workers' committee, and the union has never held a union activity or protected workers' rights. Finally, the factory "passes" external audits, by getting the workers to lie about wages, overtime pay, and safety conditions. And this situation goes on despite the existence of The New Contract Labor Law.

There is an informal "quiet" rule now, since the recession began, which says, "You may do anything with workers but fire them," since there is so much unemployment. They use that to take advantage of the workers once again. Just like all the audits of Wal-Mart's suppliers, the Hantai shoe factory pushes the workers to their limits simply because they can.

But when it wants to, Hantai will also do all it can to get the women to quit. They try that when they are not busy. Management will "verbally abuse" the workers and beat them until they feel forced to leave, or their lives are in jeopardy. The company will reassign workers to jobs they are not familiar with, and they leave when they fail to do them correctly. Then the employers fail to pay the mandatory severance pay. The employer will not lay anyone off, they will "just quit."

The women are fortunate to have a job at all. About half of the 24 million people unemployed all over China will not find jobs this year. The economic stimulus, large as it is, cannot produce enough jobs for all the people who need them. That is the same for college graduates. But, more importantly, although Wal-Mart has vowed to "establish corporate responsibility standards for its Chinese supply chain," it has reneged on its responsibility. Some workers in contracting plants make only 51 cents an hour, 60 percent of the minimum wage—another violation of the labor code.

Yet, what is even harder is the regimen.

"Workers . . . are prohibited from talking, listening to music, even raising their heads or putting their hands in their pockets (to keep from stealing) when they are at work. Workers are fined for being one minute late, for not trimming their fingernails—which could impede the work—and for stepping on the grass. Workers are searched on the way in and out of the factory, and workers who hand out flyers or discuss factory conditions with outsiders are fired."

They work as they sit on stools, 12 hours a day. They handle "five hundred computer keyboards an hour," one every 7.2 seconds. A woman is allowed just 1.1 seconds to put each key in place. They are not permitted to go to the bathroom unless there is a break. All overtime is mandatory; they have two days off—once a month. Women are at work 81 hours a week, when not in their overcrowded dormitories. They work about 34 hours of overtime, "which exceeds China's legal limit by 318 percent."

This exceeds the degradation of the women in Lowell, Massachusetts at the end of the 18th century, when women made textiles. The reason for this is that the purchasers of computers in America give them a "very short time" to deliver the products. The managers are under constant pressure. They will be penalized if they don't deliver on time, and thus so will the workers. Even the manager has a stressful job. He was quoted as saying, "Well if they press me too hard, I'll just give up."

In this Chinese plant they get wages of 64 cents an hour, which does not come close to the level needed for subsistence. Is that because at the Wal-Mart factory they produce shoes, which are a "low-end" item? But at the Meitai factory they make "computers" which are "high tech."

Foxconn is a company that makes computers and ipods and such, and employs 120,000 workers in several plants. It has been continually in the news for having 12 young workers commit suicide. Like the Meitai factory in China it has no union, and it has many of the same conditions. Workers typically are subject to the pressure of getting production out as fast as they can. They work long hours, and for little pay. At Meitai they "feel like [they] are serving a prison sentence." Management tells the women when they are hired, "love the company like your home," and "continuously strive for perfection," and to "actively monitor each other." (It actually tells them to spy on each other.) This is a message much like Hantai delivers—or Foxconn.

It is not very different from Hantai factories, except for the publicity. Like the Meitai factory in China it has no union, and workers typically are subject to the pressure of getting production out as fast as they can. It is no wonder that at Foxconn young men and women threw themselves off the roof.

Managers—The Men

Wal-Mart has a very different way of treating managers in its stores in China than they do in the United States. For in China, store managers are exclusively male. It has had to base its treatment of men on aspects of the Chinese culture. It is necessary to create a belief among managers that Wal-Mart has values that are consistent with the Chinese culture and Chinese traditions.

David J. Davies exemplifies how "the Wal-Mart concepts" have done that. The best way to describe this phenomenon is to show how a portrait of Sam Walton mirrors a view of Mao Zedong. Davies shows that Sam Walton's ideas can resemble a view of an older China.

"The largest poster featured the benevolent image of Sam Walton, dressed in a dark formal suit and conservative burgundy tie; his corporate image was softened by the simple working-class Wal-Mart baseball cap sitting slightly askew high on his head, in rural American style. An everyday red, white, and blue Wal-Mart employee nametag was pinned over his heart. Walton's right hand is raised in a partial wave of greeting and his face has a muted expression of pleasant indifference . . . .Walton's pose is eerily similar to the images of Mao Zedong that circulated during the Cultural Revolution, hand raised in greeting at the top of Tiananmen gate, wearing his own symbol of unity with the masses—the armband of the Red Guard." (13)

In China, Wal-Mart needs a positively motivated staff of managers so that they can perpetuate the Wal-Mart culture. This is not a hope or a wish, but something that Wal-Mart expects of its managers at the highest levels. Identifying Mao Zedong with Sam Walton is a way to do this. The purpose is for the managers to identify with Wal-Mart; that makes them feel they are "new Chinese men." They must know there is a different "way of life" from one that is filled with corruption, bribery, and fraud as Chinese society is—one that is free of the "stress and uncertainty" of the Chinese freewheeling (and often corrupt) market economy.

Having managers with an identification with Wal-Mart means giving them a route to a different "way of life." Then one will be loyal to the rules of Wal-Mart. Loyalty is the key to the process. That is the way Wal-Mart trains its managers in the U.S., and they are loyal to the American "Wal-Mart way." (14)

One subject, a Chinese manager who was named "Steve," said in all honesty, "Sam Walton studied Mao Zedong for five years before he opened Wal-Mart." Indeed, he explained that there are some facets of Walton's life that "fit" with Mao Zedong. Like Mao, Sam Walton was born poor "and started out with a base of committed colleagues." Walton's colleagues were "working class"; they were like Chinese functionaries that "emerged since China [has been] integrated into the global economic system." All of the managers, his colleagues, must be enamored with the new culture.

And managers are happy, of course, to have the opportunity, by working at Wal-Mart, to become wealthy and successful entrepreneurs. It is a theme that "unites employees' work performance with a personal and social morality." They are proud to share in the culture.

It is ironic that the "ten laws" of Wal-Mart are similar to those of the Red Army, or to the "Ten Commandments." In that sense they are a religion. How can they represent the Chinese culture, a culture which is "reminiscent" of revolutionary communism? Or is it reminiscent of contemporary Confucianism? By counterposing the Wal-Mart way to the corruption in the business environment, the Wal-Mart way provides a "moral injunction" that the manager not take any gifts in his dealings with agents of other companies or within Wal-Mart. It is "wrong," and borders on the irreligious; like violating the Ten Commandments. (15)

This ideology is internalized in the Wal-Mart manager. After a time, men's colleagues confirm this moral perspective. At the same time the store also becomes "my Wal-Mart" in that all the managers demonstrate the "spirit of ownership."

"Wal-Mart culture is American culture!" The managers feel they are living the lifestyle of Americans, and the American family. "Chinese here at Wal-Mart live an American lifestyle and many really take American culture into their work habits, their individual lifestyle and their honesty." They do all writing in English. They are given American names, names like "Steve." An American name "is a marker of professional status" marking a worker's position as a modern Chinese, working in a global economy. Wal-Mart appears to be non-hierarchical; it's like America. Wal-Mart is democratic—one can talk to anyone; and anyone can talk to you. (16)

Managers cannot be fired unless one commits the sin of failing to be honest. "Honesty" involves "theft, offering kickbacks, or violations of the gift policy." In China, Wal-Mart tries to be virtuous by not firing anybody, in stark contradiction to its policy in America. Managers are not fired for this, neither are the sales women fired—they quit. "In other words, the corporation creates, trains, or empowers individuals (men) who carry out extraordinary work." (17)

But there is a fly in the ointment. Wal-Mart is so American that it is ruled by the sales figures, something that no one can control. "At 11 p.m., an hour after the store closes, store managers are notified of the volume of sales, the number of customers, and the customer's average total purchase and other information." Managers, like the Americans, are under severe pressure to fulfill the store's goals. Yet, fulfilling the goal means "how much you sell." Since there is no "punishment" for not selling enough, the employee must be motivated by something other than money. (18)

In spite of all the good aspects of being a Wal-Mart manager, there is a sensibility that being a good and virtuous employee comes at a steep price. The Chinese managers subject themselves to "a burden of supervision and discipline that extends to their personal lives." In that sense they do have the "iron rice bowl" in that they are loyal to Wal-Mart, that is their home; they are there for a lifetime and they can never be fired. Therefore, they don't need a union. (19)

Thus, there is an intrinsic need to internalize Wal-Mart's commandments. Wal-Mart is an authoritarian enterprise. It requires that the rules that one follows are not just accepted, they must be deeply internalized. That is the way the Chinese ethic is transformed into what "works" for Wal-Mart. (20)

The Harmonious Society

In China the union, the ACFTU, does not see itself as the carrier of "class consciousness." China has no public ideology of workers being pitted against their bosses to ensure they get a "fair share" of the productivity that is produced. In China the purpose of the union was to bring about a "harmonious" society, as the ACFTU claimed. What, then, do the Chinese employers see as the ideal relationship between capital and labor? (21)

The ACFTU and the Chinese workers see the union not as an advocate for labor, but at best a "bridge between management and labor." The union is not a defender of workers' rights; it "seeks to facilitate a compromise between two sides." (22) At its worst, the union defends management and not the workers. China is still far from a "harmonious society." "At least one strike involving more than 1,000 workers occurs every day in China's manufacturing hub, in the Pearl River Delta area, underscoring rising labor unrest in the country." These spontaneous strikes have nothing to do with the official union, which seeks to bring about harmony. (23)

There is also an ACFTU booklet called "Implementing Regulations" . . . which further defines the union's new role "creating a responsible, empowered, and battle-ready union that can protect workers' rights." That is rhetoric, not reality! At Wal-Mart, as at every other firm, the situation does not lead to "a harmonious society," but one of increasing anger or cynical acceptance.

When the Union Intervenes

The ACFTU does do some things for the workers, at various times and in various ways. For example, when an employer does something against the state, i.e., when the workers don't get their wages or when employees are laid off, then, in some cases, the ACFTU intervenes on behalf of the worker.

Wal-Mart was expanding and it had a plan to reshuffle its mid-level managers. Not only was it doing it in Changchun, but it was doing it in Changsha, Dongguan, and Fujian—affecting over 100 people. In fact the displaced managers believed, quite rightly, that this was a ploy to reduce the labor force in some stores, due to a "reorganization," which Wal-Mart does all the time. (24)

As Wal-Mart was expanding it needed to move some managers to other stores, to a province far from Changchun. It gave the men some choices. They could move to a far-off location where the other stores were located, they could take a cut in pay, or they could leave the company. (25)

In the United States, moving isn't normally a problem. The average family moves at least every five years. But in China it is. The Chinese have their families in one town or city, and moving is tantamount to saying goodbye to the families forever. And the third option is to let them go, with compensation.

This kind of decision had never been made before by Wal-Mart, and it left the other managers who remained in the store, aghast. Moreover, the management of Wal-Mart had not given the managers any detailed information about the other stores in the area. It is as if Wal-Mart is "firing them" no matter which option they take. "The Company wants us to leave, because few will find the first two options acceptable," said one manager. "We don't think it is right for the Company to announce such a decision without consulting the workers."

Then, with nowhere to go, the managers consulted the Shenzhen Municipal Federation of Trade Unions, the local branch of the ACFTU for help. The federation reported this situation to the ACFTU. (26) It was resolved in the managers' favor when "three mid-level executives came to my office this morning and told me the plan was shelved, and they had resumed their work," said Yang Fenzhi, the Director of the Law Department of the city's Federation of Trade Unions. Thus, sometimes workers in China get the benefit of having the union work for them, and sometimes they save the workers' good jobs.

At this time the workers are suffering from rising inflation and low wages, and at the same time a shortage of low-wage workers. This is because the new generation of workers will no longer work for such low wages. There is also the fact of the global economic crisis. But the 66 million stimulus packages launched in 2008 are all but spent and men are now working for months on railways with no pay. Rapid inflation has put a squeeze on bank lending, and has prompted businesses to stop paying wages to blue-collar workers, even in the state sector. (27) And because of this, there are more strikes and protests since the workers have no other way (collective bargaining) of getting what they want. There were, by rough calculation, about 30,000 collective protests in 2009. Yet 66 percent, almost two-thirds of the cases accepted by both mediation and arbitration committees, actually increased by 3.8 percent. The local branches of the ACFTU had actually resolved cases of workers not being paid, through a process of mediation rather than coercion.

The protests have made the government aware of the horrific consequences of not being paid, or of getting half of one's wage on payday. This has been carried by the media all throughout the world, and it has generated some victories. Some workers have gotten serious increases in pay. In Chengdu and in some other provinces this year, the "average salary" has risen to $325, up 21 percent from the previous year. (28)

But some other did not get a raise in pay. The raise had been put "on hold." The Pearl River Delta is the seat of manufacturing for the export sector, and Hong Kong "claimed that an increase in the minimum wage would add seven percent to their overall costs." A whole sector of China was sacrificed to their needs. Yet:

"The Chinese authorities are searching for other ways, apart from raising the minimum wage, to deal with the increasing number of labor disputes across China. The official ACFTU has once again emphasized the need for employers and employees to negotiate collective wage agreements, a program reportedly endorsed by the ILO's Asia Director, Sachkiko Yamamoto, who told the China Daily that collective bargaining could help workers 'enjoy a fairer share of the country's booming economy." (29)

There is reason to doubt the Chinese government. But last November there was a new message. For the Chinese government to say (and there are some in the ACFTU who believe in it) that there should be collective bargaining, was a "revolutionary" statement. Wal-Mart was not mentioned in the strikes that prevailed. Perhaps there were no strikes or protests at Wal-Mart because the only thing Wal-Mart is fearful of is the ACFTU. It does as it is bid. Wal-Mart tries very hard not to disturb its relationship with the union.

The basic relationship of Wal-Mart to the union is one of acquiescence. It appropriates the customs of Chinese culture. By supporting gender differentiation, as the immigrant workers in China do, it pays low wages to women while it sees men as the real masters of Wal-Mart. It sees them as managers and it educates them to be intensely loyal. That is exactly what it does in the U.S., and that kind of institutionalized stereotyping led to a massive class-action gender discrimination lawsuit in America. But Wal-Mart takes care of its people, so they do not strike at all. It pays low wages to the women in the factories, because that is the norm in China, and it chooses young women who are passive. The young women workers are right about their lives in the factories: they need higher wages and they need more respect.

The International Labor Organization

A very new thing in China is the focus on the promotion of collective bargaining. "The ACFTU has been actively working with the International Labor Organization for ten years to enhance the capacity of union negotiators and trainers, at the enterprise level." And the ACFTU has made an effort to promote collective bargaining at the sectoral and regional level. These are vital steps for the Chinese. Because without this there will be no way to arrest the number of labor disputes. The disputes tend to engage in massive protests and large demonstrations, because labor has no other means of expressing itself. According to the Ministry of Human Resources and Social Security, the number of labor dispute cases had doubled from 314,000 in 2005 to 690,000 in 2008. That is an indication of how serious this is. They have come to realize that "the harmonious society" will not be reached until there is a union, with collective bargaining.

"In an emerging capitalist economy labor's adversary is management, but to the extent to which, and the means by which, unions can represent labor to counter management are decisively defined and circumscribed by the state." (30)

There is the same conflict with the Chinese today. There are people of various opinions in the ACFTU working in the traditional structure, who are open to new ideas. The ACFTU is learning about collective bargaining, but has learned to work within a state structure. In

China, Wal-Mart made a pledge to China Labor Watch (an investigative and publicity arm of the labor movement in the Chinese factories) on July 29, 2008, that Wal-Mart would conduct "an investigation to assess [the] "violations" that China Labor Watch discovered in its first audit—and it did find many violations. Indeed, there are actually many new violations in the Hantai company. Wal-Mart promised that it would treat all of its workers with the "respect and dignity they deserve." Yet, one year later, Wal-Mart had not fulfilled its promise. China Labor Watch has written to Mike Duke, the president of Wal-Mart about this, and he hasn't responded as of this writing.

In 2014 there are some new problems at Wal-Mart. This one is a problem of the low wages, and the refusal of Wal-Mart to raise them. "When a small strike involving about 40 workers broke out, in Shenzhen, because of dissatisfaction with the pay rise scheme, which would also cancel the housing subsidy and the bonus, (emphasis mine) more than 40 workers went on strike at the Shenzhen distribution Center. And the management cracked down." (31) " "Wang Shishu (one of the people to protest) noted that the trade union agreed on a contract deal with the company in 2012. But from the workers perspective it wasn't high enough, and they generally were not in accord with the pay raise mechanism. The workers didn't think the trade unions represent them since they are not democratically elected."(32) When, eighteen year ago, when Wal-Mart first came to China, the wages at Wal-Mart were considered high. But the economy has grown, and the wages have only risen 73 cents an hour. The economy is now "eleven times as big" (33)

No one at the company was available for an interview on the topic, about how Wal-Mart treats its workers, said Kevin Gardner, Wal-Mart's Senior Director for International Corporate Affairs. Both activist and academics have found that the abuses in China are similar to the United States—low wages, worker intimidation , gender based discrimination, unpaid overtime, replacing full-time workers with part-time (who have lower hourly wages and don't receive any benefits) , firing workers who complain or organize.

At this point, 2014, there is a new problem at Wal-Mart in China. Besides pointing out that Wal-Mart has sold tainted meat, it has sold "donkey meat that contained DNA from other animals, like foxes.(34) Wal-Mart has once again, has fired workers another worker who protested in the pay raise scheme.

Footnotes

1. "Wal-Mart to Open 100 More Stores in China by 2015," Reuters, October 26, 2012.
2. David J. Davies, "Wal-Mao: The Discipline of Corporate Culture and Studying Success at Wal-Mart China," The China Journal, No. 58, July 2007.
3. Mei Fong and Ann Zimmerman, "China's Union Push Leaves Wal-Mart with Hard Choice," The Wall Street Journal, May 13, 2006.
4. "China Says Foreign Company Union Drive Not Over," The New York Times, October 18, 2007.
5. "Trade Union Gets into Wal-Mart," About ACFTU News, August 10, 2006.
6. "Wal-Mart Signs Its First Collective Wage Agreement with Employees in China," China Labor Bulletin, July 16, 2008.
7. Han Dongfang, "China Brief: Labor Law Strengthens Chinese Unions," Jamestown's Foundation China Brief, July 30, 2008.
8. Marc Blecher, "When Wal-Mart Wimped Out; Globalization and Unionization in China," Critical Asian Studies 40:2 2008, 263-276.
8. The whole story of Wal-Mart and the ACFTU is explained in a series of articles written by the China Labor News Translations (CLNT) e.g. "Trouble at Wal-Mart: The Rocky Road to Labor Reform in China," October 15, 2008.
10. Anita Chan, "Organizing China's Wal-Mart. The Chinese Trade Union at a Crossroads," no date.
11. Anita Chan, "Wal-Mart Workers in China," International Labor Rights Forum and the National Labor College, Washington D.C.
12. Ali Farhoomand and Iris Wang, "Wal-Mart Stores: 'Every Day Low Prices' in China," Asia Case Research Center, 2006.
13. David J. Davies, in "Wal-Mart in China", edited by Anita Chan, ILR Press, Cornell University Press. Also see: David J. Davies, "Wal-Mao: The Discipline of Corporate Culture and Studying Success at Wal-Mart China," The China Journal, No. 58, July 2007.
14. "Carrefour and Wal-Mart's Differing Expansion Strategies in China," Euromonitor International, March 22, 2008.

15. Robert Weil, "City of Youth; Shenzhen, China," Monthly Review, June 28, 2008.

16. Catherine Bodry, "Five Ways Wal-Mart in China is Way Different (and Way More Intense) Than at Home," Gadling.com, November 20, 2009.

17. Chris White, Labor Lawyer and Researcher at Flinders University School of Law.

18. Japan Focus, September 28, 2006.

19. "Wal-Mart Willing to Talk to China's Official Trade Union," BBC Monitoring International Reports, Global News Wire-Asia-Africa Intelligence Wire, Financial Times Information Limited, August 9, 2006.

20. People's Daily (October 8, 2003) and Japan Focus (September 8, 2006).

21. P. Pameswaran, "Labor Unrest Growing in China," January 15, 2008.

22. "It's Over! It's Over! Come Quick and Save Wal-Mart's Union," China Labor News Translations (http://clntranslations.com).

23. Han Dongfang, China Brief: Labor Law Strengthens Chinese Unions, Jamestown's Foundation China Brief, July 30, 2008.

24. "Wal-Mart China Begins Management Reorganization," Supermarkets, April 22, 2009.

25. "Wal-Mart's Reshuffle Plans," Xinhua, March 12, 2009.

26. Li Chang, "Unity is Strength, The Workers' Movement In China, 2009-2011," China Labor Bulletin, Research Reports 2011.

27. "Companies' Cash is Drying Up, With Dire Consequences for Their Workers." The Economist, October 19, 2011.

28. "Chinese Migrant Workers' Wages 21% Up Last Year," The China Daily, February 29. 2012, and "After Struggling for Two Years, 77 Migrant Workers Successfully Get Their Back Pay, More Than 550,000 Yuan ($87,300) on January 11, 2012." Wang Zhenghua, "Workers Face Uphill Fight for Rights," China Daily, February 20, 2012.

29. Guangdong Reportedly Postpones Minimum Wage Increase," China Labor Bulletin, November 9, 2011).

30. Feng Chun, "Between the State and Labor: The Conflict of Chinese Trade Unions' Double Identity in Market Reform," The China Quarterly, Number 176, December 2003.
31. The American Prospect—As Wal-Mart Swallows China's Economy, Workers Fight Back, by Esther Wang, April 23, 2013
32. Wal-Mart Empire Clashes with China , by Michelle Chan, The Progressive, 2014
33. Chinese Workers Fight Wal-Mart for Better Wages, Marketplace World, Rob Schmitz, January 22, 2014
34. Adam Jourdan, Wal-Mart Recalls Donkey Product in China After Fox Meat Scandal Did , Reuters, January 2, 2014

9

FDI in India

Food is a major problem for India. Feeding a nation of 1.1 billion people is not simple, especially for a country that is backward technologically in many areas. What many Indians realize is that Wal-Mart may hurt them right in the stomach if food costs them more, such that the poorest of them cannot eat. After all, the "dalits," the undesirables, have a right, if not to have the finest jobs, then at least to eat.

Since 1991 India has begun to industrialize. As soon as Wal-Mart became focused on India, a great debate was started over Foreign Direct Investment (FDI). The debate was about whether foreign retailers as well as domestic retailers could own supermarkets in India, and whether FDI would finally come to India.

In December of 2006, John Menzer, the CEO of Wal-Mart, met with Manmohan Singh, Prime Minister of India. Menzer asked for permission to open a liaison office in New Delhi, to source materials. It had already been sourcing in India since 2001, without an office. But in view of its much later agenda—to open stores—Menzer wanted to use this meeting to lobby the Indian government to open up FDI.

Singh was not only concerned about opening India to FDI. The Indian government was more "protectionist" and less of a "free trader" than the United States. It was Singh's goal, who had been a former

Finance Minister, and that of his party, to look for a way to keep Western nations out of India. He was looking for an:

". . . incremental mode that creates new jobs that does not replace or displace employment in small neighborhood shops. He might limit companies such as Wal-Mart to India's six biggest cities and allow them to open only one store a year in each city, with not less than 100,000 square feet, so they can't be located in inner cities' neighborhoods where real estate is expensive. At least half of the retail space would have to be allocated to food to stimulate the development of upstream agriculture, and the percentage of foreign equity would be limited at first . . . probably to 26 or 49 percent." (1)

This certainly was in no way acceptable to Wal-Mart. In comparison to Wal-Mart's haste, Singh was cautious about having Wal-Mart in India. He wanted to make a very limited decision before finally opening the door to foreign retailers. With Wal-Mart's competitive policies, it could run the traditional retailers into the ground.

At the end of these discussions, Wal-Mart got its liaison office, with 120 employees. But that's all it got. Wal-Mart, at the time, was in a precarious position. It had just been forced to sell two subsidiaries, one in Germany, and the other in South Korea. Indeed, Wal-Mart had lost $1 billion trying to keep its stores in Germany. Wall Street was also dismayed, and was beginning to breathe down Wal-Mart's neck.

Since it appeared that Europe was closed to them, Wal-Mart thought it would try underdeveloped markets and was eager to explore them. Wal-Mart realized it could only be successful in BRIC countries. Wal-Mart looked at Russia, and then it looked at Australia, both of which it ruled out for various reasons. India was the last big market! Wal-Mart was already buying $1 billion worth of goods from India for its international stores, and its eyes became fixed on India's seven percent rate of growth. It had aspirations of having perhaps 500 stores there in the future.

India and China were the two "big emerging markets." Wal-Mart had already opened stores in China and was doing fairly well there, with 70 stores and 100 more in Trust Mart, which it had just bought.

India was the second most populous, and fourth largest market on earth. Someday they believed it would become the "jewel" in the corporate crown of Wal-Mart.

But the maneuverings of Wal-Mart, its history and culture, did not help bring about FDI. In fact, two years later there was not a new law. Mohan Guruswamy, head of the Centre for Policy Alternatives, a New Delhi think tank, came out with a new report with estimates that eight million people would lose their jobs if Wal-Mart or similar stores took just 20 percent of the retail trade—much like what happened in South Africa six years later. This could unleash a "pipeline of cheap Chinese goods," that would hurt Indian retailers and food purveyors. (2)

Wal-Mart's response was to meet secretly, with Sunil Bharti Mittal, a large Indian entrepreneur. He and John Menzer of Wal-Mart made a decision to open retail stores together. It was done, a fait accompli. Bharti would open the stores and sell to the public, and Wal-Mart would supply the stores, using its infallible logistics system. This was legal, but did not accord with Indian law and culture.

Sunil Bharti Mittal is one of India's leading businessmen, one of the country's leading manufacturers and exporters of mobile phones—, something very much needed in India since there are no telephone lines in India's homes. Mobile telephone lines are very practical, and very cheap. He had joined with some foreign actors in his investments and it made him a billionaire; and one of a handful of wealthy men in the business community. (3)

While India had a policy of no FDI for supermarkets, according to Indian law Wal-Mart could open "single-brand" stores, giving it 51 percent ownership. But India would not allow "multi-brand retail stores" like Wal-Mart into the country. Wal-Mart could sell to other retailers, but could not, in and of itself, be a retailer. That was the law!

What Wal-Mart and Bharti did then was completely without precedent. It was in accord with the law, the letter of the law, but not the spirit. Wal-Mart appears to have managed to get in "under the table." Wal-Mart was ready to open supermarkets, and their talks suggested that Bharti was ready to look for a supplier.

When the outcome of these maneuvers became apparent, FDI became a highly charged issue. India wanted to give its own domestic retailers the advantage of being the first to open their stores; before they would "possibly" admit the foreigners, following the policy of Mahatma Ghandi. It was to keep India "closed" to foreign investment.

But India wanted to fuel its exports and its exporters wanted to sell their goods. "Wal-Mart promised to buy $1.5 billion worth of goods from India, almost 50 percent more than they had bought from India in the past—on the condition that India would open its doors to Wal-Mart's supermarkets," said Menzer, in the usually aggressive way that characterizes Wal-Mart:

"Wal-Mart [was] no longer prepared to wait but was prepared to make its foray into India, with an Indian joint-venture partner to "take advantage of this market while it's still developing." Its new partner, Sunil Mittal Bharti, was of the same mind, and said he would build 500 supermarkets." (4)

"Wal-Mart is extremely bullish on India, so bullish that it was to the extent of being desperate." (5)

In November 2006, Mukesh Ambani, who was a domestic retailer and head of the top energy company of India, "opened 11 western-style supermarkets simultaneously, in the southern city of Hyderabad." His stores, "Reliance Retail [are] already planning to take a lion's share of the market ahead of the entry of foreign competition." (6) The domestic lions wanted to open their supermarkets fast, before India could have a chance to open the country to FDI. Ambani's plans were to sink $5.6 billion into opening 4,000 stores in 1,500 towns and cities of India over the next four years. Indian companies had never plunged into the retail market the way Reliance was doing:

"Reliance is betting that their supermarkets will provide 'a welcome relief' for young upwardly mobile couples seeking refuge from the loud, crowded dust-clogged marketplaces (in many, cows still plod along disrupting traffic).They also threaten to displace a significant proportion of the 54 million Indians who work in the country's retail sector, in some 12 million small shops." (7)

Another Indian grocer, Kishore Biyani, was also opposed to FDI. The CEO of Pantaloon Retail, Big Bazaar Hypermarkets, and Food Bazaar (food and groceries) stores, Biyani already had 100 stores that would be in competition with Wal-Mart. He was also among the largest owners of retail stores in India. He said that Indian supermarkets "should not be given away to foreign players while they have much new to learn before competing with Indian stores." (8) And he assured his compatriots he would open 100 more stores. He is quoted in Fortune Magazine as saying, "Make it difficult—then the foreigners would have to pay more . . . Why should we make it easy for them?" (9) Sixty-five percent of Indians were rural, and were poor farmers. "Organized retail" in the form of modern retail supermarkets (and very small supermarkets they are too), represented only 3 percent of India's retail sales. But their sales were expected to rise to 15-18 percent by 2010-2011. Domestic supermarkets (and hypermarkets) were growing at the rate of 30 percent annually. The "organized" domestic, food retail industry said it could provide 10-15 million jobs over the next three to five years. But at present, "the organized sector was only $8 billion, compared to the $305 billion that was the unorganized retail sector, the small family shops called "kiranas." (10)

Yet Singh's and India's answer was still "No" to FDI. Politically he could not say "yes." The Communist Party, which was allied with his party, was opposed to it. Singh needed the Communists aligned with the Centre of Indian Trade Unions (CITU)—the trade unionists, in the country—in order for him to have a ruling hand. The Congress Party couldn't pass a bill without the Communists' ten percent of the vote. The Communists voted along with the Congress Party and that represented, 44 out of 454 members, almost ten percent. They were small, but crucial.

The Commerce Minister, Kamal Nath, was not in harmony with the Prime Minister. He was more in step with the ideas of the "free traders" and neo-liberals. The Commerce Minister's policy was to bring organized retail into India. They went on to disagree, to create a feeling of indeterminacy that was to keep the government and the country on edge. Would there be or would there not be FDI in India?

The Communists

The Communist Party (CPI(M)) was opposed to Wal-Mart, and opposed to approving FDI. India has a freely elected democracy in which the Communists claimed a cultural commitment that "opening the country to FDI would undermine the Indian tradition of local self-reliance espoused by Mahatma Gandhi, and to change that tradition was wrong." India would develop naturally as it came of age. More importantly, they also contended economically, that 70 million people were making a living through their own homegrown retail operations, the kirana stores. Opening the country to a host of foreign multinational chains at this point, would make the small stalls, selling homegrown fruits and vegetables and other sundries, obsolete.

Sonia Gandhi

It was Sonia Gandhi, actually an Italian–born leader of the Indian National Congress Party and the daughter-in-law of Indira Gandhi and Rajiv Gandhi, who was the mix in this cake that made Foreign Direct Investment flop. After toppling the fundamentalist Hindu nationalist regime of Atal Bihari Vajpayee and his Bharatiya Janata Party in 2004, she nevertheless refused to become Prime Minister of the traditional Congress Party after she was elected. She saw the election as a victory over Hindu Fundamentalism and proved that "bread-and-butter issues would triumph over religious frenzy." She gave up the Ministry to former Finance Minister, Manmohan Singh, "a gentlemanly Oxford-educated economist" who saved India from the economic crisis of 1991 by saving the rupee's value. The two were very close and administered India together. They now made some major decisions for India.

So Sonia Gandhi wrote a four-line letter to the Prime Minister, saying:

"Several Indian newspapers, including The Economic Times, reported that Sonia Gandhi, president of the Congress Party which leads India's coalition government, has asked Indian Prime Minister Manmohan Singh to reassess how further relaxing foreign direct investment rules could affect the country's family-owned retail-businesses." (11)

"The supermarkets and hypermarkets would destroy the small kirana shops," she said, and India would have more unemployment. And in India where there already is significant unemployment—there is famine—and suicide. And Mohan Guruswamy et al., a well-known academic consultant, agreed with her:

"The retail industry provides some semblance of a social safety net, in the absence of any unemployment benefits. Thus the ongoing increase in individually owned shops (kiranas) is almost entirely due to the jobless growth and deindustrialization, largely due to 'efficiencies' of the last decade." (12)

The existence of kirana stores prevented people from being unemployed. "Unorganized retail" is actually "the largest contributor to India's estimated GDP". But the average size of kiranas is only 50 square feet, and includes 150 million of India's people. "It is very unorganized, fragmented, and has a rural basis." (13) The fear that "organized retail" supermarkets would open in the urban centers was enough to push the farmers and peasants to protest.

The Indians spend 40 percent of the $258 billion in their annual budget for food, which they buy in small shops and bazaars—kiranas. This sum is far more than is spent by Americans or Europeans, who spend only 8 percent of their budget on food.

Then there was the response from the trade unions regarding FDI. The CITU, which was linked to the Communist Party, also said "No" to FDI. Indians go to the kiranas to shop. And, as Indians would say, "shopping is a tradition." There are 50 million CITU members who would potentially protest the opening of India to FDI and Wal-Mart's entry into India.

The Indians knew relatively little about Wal-Mart except that the giant retailer controlled at that point 6,956 retail units worldwide, and sourcing for over 60,000 suppliers in 70 countries. It dealt in literally thousands of brands and served about 176 million customers weekly, in 13 countries. To them it was only a "massive empire that would take over their businesses." Many understood that India could well be the next frontier. And Wal-Mart was coming to India to compete with others like Ambani and Biyani and the like,—and of course the kiranas.

Wal-Mart had already announced they would open 75 hypermarkets and 500 supermarkets, but a major businessman like Ambani was competitive. He bragged a bit but, along with several other large supermarket owners, he was "girding his loins" for the coming competition with Wal-Mart.

The Indians also didn't know much about Wal-Mart's baser side, about its clear anti-union and anti-worker stance. In a country like India which had 50 million union members, no one knew of the many reports that had been written documenting the economic and social degradation which occurs when Wal-Mart "comesto town," or of the many lawsuits that it faced, or the difficulties it had with its workers.

Carrefour, Wal-Mart's greatest competitor, was willing to wait for FDI. Carrefour did not try to enter "through the back door" to enter India as Wal-Mart did. It would wait until the FDI issue was resolved before it was prepared to enter. Thus, reports appearing in the Indian press vilified Wal-Mart.

Wal-Mart was claimed to be guilty of two things. First, it was accused of "getting in through the back door." And, secondly, its poor record of treating employees badly appeared to continue.

Wal-Mart was waiting with bated breath. Wal-Mart had every confidence that the laws would change—because Wall Street and the U.S. government were anxious for it to happen.

On November 28, 2006, Sunil Bharti Mittal and Wal-Mart announced that they had arrived at the decision to enter India. (14) The announcementwas met with surprise and shock. Wal-Mart and Bharti Mittal had a press conference; they would build supermarkets together. Bharti would take care of opening the retail stores and running their management, and Wal-Mart, since that was its forte, would take care of the wholesale logistics.

Needless to say, the supporters of FDI in the Indian government were irate. The day after the announcement, the Commerce Minister, Kamal Nath, said "he would examine whether 'permissible limits' with regard to foreign investments were adhered to." He was told that in the joint venture between the two businesses, Bharti would operate the stores, while a surrogate of Wal-Mart would arrange for procurement, inventory management, and logistics—i.e., deal with the wholesale supply chain. (15)

He found that Wal-Mart had gotten around the rules of India's FDI and it was legal. Wal-Mart had pulled off a coup as it got around a technicality in the law. But it had followed the rules—in part. There was little the government could do to stop it. It was legitimate!

The pro-Wal-Mart faction was delighted to see this happen, because it signaled that the rules concerning FDI would no doubt be changed. But, with or without Bharti/Wal-Mart, the domestic supermarkets persevered.

There were no "Wal-Mart lobbies" in India to protest Wal-Mart. Instead, there were the large number of small kirana owners and farmers, and the relatively large Indian retailers like Ambani and Biyani who, as I said, feared unequal competition. (16)

Finally, the Service Employees International Union (SEIU) came to India for a visit. It is an American union that is active on the issues that touch on Wal-Mart, and it was actively opposed to seeing Wal-Mart ensconced in India. Also, in talks with the CITU in India in December, the SEIU took part in a massive protest against the opening of FDI, and said "No" to Wal-Mart. (17) The protest organized was so big it nearly shut down Calcutta's airport. There have also been many additional protests since then, many in supermarkets, every time Wal-Mart starts a new endeavor.

In the spring of 2007, Wade Rathke, of Acorn, came to India. Rathke turned the question to supermarkets, wherever they were. Rathke is an American, who had studied Wal-Mart. He had organized against Wal-Mart in the U.S. and in Latin American countries. He told his Indian audience that Asian countries like Japan, Thailand, and Malaysia had found ways to make sure they were not victimized by neoliberal forms of modernization. These countries had imposed "restrictions on multinational retailers—including zonal restrictions, sourcing requirements, and the number of stores a foreign retailer could build at a certain locality."

"In Thailand," he said, "60,000 small traders were forced to shut down . . . I wouldn't want to see the same thing happen here. Wal-Mart and all the 'big-box' stores can very well afford to sustain losses for a number of years if they have to." And they can afford to engage in "dumping," he said. (18)

Any other retailer would have "gone home on the next train," but Wal-Mart was determined—it would make the government carefully rethink its position on FDI. As it came closer and closer to the opening of the new stores in the summer of 2007, Sunil Bharti and Wal-Mart were delaying. They were "discussing business plans." They apparently had problems finding stores that were affordable, finding a way to implement their logistics without stepping on anyone's toes, and working out what each of them should be responsible for. So far the Bharti/Wal-Mart stores seemed to become a fait accompli, since there was no legitimate reason why they should be removed.

Bharti, rather than Wal-Mart, spoke to the press, and Bharti kept Wal-Mart in the background. They were now to open at the end of 2008, not 2007, but they were still "discussing business plans." Upon investigation by the Commerce Minister, as their joint venture became more credible it seemed that it would become a reality in India.

Bharti Mittal immediately made the announcement that they would open one store—not 500 stores, but one store. The tone of the official dialogue changed. "There is no ban on foreign companies making wholesale purchases from India to support their global supply chains," they said. Certainly Wal-Mart had expertise in the field of procuring goods. So they said, "Wal-Mart will not own stores, but it will have a presence in India." (19) Wal-Mart had also decided to sell all its food products to all the kiranas, who then would have prices as low as Wal-Mart stores. This was, of course, a goodwill gesture, and one that would pay off in the future.

Wal-Mart and Bharti maintained that what would transpire "would become apparent" once these stores were about to open. They would not reveal the plans, or where they were to be. They now also kept all their business plans a secret; the stores could not be criticized for whatever they were doing.

Then Kamal Nath reiterated their plan. "What I have read is that Wal-Mart is going to invest in the logistics management . . . , which is the supply end of it, and which is needed." He said, "We have made it clear that small shop owners should not be affected . . . . They should not be displaced." He also said, "We want investments in the back end." With 40 percent of the food being wasted before it gets to the market, the country needs supply chains to bring the food from the farmer to the marketplace as quickly as possible. Right now it takes a day and a half, instead of ten hours as in America, to do that. (20) At the same time, Tesco and Carrefour, two of the largest supermarkets, were also talking with Bharti and other would-be business partners. Each was already "waiting in the wings and actually negotiating with several Indian companies as potential partners." (21) Wal-Mart was seen as a "test case," to see how the rules of India could be bent to its wishes. Wal-Mart said only "it is conducting feasibility studies." But, as far as FDI was planned, industry experts believed that "further relaxation in retail FDI norms must come first."

How to Get It There

Wal-Mart actually faced problems in getting the food to the people. First of all, there was a "complex tax system" in India which varied from state to state, making it difficult to get produce and products across state borders. In addition to standing on long lines in the traffic, the truckers had to bribe the officials. This alone would make it problematic to do business. Second, there was the need for refrigerators and freezers, "cold chains," in trucks and trains. The country only had 1,500 refrigerated trucks, so one-third of the produce rotted before reaching customers. Wal-Mart, with its billions of dollars, promised to make sure that the "cold chains" would appear, and the price would be affordable. (22)

Wal-Mart first had to deal with India's lack of technology. Without the money to repair them, India needed wider roads that allowed for trucks to get to the stores in a reasonable time. There were often water shortages. There were also power outages each night, and there was an electricity shortage as well. (23) Third, there are few electrical power-er stations in India. When the insufficient electrical power goes off, hospitals, hotels, and supermarkets—and any other place that needs electricity around the clock—uses a private electricity generator. Those who don't have one will find the food in the freezer melted. China, by contrast, has a reliable supply of electrical power, despite the pollution. They get it from their generating plants. It burns fossil fuels at best, and China's air is polluted—but at least the electricity runs.

Fourth, there are corrupt officials and middlemen who run the current purchasing and distribution system. Fifth, the investments in the supply chain are "hamstrung" by the lack of refrigerated trucks and warehousing. They need to cut out the corrupt middlemen, who take a slice of everything that goes from the country to the city, all of which helps to raise the price of food. (24) "In reality there are six to eight levels of intermediaries between the farmer and the final consumer." And billions of square feet of new warehousing space will have to be built, with cooling units to accommodate fresh fruits and vegetables.

Wal-Mart—The American Ruling Class

Still, the question remained, Wouldn't Biyani and Ambani, as well as Wal-Mart, put the kiranas out of business? That was a question which never disturbed the anti-Wal-Mart haters. All their hatred was for Wal-Mart. Yet some of the kirana owners said, in contrast, they would charge less than the large supermarket—domestic retailers, as well as Wal-Mart.

Yet 50 Reliance supermarkets had opened in 20 Indian cities since the rollout began in November 2002. Plans called for 2,500 domesti-cally owned outlets in the next four years, including 500 hypermarkets.

The American Wall Street retail experts said, optimistically, the or-ganized retail industry in India would reach 35 percent of the market by 2015—up from the present 3.6 percent in 2002. They said that by 2012 India may have 14 times as much space dedicated to organized retail as it does today, and one million more retail jobs than it does today—hypermarkets, supermarkets, shopping malls, and convenience stores may dot the landscape. Their predictions were way off course; this was definitely not what India wanted. But the government was not afraid of all supermarkets, they were only afraid of Wal-Mart.

Then, when a group of 5,000 Indian vegetable sellers and street vendors, armed with rods and sticks, attacked three stores owned by Reliance Retail, a domestic corporation, about a dozen people were hurt in the eastern city of Ranchi. "The vegetable vendors were 'agitated' because Reliance outlets are selling vegetables at prices which are much lower than the market price, and are driving away their customers." (25) Although they did not realize that this wasn't Wal-Mart; they thought all mass retailers were Wal-Mart, and Wal-Mart was evil.

What did Reliance's owners do? "The company, in defiance, tightened security and announced it would open 1,500 more stores by 2009. (26) It behaved like the worst of foreign multinationals. It acted that way because Biyani was aggrieved that Wal-Mart got into India "under the table."

And when Wal-Mart executive David Duke came to India to prepare for the American retail giant's planned market entry, his visit was protested. The protesters burned an image of Wal-Mart in effigy. (27) All mass retailers took on the image of Wal-Mart:

"Fearing the loss of livelihood, traders, farmers, and small shopkeepers oppose plans by foreign and local companies to introduce western-style super marts into India's fragmented $350 billion market. Farmers worry the influx will lead to prices being dictated by a handful of large retailers." (28)

As Mukesh Ambani said, the goal was to make it harder. In addition Ambani, to compete, had revolutionized the supply chain at a very high cost to himself. He had a whole fleet of airplanes ready to whisk away the fruits and vegetables from the farms to the stores. He already had a monopoly on milk, and he was investigating the Wal-Mart logistics.

But Wal-Mart wanted a cheaper solution to the "logistics" problem, which might really lead to lower prices. At first, Wal-Mart tried to arrange one alone. "As per information furnished by Bharti in January, it is working with Wal-Mart for setting up back-end infrastructure like cold chains, logistics, sourcing, and merchandising for cash-and-carry wholesale operations." Bharti also said he would build supermarkets, hypermarkets, and malls. For Wal-Mart to compete, "Wal-Mart, the world's largest retailer, will also offer rock-bottom prices in India."

"Suspicion of the United States is part of the larger suspicion of everything that goes against the grain of half a century's indoctrination." Because America had the world's greatest chain of stores, it was easy to stir up resistance to this competitor, by saying that Wal-Mart will fill its stores with Chinese goods. (29) And that was the truth!

The Opposition

Much of the conflict was between Wal-Mart and the Indian supermarket owners, their traditional competition. The people wrote saying that FDI "can't be allowed at any cost" because the government is "against the very spirit and heart of this movement."(30) And seven more retail groups entered the fray; groups from Birla, Tata, and Ambani, who invested over $1 billion in stores. These stores all compete with one another. "Retailers like Metro, Reliance, and Bharti/Wal-Mart, as well as the Future Group, are either floating business-to-business ventures (cash-and-carry), or roping kiranwalas in as franchisee partners to get the first mover advantage." (31)

The Communist Party and the CITU were ready to act. Fifty million CITU members were ready to protest Wal-Mart's entry into India. On a Thursday in February 2007 they would all take part in a massive protest against the expansion of FDI. (32) "The Communist Party had proposed that the government implement a system of licenses for retailers and set a limit on the number of outlets that a company could open in a city or province." (33) There was also conflict among the farmers, the kiranwalas, and the major supermarket owners. And the farmers would need some type of legal protection.

All of this took shape as a political debate in India. In many countries the fear of becoming tied to the capitalist world, fear of being overtaken by the WTO, global capitalism, and neo-liberal formulations is a threat. They believed it would change their lives for the worse. They felt they will be uprooted, extinguished! For the most part they may be right! These people, who take their land and leave them unemployed and stateless, often lead impoverished people in India to commit suicide. It is foreign neo-liberal capitalism that they deplore.

For the poor Indians, the real fear is not only the fear of unemployment. It is the fear of a food shortage, of starving to death, and of suicide. Manmohan Singh wanted to "go slowly" because it was the farmers and the kirana owners he most wanted to protect, because they were the heart of the country.

Best Price Modern Wholesale

Wal-Mart opened only one store in June 2009. It was not the store they planned, and it was only one store—it was not 15. And it was not a retail store that sold to the public. It supplies the retail businesses, as it had said, not consumers. It caters to "restaurant owners, hoteliers, caterers, fruit and vegetable 'resellers,' offices, and institutions, and—wouldn't you know—kiranas. It is called Best Price Modern Wholesale. Its name was changed, so it wouldn't be identified with the infamous Wal-Mart stores.

Best Price Modern Wholesale is in Amritsar, in the northwest of India, far from New Delhi or Mumbai. It has been inordinately successful! "In recent weeks crowds have swarmed the store, located on the Grand Trunk Road, the ancient and fabled trade route that stretches across India and into Pakistan," a strange spot for a Wal-Mart store. (34)

Best Price Modern Wholesale has avoided antagonizing anyone, and Wal-Mart and Bharti have "eased the tensions among the merchant associations and left-wing political parties" by following the government's rules. This is their typical behavior when they are under threat.

They are allowed to sell only 6,000 items, and to grant access to the store to up to three friends and family members. It is a "membership" store and "many others are clamoring to borrow membership cards for a chance to benefit from the low prices." It's something like a Sam's Club. The store is 50,000 square feet—not too large, but not too small.

Its wholesale operations in India are subsumed under a joint venture with New Delhi-based Bharti Enterprises. The U.S. company's retail presence is also restricted to providing back-end support for Bharti's chain of 25 Easy Day grocery stores that opened in 2009.

Kishore Biyani has 114 retail supermarkets, while Aditya Birla has started 548 stores since 2007, and Reliance Industries' Mukesh Ambani has built 940 stores across the country in 18 months. But at this time Wal-Mart has only 15. It doesn't seem to be too bothered by that, because business is so lucrative. It has 70,000 customers and it started with 35,000. Sales exceeded expectations, by almost 70 percent. "If its Indian team can find more land, it will set up 15 more stores," said McMillon, the CEO of Wal-Mart's International Operations. And by now it has 16 stores. But Best Price Modern Wholesale (the cash-and-carry opportunity) creates a much larger, $400 million opportunity. After China, this is the only country where it sees enough potential to plant at least 1,000 of the Best Price Modern Wholesale stores. (35)

While India has hordes of middlemen, each taking part of the profit, the farmers who sell to the store have become essential. They make 5-7 percent\ more when they sell to Wal-Mart stores, and Wal-Mart picks the produce up from their fields. (36) Wal-Mart is trying to make agricultural goods into a product that can be sourced.

That's what it has done to agriculture around the world. It is trying to change business models, by using its hyper-efficient practices to "improve productivity and speed the flow of goods." Raj Jain, the president of Wal-Mart India, says Wal-Mart has worked with 110 farmers from Punjab "to source fresh vegetables" for its stores, and added, "they had been training these farmers on modern practices to get maximum yields with lesser investment." (37)

Ultimately, Wal-Mart wants to make India a "sourcing hub." For all these agricultural products India will make or grow "hundreds of millions of dollars" worth of products to sell to nearby countries. (38) Wal-Mart has now truly become the "new landlord" of the realm. Douglas

McMillon, the CEO of the company's International Operations said, "We have a $4.8-$5.3 billion fund earmarked for our international business—India can use as much of it as it wants."

In 2011, already something had changed. Not only Wal-Mart had gotten in "under the table," but other multinationals "are investing, to top surging demand," as well. In fact, new Indian retailers "have been setting up separate retail and wholesale companies to get around the restrictions on foreign investment." American venture capital partners invest in the wholesale operations, selling goods and services to retail firms, while many indigenous firms set up retail companies. (39)

The pressure in Washington is tremendous. The United States is pushing India hard for India to open FDI. (40) In a speech at the Asia Society, Assistant Secretary of State Robert Blake said, "The U.S. has called upon India to open up its markets and further liberalize trade policies in order to strengthen bilateral ties." The Indian retail market is valued at $500 billion today; it is scheduled to rise to more than $800 billion in 2013. Hillary Clinton, Secretary of State, also pressured Wal-Mart to open its FDI. (41)

Even Rob Walton, Chairman of the Board of Wal-Mart, started pressing the U.S. government and India to persuade India to open FDI. Rajan Bharti Mittal wants it to open, too. The son of Sunni Bharti Mittal, and Chairman of Bharti/Wal-Mart said of Wal-Mart's business, "During 2010 we plan to extend Best Price Modern Wholesale across India, with seven stores, up to 100,000 square feet." (42) And Wal-Mart is beginning to outsource from India, since it is considerably cheaper than China. Tesco already has a joint venture with Tata and has opened a store. Is there any reason not to think that FDI will be opened soon? The answer is "No—not yet." The Indian government will grow—at 10 percent, so Wal-Mart hopes—but not with FDI in retail.

The Coming of Wal-Mart, and the Question of FDI

Surprisingly enough, in November 2011, "The long–awaited decision by Prime Minister Manmohan Singh had come—the long-awaited coming of FDI. It would allow retailers who sold multiple brands of products to own 51 percent of their Indian operations, with the rest held by an Indian partner." The government decided that foreign businesses, like supermarkets—even Wal-Mart—would be allowed to operate in India.

What motivated them to do it? Food inflation was destroying the nation. It was hovering near 10 percent, due to almost 35 percent of fruits and vegetables spoiling and rotting before they got to market. This was the result of an "antiquated food system": the absence of cold storage, bottlenecks, and the six stops the food had to get through, before it got to market. Poor Indians were starving.

A fierce hostility broke out in the government about the law to allow in the Western supermarkets. Small traders wreaked havoc, with demonstrations all over the country to protest the move. In the north, politicians "pledged to physically attack the stores." And ". . . a leading opposition politician has already threatened to set fire to any Wal-Mart store that opens in India." It will also hurt some "tens of thousands of small traders as well as poor and middle-class consumers." the leader of the government allied with Singh, the DMK party said. The opposition made it clear that Wal-Mart was not welcome in West Bengal, Jharkhand, and Uttar Pradesh by protests from shop owners and farmers. And they passed a law to that effect.

The small shops some of the kiranhas, are convenient and give credit. Most Indians do their shopping there. They operate with little overhead and "razor-thin margins." And yet, Tesco, Carrefour, and Metro agreed if FDI occurred, they would have to let Wal-Mart in. There were also expressions of happiness from policy makers with the view that "they might be more willing to open the broader economy further." (43) Goldie Dhama, Associate Director of PricewaterhouseCoopers, said, "There will be substantial investment in back-end logistics such as cold and supply chains, lack of which results in wastage of 30-40 percent of the total produce," and "it will ease inflationary pressures," and the new big boxes will appear only in the big cities. (44)

However, the new policy came with restrictions on Wal-Mart: 1) prior approval of the Indian Foreign Investment Promotion Board (FIPB); 2) at least 30 percent of the products would have to be sourced from small producers and industries; 3) a minimum of U.S. $1 million, with at least 50 percent of such foreign investment in back-end infrastructure; 4) stores could only be in cities with at least one million people [53 cities]; and 5) the Indian government would have the first right of procurement. (45)

One month later, in December 2011, the government changed its position. It did so because the compulsions of coalition politics and also partisan opposition made Congress put the decision "on hold"—until it could reach consensus. Congress was having a terrible time convincing the opposition members of Congress to accept this.. In addition, the government was threatened with falling, if it was enacted. Coalition politics also put a stop to FDI, for the moment. The government said, "The central government has decided to keep on hold its decision to allow foreign equity in retail until a consensus emerges on the issue." (46) According to Manmohan Singh, who obviously changed his position on it, there would be a consensus about FDI as soon as the opposition parties could be convinced.

The Trinamool Congress, (TMC), which was an opposition party, was the party that defended the poor peasants in the rural areas. Started in 2006, it was fiercely against the decision to allow FDI. TMC allied with Singh's government. But when a state agency claimed that a land development authority was removing 70,000 people from their homes, TMC fought against the land grabbers, and won. (47)

Mamata Banerjee became the leader of TMC, and allied herself with the Bharatiya Janata Party to oppose FDI. They became adamant in their demand for the rollback of FDI in the retail sector, and the United Progressive Alliance (UPA), the leading party, was in the minority in the government for a rollback of FDI. It promised to close the government, and the government was closed for eight whole days while all the ministers tried to sort it out.

Therefore, it was somewhat disingenuous when Anand Sharma, the Minister of Commerce and Industry, spoke to the leaders of Wal-Mart and Metro and intimated that there would be FDI in India. He said, "It was just a pause. (48) The decision has only been put on a temporary halt . . . .and the government is committed to take forward the reform agenda." (49) And if it does, the supermarkets were planned to meet the needs of the middle-class.

It was very fortuitous, that just as the story of Wal-Mart's bribery scandal was being investigated in Mexico, Wal-Mart had discovered in its investigation of bribery in Mexico that its behavior had led to other kinds of "corruption" in "some of the retailer's most important markets." (50) Singled out for further study were India, China, and Brazil. After a year of waiting, it may have been fortuitous, as this story came to public attention, as:

"India ushered in the biggest economic reforms in two decades on Friday, allowing big foreign retailers like Wal-Mart, foreign broadcasters, and foreign airlines to invest in the country, among other reforms." (51)

As that happened, Rajya Sabha, a member of the Upper House of Parliament from Kerala, "blew the whistle" on Wal-Mart. He submitted a petition in 2010, which revealed the details of how Wal-Mart invested $100 million in Cedar Support Services in 2009. Then the name of the company was allegedly changed from Bharti Holding Enterprises to Cedar Support Services.

It so happens that Cedar Support Services is a 100-percent holding company of Bharti Holding Enterprises. The name was changed to protect it, as a company which was supposed to be a real estate "consultancy." Foreign real estate consultants are allowed to be in India, and have 100 percent FDI. But the money was allegedly used to fund the retail operations of Bharti/Wal-Mart. (52) And the Reserve Bank of India, which should have been informed of this investment, was never told. More to the point, an income of Rs 8 lakh (or Rs 800 thousand) was ostensibly shown in 2010, but did not have one employee to offer consultancy. But Wal-Mart has denied any wrongdoing. The corporation is under investigation by the Directorate, a part of financial services.

Nevertheless, the government has decided that India will let

Wal-Mart in—with stipulations! India is the victim of a growing crisis. It is under pressure to "boost employment and improve the country's infrastructure." The peasants starve because India does not have the capacity to get a large part of the food supply into the cities to feed them. Whether the supermarkets can do it is questionable. Can they get the food to feed the poor, or will supermarkets become a middle class institution?

"Supporters of the move say the global companies will provide employment for thousands, help farmers cut out middlemen and contract directly with the companies, and improve India's supply-chain apparatus."

In India the service sector makes up 55 percent of GDP, the industrial sector 26.3 percent, and the agricultural sector only 18.1 percent. But in India there is little industry in the cities; there are no cities to immigrate to. So people stay on the land, eking out a living from the earth. India is divided into a rural society and an urban society. China has industrial cities; and peasants are constantly arriving in the cities to find work. Will the Indian supermarkets be able to solve this problem?

As of this point the answer is—not so fast! The Indian authorities, the Department of Industrial Policy (DIPP) has made it more difficult for firms entering India to do so. DIPP said that all supermarkets entering India must purchase 20 percent of all goods from small and medium sized producers. (53) That will put a crimp in Wal-Mart's plans.

And Wal-Mart is now held up by a phenomenon that has not plagued other stores. It is the Foreign Corrupt Practices Act (FCPA) which only applies to stores in the United States, not to Tesco or Carrefour. Wal-Mart is beset by this law which prevents it from bribing anyone in any country where it does business, or there will be strong and definite penalties to pay

"The U.S. Foreign Corruption Act forbids American firms from paying bribes. Wal-Mart launched a global review of corruption last year after a New York Times report on bribery at the company's Mexico operations. Its lawyers flagged India among the countries with the highest corruption risk." (54)

Therefore, Wal-Mart simply cannot give bribes to anyone in India or it will have violated this American law! The Indian bureaucracy has held up the licenses because Wal-Mart has refrained from giving the "traditional" bribes. Wal-Mart wants to open stores, but it can't do so, because all its licenses have been held up.

"More than 15 attorneys from U.S. law firm Greenberg Traurig are now working with the Indian business to help strengthen compliance, a Wal-Mart spokesman said." (55)

Thus, after all this, the United States has blocked Wal-Mart's expansion in India, when it tried to get in early by having an agreement with Bharti, which was designed to make it move in faster than any other supermarket could. Fortunately, or unfortunately, Wal-Mart is "hoist on its own petard."

What has happened with Wal-Mart's stores since that time? Actually, in 2013 Wal-Mart and Bharti have ended their relationship. "Raj Jain, it's international executive was let go". Now Wal-Mart will have its own separate stores and so will Bharti. And The New York Times had earlier reported that the joint venture "had suspended several senior executives and delayed the opening of some stores in the country as part of an internal bribery investigation." (56) Now, many were sure that the kingpin had been identified. Wal-Mart only opened six stores last year, instead of its planned twenty-two, while Metro AG, a German firm, opened sixteen

Foreign companies have found India's endemic corruption, something that has forestalled them from investing in India. But American law also requires that US firms remain free of corruption. "Executives in the United States have taken an increasingly dim view of doing business in India, with its low profile and constant legal worries." (57)

Girish Kuber, a former political editor of the Indian news the Economic Times, called the dissolution of the Wal-Mart and Bharti partnership "inevitable." It is a sad story," he said. "The reforms are going nowhere, and there is no investment coming in." (58)

Footnotes

1. "Wal-Mart: Rapping on India's Door," Business Week, May 1, 2006.

2. John Elliott, "Wal-Mart Must Wait": Dispatches: Business Reports From Around the US and the World; India Retail, Fortune Magazine, May 29, 2006. ???

3. Vivek Sinha, "The Man Behind 'em All," The Economic Times, Online, December 4, 2006.

4. Parija Bhatnagar, "Wal-Mart's Hot on India," CnnMoney.com, July 6, 2005.

5. Mayur Shekar Jha and Chaitali Chakraverty, "How Wal-Mart Edged Tesco Out," The Economic Times, November 28, 2006.

6. Daniel Pepper, "In India, Reliance Looks for 'Lion's Share' of Retail," The International Herald Tribune, June 28, 2006.

7. "India's Retail Industry Gets a Shake-Up," The Sydney Morning Herald, November 4, 2006.

8. Vinay Kamath, "Getting Inside Wal-Mart," Business Line, June 21, 2007.

9. John Elliott, "Why There Are No Indian Wal-Marts," Fortune Magazine, May 9, 2006.

10. "Wal-Mart Enters India," Knowledge at Wharton, February 2, 2007.

11. India FDI Watch, "Thousands Protested to Oppose the Bharti/ Wal-Mart Joint Venture," October 10, 2007.

12. Mohan Guruswamy, Kamal Sharm, and Maria Mini Jos, FDI in Retail: Implications of Wal-Mart's Backdoor Entry, Center for Policy Alternatives, New Delhi, February 2007.

13. Team D'Essence, "The Changing Retail Landscape of India," White Paper Series, no date.

14. Isabelle Sender, "Wal-Mart's Ambition in India," BusinessWeek. Online, February 9, 2006.

15. "Government to Scan Bharti/Wal-Mart Deal: Nath," ,The Economic Times, November 28, 2006.

16. Balagi Reddy, "Wal-Mart Assault: India May Be Forced To Open

its Protected Retail Sector, but Wal-Mart for the First Time Will Face Real Communists in India," India Daily, July 12, 2007.

17. Ruth David, "India Union Ready to Protest Wal-Mart," Forbes. com, December 8, 2006.

18. "Activist Wants Small Retailers Protected Against Top Guns," Business Standard, April 19, 2007; K. Raghavendra Kamath, "Why Wal-Mart Should Not Enter India" Rediff News, April 23, 2007; "Wal-Mart Likely to Increase Direct Sourcing from India," Forbes Magazine, April 20, 2007.

19. Rajesh Mahapatra, "India Confident About Economic Risks," Associated Press.

20. Ashok Battarchargee, "Indian Minister Comments on Wal-Mart's Proposed Retail Venture," Bloomberg.com, November 28, 2006.

21. "Wal-Mart Enters India," Knowledge@Wharton, February 2, 2007.

22. Parija Bhatnagar, "Wal-Mart's Dilemma in India," CNNmoney. com, April 4, 2006.

23. Somini Sengupta, "In Teeming India, Water Crisis Means Dry Pipes and Foul Sludge," New York Times, September 29, 2006.

24. Somini Sengupta, "In Teeming India, Water Crisis Means Dry Pipes and Foul Sludge," New York Times, September 29, 2006. Ibid. ???

25. "Indian Street Vendors Attack Retail Chain's Stores," Reuters, May 12, 2007.

26. "PMO Wants Commerce Ministry to Speed Up Impact Assessment," India Business, March 25, 2007.

27. "Wal-Mart Manager's India Visit Clouded by Shopkeeper Protest," UNI Commerce Home page, February 22, 2007.

28. Kriittivas Mukerjee, "Farmers to Take on Wal-Mart in India," Reuters, January 3, 2008.

29. Sunanda K. Datta-Ray, "Why Indians Fight Modernization," The New York Times, September 11, 2007.

30. "Sonia Letter Has Left Nodding in Agreement," The Indian Express, February 6, 2007.

31. Writankar Mukherjee and Anuradha Himatsinka, "Retailing Giants Now Stock Up on Mom's and Pop's." The Economic Times, May 21, 2007.

32. "FDI After Sonia's January 11 Note. PM Talked to Kamal Nath," The Indian Express, February 6, 2007.

33.Bibbudatta Pradhan and Saikat Chatterjee, "India's Communists Seek Restrictions on Big Retailers," Bloomberg.com, May 30, 2007.

34. Emily Wax, "India's First Wal-Mart Draws Excitement, Not Protest," The Washington Post, July 16, 2009.

35. "Wal-Mart Has BIG plans for India; Do we have Enough Space?," Moneycontrol. October 29, 2009.

36. Vikas Bajaj, "In India, Wal-Mart Goes to the Farm," The New York Times, April 12, 2010.

37. "Bharti-Wal-Mart to Open 5 More Cash and Carry Outlets in India," Value Notes, March 31, 2010; and Vikas Bijaj "How Wal-Mart's Wooing Indian Farmers," New York Times, News Service, April 12, 2010.

38. "Wal-Mart to Make India a Major Sourcing Hub," (Reuters), The New York Times, 2010.

39. Jason Burke, "Indian Government's Plan to Allow in Western Supermarkets Triggers Fury," The Guardian, (UK) November 28, 2011.

40. Sandeep Dikshit, "Open Up Markets, US Tells India," The Hindu, March 21. 2010.

41. "Wal-Mart Set to Launch Amritsar Store on Saturday," Reuters, May 28, 2009.

42. "Bharti Wal-Mart Rolls Out Second Wholesale Cash-and-Carry Store," The Indian Express, April 13, 2010.

43. Vikas Bajaj, "India to Ease Retail Rules for Foreign Companies," The New York Times, November 24, 2011.

44. Sangeeta Singh and Sapna Agarwal, "Cabinet Likely to Approve FDI in Multi-brand Retail," Livemint, November 23 , 2011.

45. Pepper Hamilton LLP, U.S. India Report, November 30, 2011.46.

"Opposition Not Convinced About Mamata Claim on FDI on Hold," India Today, December 3, 2011; "FDI Decision Suspended Pending Consensus: Mamata quotes Pranab," India Today, December 3, 2011.

46. "Opposition Not Convinced About Mamata Claim on FDI on Hold," India Today, December 3, 2011: "FDI Decision Suspended Pending Consensus: Mamata quotes Pranab," India Today, December 3, 2011. Ibid.

47. "FDI in Retail: BJP Insists on Rollback, Asks Sonia to Explain her Stand," India Today, December 1, 2011.

48. Ibid.

49. "Suspension of FDI in Retail Just a Pause: Sharma to Global CEO's," The Business Standard, Davos, January 27, 2012.

50. Stephanie Clifford and David Barstow, "Wal-Mart Inquiry Reflects Alarm on Corruption," New York Times, November 15. 2012.

51. Heather Timmons, Hari Kumar, and Pam Posh Raina, "India Opens Door to Foreign Investment," The New York Times, September 14, 2012.

52. M.P. Acuthan, "Wal-Mart and Bharti Have Hoodwinked the Government," member of Parliament from Kerala, no date.

53. Krista Mahr, "This Time We Mean It: India Clears the Way For Wal-Mart and Friends," World Time, September 17, 2012.

54. Sandeep Phukan, Government Blinks after Wal-Mart's Reported Inability to Meet Norms, and Government Relaxes FDI in Multi-Brand Retail, NDTV Profit, July 30, 2013 and August 1, 2013

55. Nandina Bose, Red Tape and Graft: India, No Supermarket for Wal-Mart, Reuters, July 8, 2013.

56. The Bharti-Wal-Mart Breakup: Where Does FDI in India Go Next?, Knowledge@ Wharton, November 1, 2013.

57. Wal-Mart's India Departure, a Sign of Things to Come?, CNBC. com, October 11, 2013.

58. Gardner Harris, Wal-Mart Drops Ambitious Expansion Plan for India, New York Times, October 9, 2013

10

South Africa—A Long, Drawn-Out Battle

By 2011, Wal-Mart decided to buy a 51 percent share of Massmart in South Africa. But in 2009, Jacob Zuma, the President of South Africa, had said in his inaugural address, "The creation of decent work will be at the center of government policy." And that created a problem. (1)

One of the basic problems for South Africa was resolving the crisis that apartheid had wrought. At that time, as Zuma put it, "Jobs are being lost in every economy in the world. We will not be spared the negative impact." He said, "However, the foundations of our economy are strong and we will need to build more than ever before." (2) Unfortunately, they would have to reckon with Wal-Mart.

South Africa ranks among the ten countries worldwide with the lowest level of employment. About one-half of South Africans of working age need jobs because the economic downturn destroyed a million jobs, and employment creation only returned at the end of 2010. Since that time the economy began to grow again, but the unemployment rate was still high, "officially," over 25 percent—and 40 percent of the people when discouraged jobseekers were counted. (3) In South Africa, will employment save the formerly disfranchised? That alone will solve much of South Africa's problems.

Yet, Doug McMillon, Wal-Mart's International CEO, made a fantastic statement when Wal-Mart came to South Africa, about "The combined Wal-Mart/Massmart entity he was planning, to honor pre-existing union relationships and to abide by South African labor laws." (4) But, there were a host of other retailers in South Africa who had been approached by Wal-Mart. All of them refused to merge with Wal-Mart—except for Massmart, the third largest supermarket in South Africa. Perhaps those other retailers failed to see how Wal-Mart could add to the well-being of South Africa. Or perhaps they feared the cut-throat competition it would bring.

Massmart had been looking for an opening to "hook up" with Wal-Mart before 2006. It was quietly searching out "an internationally competitive" store, to take Massmart over or to merge with it. But as early as 1990, without anyone knowing it, Grant Pattison, the Chief Executive Officer of Massmart, had an auspicious chance meeting with Wal-Mart—he was not to leave it to fate.

He also:

". . . targeted Wal-Mart, Carrefour, Tesco, Metro, and Kingfisher for a while and met with all those companies just to make sure that, when the day came and they wanted to make the phone call, they had my card. So, the first time they [Wal-Mart was] here, I made it absolutely clear that we were available for sale." (5)

Massmart had been vitally interested in a relationship with Wal-Mart as early as 1990. But Wal-Mart and Massmart only began their talks in 2006. Rumors of Wal-Mart's interest in Massmart began to surface in 2008.

When Massmart understood that a deal was in the making with Wal-Mart, Massmart started to act "competitively." Dividends flew out of Massmart South Africa, at a much higher rate, from 19 percent to 47 percent, and the salaries at the stores were lowered from 47 percent to 33 percent.

The stores inevitably had a poorer and poorer relationship with their employees. At Massmart there was a marked shift of "aggressive rebranding, restructuring, re-engineering, and repositioning," which ultimately led to 700 permanent and 800 flexi-time workers losing their regular jobs. (6) Suddenly, "disputes that would have been settled amicably in the past, now reached deadlocks on shop-floors." (7)

Although some of the union's people did not initially comprehend from where the hardening of Massmart's attitudes came, Massmart was changing its rules rapidly, dramatically, and aggressively for the workers. It was getting ready to be "lean and mean" for Wal-Mart.

This behavior generated much fear and anxiety—just as in France's Carrefour when Wal-Mart came to Germany. Carrefour merged with Casino because they believed Carrefour would be bought up by Wal-Mart.

In South Africa the unions, particularly the South African Commercial, Catering and Allied Workers' Union (SACCAWU) and three government ministers as well, were so angered that they furiously prepared for the onslaught. The other retailers, Shoprite and Pick 'n Pay, two supermarkets, knew about Wal-Mart and they were fearful. They knew that Wal-Mart could put them out of business or, at the very least, generate painful competition.

For the people who worked at Massmart stores, they knew it was sure to lower wages. They also feared it would create a good deal of unemployment. The union estimated that as many as 4,000 jobs in general merchandise and in food industries and beverage production would be lost. (8) "For instance, there would also be a loss in the agro-processing industry, electronics, plastics, and household goods, as well as clothing and textiles" (9)

SACCAWU became the initiator of the Anti-Wal-Mart Coalition. The Anti-Wal-Mart Coalition called a meeting of the Congress of South African Trade Unions (COSATU), which is the over-arching branch of all the South African unions (as the AFL-CIO is to the United States). They also incorporated the UNI Global Union in the campaign. The UNI is an umbrella organization of many unions, worldwide. It is launched from Germany (UNI), and is a union in Germany. Overall, it has 20 million members all over the world who are united to ensure that unions around the world have legitimate and fair union practices.

They are now involved in a campaign to get Wal-Mart to agree to sign a legitimate union contract for all is members. They want a contract, a Global Union contract. That may seem like a bold initiative, but UNI members feel such an organization must be started, to protect all the workers of the world.

The goal of the Anti-Wal-Mart Coalition at first, naturally, was to keep Wal-Mart out of South Africa, to get the biggest supermarket in the world to "go home." South Africa, after all, was a land that was terribly poor, with high unemployment. It had suffered from apartheid, and the Blacks were poor. Forty percent of them lived in the slums.

SACCAWU, itself, had established a vast South African union of 80,000 members. It was militant and strong. It had fought the apartheid police, and had struggled against the reigning government. It supported lengthy strikes, demonstrations, and protest meetings, all throughout South Africa, which lasted for weeks and where many Blacks were killed.

Long after apartheid had ended, SACCAWU continued its fight against the residue of apartheid. It had been trying to get the Blacks incorporated into South Africa, and to end all forms of discrimination. And it was engaged in that when Wal-Mart appeared in 2009.

SACCAWU raised its struggle against Wal-Mart when it discovered that Wal-Mart was coming to South Africa. As it learned more and more about Wal-Mart, it held education sessions to let everyone who would listen know, whether or not they were employed at Wal-Mart, about how it operated, and just how Wal-Mart was anti-union. Even the workers in America were not unionized. Of all the "associates" in the United States that were employed in Wal-Mart's stores, not one single store had a union.

The fact that Wal-Mart sourced its products throughout the world was an impediment even to the United States—it was responsible for putting millions of people in the lowest of low wage jobs, and they feared outsourcing would do this to South Africa. It was also a worldwide importer, and with just one percent of its imports, it could cause the loss of 4,000 jobs in South Africa. (10)

If Wal-Mart, the largest company in the world, was to start spreading its tentacles all over South Africa, which it said overtly that it definitely would, Wal-Mart would "provide a platform for growth and expansion in other African countries." (11) Wal-Mart might end up all over Sub-Saharan Africa spreading unemployment, like a disease.

Massmart had 290 stores in 13 countries, as well as eight wholesale and retail chains. The stores were in every part of Southern Africa. They were in Namibia, Lesotho, Botswana, Mozambique, Malawi, Mauritius, Zambia, Tanzania, Uganda, Nigeria, and Ghana—and even in Zimbabwe. Wal-Mart has planned 40 more stores next year, and who knows how many after that.

Wal-Mart's bid for Massmart was an attempt to gain a "first-mover" advantage in Africa. As Wal-Mart explained to its stockholders, South Africa was to be the next big growth market, or "The Gateway to Africa." (12)

Such a scenario could make manufacturers of small businesses and retail stores—not only in food, but in textiles and clothing and in agriculture and agro-processing as well see their demise, thereby destroying what there was of the middle class. It could lead to just what Jacob Zuma, the President of South Africa, was trying hard to avoid. But for the executives of the company, the merger of the two supermarkets would be "the company's greatest acquisition in more than a decade." (13)

An Anti-Wal-Mart Coalition was born. It was composed of SACCAWU and the three ministers of the government, and any person who was incensed about the coming of Wal-Mart. They decided that if Wal-Mart prevailed, if the merger went through, the South Africans would see, as promised, "The mother of all protests."

Yet, the price that Wal-Mart offered was 26 times Massmart's entire earnings; Wal-Mart paid $4.6 billion for Massmart. Wal-Mart has the resources—regardless of what it costs. But, as the Wall Street Journal said, "The deal would give the Bentonville, Arkansas giant a critical foothold to expand in Africa, and allow Wal-Mart to beat European multinational rivals Carrefour, Tesco PLC, and Metro AG into the potentially lucrative Sub-Saharan market. (14) At the same time, it would place Wal-Mart into a politically combustible region." (15) However, it will take a long time and much effort to "earn the cost of capital." But Wal-Mart was ebullient, very satisfied with the potential deal, and anxious to press forward.

Ever since Wal-Mart has announced its takeover bid, there have been "$15 billion worth of deals announced all over Southern Africa." (16) It seemed to Wal-Mart that its entry into South Africa was the lynchpin that would begin South Africa's investment frenzy.

Despite the cheers of Wal-Mart, The Norwegian Pension Fund disinvested in Wal-Mart, and so did the neighboring countries of Holland and Sweden. (17) When Norway disinvested it said, "Its business operations [consist of] a manner that contradicts internationally recognized human rights and labor rights standards, through its suppliers in Asia, Africa, and Latin America, and in its own operations," and it "risks complicity in serious or systematic violations of human rights." (18)

Did Wal-Mart make a good deal? South Africa is plagued with high crime and unemployment, and marked with a heavily unionized workforce known to be organized, and sometimes lengthy, strikes that lasted for weeks.

Finally, if Wal-Mart acquired Massmart, Wal-Mart said it would have to do a lot to make the stores profitable. This appeared difficult for most supermarkets, but it was not a problem for Wal-Mart. For with its massive profits, with some long-range planning that could be done easily. And that's what it hoped to do.

They said the South African market was highly competitive. Wal-Mart had failed in Germany due to competition, but it had entered South Africa with euphoria and high hopes. Would it fail again? Wal-Mart pulled out of the German markets because the German court would not allow Wal-Mart to sell milk below cost. Wal-Mart must operate this way. It cannot succeed as it does without selling below the market price. Wal-Mart has learned never to raise its voice when there is conflict. What it does, it does it quietly, behind the scenes.

As this conflict escalated, Wal-Mart used its ingenuity. Wal-Mart filed the case with the Competition Commission, hoping that the government would finally give its blessing and make the takeover legitimate. The date was scheduled to be in the future, seven months later, in March, 2011. The merger was "on hold" until that day. SACCAWU filed a separate appeal on the grounds that the Competition Commission failed to take adequate consideration of the public interest.

But, well before the decision of the Competition Commission, Wal-Mart raised the issue with World Trade Organization, (WTO) as to whether it could trade only internally. (South Africa was a member of WTO as well.) The answer was clear: trading with the internal market only, (which is what the opposition wanted) and not from its overseas supply chain, could only violate the country's trade obligations. In short, Wal-Mart's and South Africa's membership in the WTO could act against South Africa's own trade interests. That was the verdict and Wal-Mart was relieved. That is what often happens with countries; the WTO can often impair their own development.

For, "if buying locally from South African producers only became a condition of the merger, Wal-Mart would have to drop the deal." (19) But SACCAWU continued to hold its protests, and the continued strength of the opposition surprised Wal-Mart.

A Decision

The Competition Commission was a quasi-judicial body charged with protecting the public interest in large public mergers. It wanted to get this hearing over with. The Competition Commission was merely placating the forces of the opposition. They were anxious for the merger to take place. They knew Wal-Mart would win as the shareholders voted to accept Wal-Mart's bid for Massmart.

The Competition Commission decided that it would make a decision whether to approve the merger, approve the merger with conditions, or prohibit the merger outright. It rendered its verdict on May 31, 2011.

This first verdict was Wal-Mart could go through with the merger, but it was subject to two conditions. Since the South Africans', three government ministers', and SACCAWU's opposition was so strong, Wal-Mart decided to make available to South Africa a $1 million Rand Fund to train workers to be "entrepreneurs" or—as Wal-Mart put it—"Wal-Mart suppliers."

The $1 million Rand payout that Wal-Mart offered was negligible, and the company leaders had very little interest in cultivating local suppliers. Although Wal-Mart does advertise its program helping farmers to grow more productively, it does so to demonstrate its goodwill. It does help some small farmers in India and Central America to grow their fruit and vegetables more productively (see chapters on India and Central America), and buys some of the produce for its stores. But the lion's share of the merchandise Wal-Mart sells in most stores comes from abroad.

South African manufacturers and farmers were erroneously told by the leaders of both partners to the merger, that the "new" (Wal-Mart/Massmart) would not be inundated by what was produced in Southeast Asia. Actually, Massmart bought about 60 percent of its goods from foreign suppliers. We will have to see whether Wal-Mart continues this level of outsourcing, or whether it begins to buy more of its products at home.

Finally, the Competition Commission decided that they would allow the merging parties to seem "generous," by giving preference for any new job which opened up, to the 700 workers who had been let go before Wal-Mart entered the scene. But what if a worker lived in Cape Town and the new retail spot was in Zimbabwe? Or, what if the worker couldn't be found, because he has gone somewhere else to find a job? Wal-Mart said nothing about this. SACCAWU wanted Massmart to give the laid-off employees their old jobs back.

Those who testified against Wal-Mart in May were people who had been asked to "enlighten" the Competition Commission about what Wal-Mart was doing now, internationally, in places like Argentina, Chile, and the U.S., and of course, there was a representative from SACCAWU.

Noel Mbongwe, Deputy Secretary General of SACCAWU, was the

first to give his evidence. He said that international organizations such as Human Rights Watch had reported on Wal-Mart's "poor record" as a global corporate citizen. Claudio Alvarez, a Chilean national who works as an attorney in that country said, "I believe that Wal-Mart is formulating a strategy to neutralize unions." (20) He said:

"Since Wal-Mart forced them to lower their prices, these small suppliers have had to restructure their costs, by reducing personnel and lowering wages and working conditions for workers." (21)

Then it was Sylvia Sasserra's turn. She was the economic advisor to the Argentine Federation of Commerce and Service Workers. She said that Wal-Mart buys its merchandise "on consignment," which means that suppliers don't get paid unless the product is sold. "If it doesn't sell, the suppliers take a total loss on the whole product." She argued:

"This means that in the event the product sells the supplier gets paid. But if the product does not sell, then it was deemed never to be Wal-Mart's to begin with . . . . The fact that the producer is responsible for the unsold products has generated a dependence and a great loss, especially in the food sector as the products are perishable." (22)

Nelson Lichtenstein, Professor at Santa Barbara, California, showed that a report from the Economic Policy Institute found that 200,000 job losses between 2001 and 2006 in the United States were due to Wal-Mart's sourcing abroad. In total that is 11.2 percent of all jobs. "Because Wal-Mart sets the pattern that other mass retailers follow. Thus, the Wal-Mart effect is undoubtedly responsible for at least 50 percent of all U.S. job losses due to cheap foreign imports during the years 2001-2006." (23)

The Fly in the Ointment

The four government ministers who were opposed to the merger were: the Minister of Economic Development, David Levin; Minister of Trade and Industry, Rob Davies; Minister of Agriculture, Forestry, and Fisheries, Tina Joemat-Pettersson; and Minister of Economic Development Department, Ebrahim Patel. There was a request from the three departments and three unions: SACCAWU; the Southern

African Clothing and Textile Workers Union (SACTWU); the UNI Global Union; and the United Food and Commercial Union, of the United States, who were involved. They all asked the Competition Commission for a postponement of the meeting, until June.

The Anti-Wal-Mart Coalition was stymied when the information about what Wal-Mart was planning to import wasn't forthcoming. That is what made it so terribly difficult for the opposition. Yet, the Competition Commission agreed that it was not necessary.

David Levin, the Minister of Economic Development, took the lead. He first had a meeting with representatives of Massmart and Wal-Mart, at which time they were very "receptive," and showed a "clear willingness to cooperate." But Wal-Mart was extremely deceptive. The deception was provided in the testimony from SACCAWU, when Noel Mbongwe said at the hearing in May:

"The merging parties' (Wal-Mart and Massmart) related strategy adopted at the hearing pursuant to which Wal-Mart refused to provide meaningful data on its plans and intentions post-merger, on the basis that the local management of Massmart will retain authority to make such decisions despite Wal-Mart [emphasis mine] assuming control of Massmart, and Massmart refused to provide evidence of its likely intentions, claiming its inability to predict its actions post-merger—and subsequent to consultation with Wal-Mart." (24)

But, Wal-Mart/Massmart already had their plans ready.

In addition, Wal-Mart's witness blindly disclaimed any knowledge of its U.S. operations—which is very easily known—and, as a result, cannot credibly dispute or contradict the evidence in the record relating to Wal-Mart's labor problems and employment practices. (25)

The hearing was postponed until May 1, 2011. In the two months that followed, Levin tried to get the documentation in two different ways. He sent a letter to Goldman Sachs asking for "information relating to sales and procurement" of Massmart, and another one that asked for information about "Massmart's competitive strategy post-acquisition, sourcing and suppliers, and labor." He received an answer two months later, which was too late for him to speak to the Commission.

He also induced a third person to confer with Massmart, trying to ascertain the information he needed to testify against the two merging parties:

"Nevertheless, he wasn't able to get that which he needed to prosecute Wal-Mart and this was because of 'The denial by the Tribune of requests for discovery related to the issues of comparative labor terms and conditions, wage levels and relevant procurement-related information from the merging parties.'" (26)

On May 31, 2011, the Competition Commission issued its finding. Wal-Mart's position was left as it was; Wal-Mart and Massmart could merge. The Competition Commission declared that the merger between Wal-Mart and Massmart was to go through, of course—except for the two conditions that Massmart/Wal-Mart had suggested at the outset:

"By this time the government was getting riled about the merger. Jimmy Manyi the Government Director of Communications, said at a National Press Club briefing, 'Manyi likened South Africa's economy to that of a 'teenager' competing with 'veteran' developed countries, whose economies had 'not been stifled by apartheid.'" He said, "The merger of the two supermarkets was a 'complete whitewash!'" (27).

Grant Pattison, the CEO of Massmart, was quoted as saying "We are fully supportive of local manufacturing, but it would be disruptive of the competition process, championed under the Competition Act, to impose local procurement targets on one retailer to the exclusion of its competitors." (28) By July 20 the three ministries of the government appealed the merger when the two merged, partners said they would never agree to "a guarantee of local procurement limits" placed on the companies. But Economic Minister, Ebrahim Patel, defended the appeal by saying "There is clear and compelling evidence of probable job losses or deterioration in the working conditions of South African workers, due to increased imports as a result of the proposed transaction." He also said, "A 1 million rand supplier development fund to train workers to be suppliers to Wal-Mart could pale into insignificance," if the merger went through. (29)

At this point the "radicalized youth wing" protested. It protested just as it did in the U.S., where the presence of Occupy was due to the same outsourcing, and the lack of jobs. Such protests occurred because like the young, and Blacks in the U.S., the South Africans are dispirited because of the bleak employment landscape. For the Blacks in South Africa, especially those who are young and just a generation removed from apartheid, do not want to have Wal-Mart in their backyard.

At this point the South African government finally intervened, directing their complaints to the Competition Tribunal. Their claim was that the retailers (Wal-Mart and Massmart) provided inadequate information about their product sourcing, such that it was unable to make a proper decision on the merger. They pointed to the serious flaws in the provision of relevant information and documents by the merging parties (Wal-Mart and Massmart). "This lack of information in turn affected the ability of the Competition Tribunal to properly appreciate the potential damage of the merger." (30) Michael Spencer, the chief executive of Business Leadership, said this was not "business friendly." In response the government of South Africa said:

"We are concerned that tens of thousands of jobs could be lost in the local factories that currently supply Massmart and other local retailers. We have intervened in the proceedings as government to support local jobs and industrial capacity." (31)

The government had intervened to safeguard the public interest! The government had asked the Court to send the matter back to the Competition Tribunal "for a more considered evaluation."

Government was pressing the Competition Commission to impose more stringent conditions, and potentially stronger ones, on Wal-Mart and Massmart. And, if the three Ministers and SACCAWU were heard and considered, Wal-Mart would have had to withdraw from South Africa. But the South African Competition Commission held fast to its decision, despite the pressure from the business community not to do so:

"But the counsel for the departments, William Trengove, argued that the Tribunal's hearing was procedurally and substantively unfair.

He said that the Tribunal did not allow sufficient time for a 'full and fair ventilation' of important public issues. The merging parties should have to provide for more information around the circumstances of the merger." (32)

And with that they called for a second public hearing, on the grounds that they needed evidence from Wal-Mart. And the Competition Commission went along—they had another hearing in June 2012:

"Despite the fact that there was overwhelming evidence of the fact that Wal-Mart was prevaricating, it had never seriously been contended that the merger gave rise to competition concerns. The merger was therefore not likely to substantially prevent or lessen competition." (33)

Doug McMillon, Wal-Mart's International Chief Executive, said his company couldn't commit to specific procurement targets requested by the government. Jeremy Gauntlett, Senior Counsel for the two supermarkets told the Court, "Allegations that Massmart would cause job losses by importing more goods remain unproven, and there's no evidence of the companies having withheld relevant information." (34)

Then the lawyers for Wal-Mart and Massmart claimed, "We submit that the review application is factually unsubstantiated and legally misconceived . . . ." (35) Had Wal-Mart or Massmart addressed the potential lowering of prices before the Tribunal, it would have addressed competition. But there was no serious debate before the Tribunal that Wal-Mart was looking at a significant lowering of prices. But, aside from all of this, the Competition Commission had never vetoed a proposal about a merger. What was clear was that the "public interest concern" was ignored by Wal-Mart, Massmart, and the Competition Commission. They supported the business interests and denied the public interest claim, and thus upheld the merger of Massmart and Wal-Mart.

As a result, the Appeals Court called for a reinstatement of the 700 workers who were retrenched by Massmart. They were not to be given "preference" for jobs; they were to be given their old jobs back, as they had demanded, and "no jobs were to be cut" in the following two years. They must ensure that existing labor agreements be honored for three years and, of course, follow South Africa's labor laws which guarantee the rights of all workers. (36)

Wal-Mart also told the South Africans that it will create more jobs. But will it? Wal-Mart refused to give, in public, its plans for sourcing abroad, saying Wal-Mart/Massmart was not sure as yet, how much it would source abroad. Wal-Mart told them that there would be more jobs as a result of the merger.

Certainly there will be more Wal-Mart jobs, and Wal-Mart will undoubtedly create new stores all over Africa. The merger will give Wal-Mart "290 stores in 13 African countries, including the chains of Game, Makro, and Builders Warehouse which is part of the Massmart empire". Wal-Mart said, "The combined Wal-Mart/Massmart entity is planning significant new store openings, which will create thousands of new union jobs in South Africa." (37)

Actually, after Wal-Mart's takeover, "All of the domestic retailers were scrambling, they were trying to streamline their costs in the face of Wal-Mart." (38)

And to appease the three ministers who had opposed the merger, "the Appeals Court has stipulated that a three-month study be commissioned by a panel of three experts (one each from Massmart, government, and labor). The study must examine the ways in which small suppliers can participate in Wal-Mart's global supply chain. The parties set up a three-way committee to let the "small suppliers participate in Wal-Mart's global supply chain." (39)

The government, the three ministers, and SACCAWU invited Professor Robert Stiglitz and Genesis Analytics Managing Partner, James Hodge, to be the ones to craft a remedy. (40) Massmart and Wal-Mart appointed Mike Morris, an economist at the University of Cape Town. Inevitably the two teams disagreed. The Stiglitz-Hodge Report said "that a large fund equal to 'many multiples of the proposed R100m would be needed to ameliorate the effect of the Wal-Mart transaction in the range of R500m-R2bn, allocated over five to ten years." Professor Morris disagreed; he wanted a smaller fund. He said, "When too much money is floating around under these conditions, the chances of corruption and waste increase enormously." (41) Naturally, the Stiglitz–Hodge fund was criticized by Massmart/Wal-Mart. It was described as "outrageous" by the Massmart/Wal-Mart team. It will be a long haul before Wal-Mart gives any money to the people of America, let alone South Africa. When Wal-Mart imports through its supply chains, doing so will inevitably lead to the smaller South African firms going out of business. And with them, the jobs of the men (and women) they've hired will disappear.

Or, will the two merged entities (Wal-Mart and Massmart) exact as much as they can from the wages from the workers, until they cannot make ends meet? Will they drive out suppliers? Will they make the workers in the supermarkets afraid of losing their jobs? We have to wait to find out. Will they cause the South Africans to lose their dignity, or be frightened because they are afraid that they will lose their jobs?

"A few players dominate South Africa's retail industries, a legacy of apartheid when many companies of all sorts pulled out or stayed away under the threat of sanctions. Three domestic chains control about 90 percent of the supermarket sector . . . ." (42)

Wal-Mart's annual revenue total, which exceeds $400 billion, dwarfs the GDP of South Africa; it is bigger than the next four retailers combined, and it has 2.4 million workers worldwide. (43)

I would wager that Wal-Mart will always act as Wal-Mart does now. Michael Bride of America's United Food and Commercial Workers Union said, "Wal-Mart has been assuring its investors—as recently as last week in Bentonville, Arkansas—it will push down costs even further." (44) And Shoprite, Africa's biggest grocery retailer, is spending $416 million to expand and upgrade its distribution center as South African merchants gear up to take on U.S.-based Wal-Mart Stores, Inc. (45)

"By coming into South Africa, Wal-Mart has set its sights on a bigger mark—the entire continent. And South African suppliers see their expansion as their ticket into a wider, even global, market." (46)

At this point the stores are not doing well. (47) However, it is too soon to tell what will happen in South Africa to the Wal-Mart/Massmart accord. An update as of 2013 reveals that "Wal-Mart is to open 90 new stores across sub-Saharan Africa over the next three years." (48)

The struggle in South Africa continues: earlier this year the Competition Commission criticized Wal-Mart's continued failure to reinstate all the workers, while the union has attacked foot dragging over reinstatements and problems over local supplier fund.

Footnotes

1. Irvin Jim, Our Case Against Wal-Mart, Presentation by Irvin Jim to Parliamentary Committee, (NUMSA) July 20, 2011.
2. Robyn Dixon, "Jacob Zuma Inaugurated as South Africa's President," Los Angeles Times, May 10, 2009.
3. Erin Conway-Smith, "Attention African Shoppers: Wal-Mart is Coming," The Global Post, June 1, 2011.
4. Scott Baldauf, "Wal-Mart In or Out of Africa?," The Christian Science Monitor, May 25, 2011.
5. Miguel Bustillo and Ross M. Stewart, "Wal-Mart Bids $4.6 Billion for South Africa's Massmart," The Wall Street Journal, September 28, 2010.
6. Massmart/Wal-Mart Merger: Statement by Labour Research Service, Labour Reearch Service, 2011
7. Gillian Jones, "Unions Fret Over Wal-Mart's Bid," The Mail and Guardian, November 4, 2010.
8. Tiisetso Motsoeneng, "SCENARIOS-South Africa to Rule on Wal-Mart/Massmart Deal," Reuters, May 9, 2011.
9. South African News Association, Times Live, August 2, 2011.
10. Scott Baldauf, "Wal-Mart : In or Out of Africa?," The Christian Science Monitor, September 25,2011. Op.Cit.
11. "Wal-Mart in Talks to Buy South Africa's Massmart." The Guardian, September 20, 2010.
12. "South Africa: The Gateway to Africa," The Economist, June 2, 2012.
13. Erin Conway-Smith, "Attention African Shoppers: Wal-Mart is Coming," The Global Post. June 1, 2011. Op.Cit.
14. Miguel Bustillo and Robb M. Stewart, "Wal-Mart Bid $4.6 Billion for South Africa's Massmart, and Paul Sonne in London," The Wall Street Journal, September 28, 2010.
15. Ibid.
16. Renee Bonorchis, "Africa is Looking Like a Dealmaker's Paradise," Bloomberg Businessweek, September 30, 2010.
17. Lloyd Gedye, "CEO Payout Just Another Brick in the Wal-Mart Deal," Mail and Guardian, May 9, 2011.

18. Lila Shapiro, "Wal-Mart Blacklisted by Major Pension Funds over Poor Labor Practices," The Huffington Post, January 5, 2012.

19. Stacy Mitchell, "In South Africa, Wal-Mart Refuses to Buy Local, Threatens WTO Action, and Wins," Huffington Post, June 1, 2011.

20. Lloyd Gedye, "CEO Payout Just Another Brick in the Wal-Mart Deal," The Mail and Guardian, May 9, 2011.

21. Claudio Alvarez, "Wal-Mart-Massmart Likely to Oppose Report," Iol.co.za, October 14, 2012.

22. Sylvia Scassera, "Wal-Mart-Massmart Likely to Oppose Report, Iol.co.za, October 14, 2012.

23. Nelson Lichtenstein, "Wal-Mart-Massmart Hearings to Resume," (www.I01.co.za, May 8, 2011.

24. Testimony of Noel Mbongwe, Deputy General Secretary, SACCAWU, The Competition Commission of South Africa, Merger of Wal-Mart/Massmart Stores, November 2012.

25. Press Release for Press Conference on the Anti-Wal-Mart Coalition Campaign, November 4, 2010.

26. David Levin, Minister of Economic Development, The Competition Commission of South Africa, Merger of Wal-Mart / Massmart Stores, November 2010.

27. Katherine Child, "Wal-Mart: We Just Want to Protect JOBS, Says Manyi," Mail and Guardian, July 25, 2011.

28. "Wal-Mart-Massmart Hearing to Resume," News 24, May 8, 2011.

29. "Wal-Mart Dismisses Merger Concerns," Fin24, August 2, 2011.

30. Jaffer Zubeida and Sidwell Medupe, "Government Seeks a Review of the Wal-Mart/ Massmart Merger Approval," South African Government Information, July 22, 2011.

31. Sapa, "Wal-Mart Merger Will 'Devastate' Local Jobs," Engineering News, October 5, 2011.

32. South African Press Association, "Wal-Mart and Massmart Resume Battle Against State Departments," Union City Press, October 21, 2011.

33. Stuart Graham, "South Africa: Wal-Mart Appeal 'Unsubstantiated',", South African Press Association, October 20, 2011.

34. Mike Cohen, "Wal-Mart's Massmart Purchase Faces South Africa Court Appeal," Bloomberg News, October 20, 2011.

35. "Lawyers Rip into State's Wal-Mart Merger Appeal," The Mail and Guardian, October 20, 2011. +36. Erin Conway-Smith, "Attention Wal-Mart Shoppers: Wal-Mart is Coming," The Global Post, June 1, 2012.

36. Ibid.

37. Zeenat Moorad, "We Welcome Becoming Part of the Wal-Mart Family," Mail and Guardian, May 31, 2011.

38. "South African Supermarket Pick'n Pay Quashes Tesco Takeover," Fresh Fruit Portal, August 14, 2012; Nonpumelelo Mgwaza, "Wal-Mart's Acts Force Rivals to Cut Prices," June 16, 2012.

39. Benzinga, "Wal-Mart Plans South Africa Expansion, Approves Increased Dividend Payout," Minyanville, March 9, 2012.

40. Amanda Visser, "Stiglitz Calls for R2bn Wal-Mart Jobs Fund," Business Daily Live," June 12, 2012.

41. Ibid.

42. Devon Maylie, "Africa Learns the Wal-Mart Way," The Wall Street Journal, September 7, 2012.

43. UNI Global Union, SACCAWU, and the UFCW, "Wal-Mart's Potential Effects on South Africa." May 12, 2012.

44. Ingrid Helsingen Warner, "Appeal Against Wal-Mart and Massmart Merger in South Africa," Modern Ghana, October 20, 2011.

45. UPDATE-2—"Shoprite Takes on Wal-Mart with $416 Million Upgrades," Reuters, August 23, 2011.

46. Devon Maylie, "Africa Learns the Wal-Mart Way," The Wall Street Journal, September 7, 2012.

47. Zeenat Moorad, Massmart's Numbers Fail to Impress Business Day Live, January 10, 2013.

48. Devon Maylie, "Wal-Mart to Open More Stores in Africa Over the Next Three Years", Wall Street Journal, August 22, 2013.

48. John Logan, The Mounting Guerilla War Against the Reign of Wal-Mart, New Labor Forum, Vol. XX(X) 1-7, December 10.2013.

11

Conclusion—The Wal-Mart Global Economy

Wal-Mart is, first and foremost, a global company. It has a total of approximately 11,000 stores in the world—5,733 in the United States, its home market. Wal-Mart was on four continents in the year 2012, and it employs 2.2 million "associates" in addition to management.

Wal-Mart began as a southern store in Arkansas, and over the years it "spread its wings." In the 1990s it expanded abroad, first to Europe, where it left its stores in Germany in eight and one-half years, with a loss of one million dollars. It soon realized that expanding in Europe would not work. There were too many supermarkets that were competing with one another. There was too much of a union presence.

So it went to Mexico and bought up Cifra, the biggest food emporium in Mexico. Wal-Mart decided it needed a new strategy, one in which developing countries were the best places to build or buy Wal-Marts. It has repeated its success there, in South America and Central America. So far, it has stores in Argentina, Brazil, and Chile, and it soon will have stores in Peru. It is ensconced in five countries of Central America. Wal-Mart is harboring hopes to get all of South America into a single network. It has access now to the whole Western Hemisphere—to the United States, which is its home country, and also to Canada. With its free trade agreements, with so many of the countries, and NAFTA-like arrangements, it will soon have the whole Western Hemisphere in its thrall.

It is in the process of beginning to do the same in South Africa, just as it has already done in the Western Hemisphere. Wal-Mart chose to invest in South Africa because there was a Massmart. Massmart is the third largest supermarket in South Africa, but it has stores all over Sub-Saharan Africa—in Namibia, Lesotho, Botswana, Mozambique, Malawi, Mauritius, Zambia, Tanzania, Uganda, Nigeria, and Ghana— and even in Zimbabwe. And Wal-Mart plans to open more stores in most of them. It will have, it hopes, an opening to all of Africa.

Only Asia is left. And Asia, the fifth continent, and the only one remaining, , is the sole continent where it makes its merchandise—cheaply particularly in China, India, Bangladesh, Viet Nam, Cambodia and Sri Lanka and other countries in that area. But in parts of Asia, laborers are rebelling. In Bangladesh the incapacity of the buildings and the abstemiousness of the wages, are making the world wake up to the horror of the situation. What they want is the certainty of a decent wage, and buildings that don't collapse, killing more than 1,000 people.

In Asia, (except for Japan) there is a lot of extreme poverty. And Wal-Mart needs to contract for the production of the products it sells in poor countries. Thus, in Bangladesh, in Cambodia, and Sri Lanka, even in India, people make the products that Wal-Mart sells. For who else can produce the low-wage merchandise for Wal-Mart to sell to the rest of the world? China is now waking up to collective bargaining. China sees it as a way to stop the massive disturbances in the streets, and the way to develop a "harmonious society."

Wal-Mart thought to locate all of its stores—and its supply lines— in most of the continents, except for Europe. At first Wal-Mart, had thought it would be a coup to take over Europe—from England to Russia. But that was not to be. Wal-Mart has stopped carving out territory in Europe. It is too crowded, and too developed, with too many supermarkets, and too many unions. So Wal-Mart chooses other locations to build stores and distribution channels, where the owners are sympathetic to Wal-Mart, and its politics are obliging.

That is why Wal-Mart is pleased about the new terminals at Lazaro Cardenas in Southeastern Mexico, and the Port of the Panama Canal. From these locales it can get its merchandise to all the cities in North and South America—and to Canada, as well. With NAFTA, and with the new trade agreements, it can move its merchandise all over South America. It can save time and money and, because of this, Wal-Mart can assure its customers that it will always have the lowest price.

Wal-Mart may say it "accepts" unions in any country where they are "part of the culture." Doug McMillon, Wal-Mart International Chief Executive, answers this question in a more self-aggrandizing way. "It's our intention to demonstrate that we are a great corporate citizen." But ultimately, this book has been a story about Wal-Mart as the "great chameleon,"—it changes its "skin" and its behavior, as it moves from country to country, in every country that I have studied.

Wal-Mart has met different situations in different countries. But, when there is a trade union in a country where it has subsidiaries, it sees "the union" as one of its first-order problems. At times in Germany, it was so hostile to trade unions that it couldn't get along with the people, the business practices, or the government. In Germany there was a major union presence, and Germany had work councils. Also one member of each trade union typically sits on the Boards of Directors in Germany, at the top of every corporation or business.

Because it could not get on in Europe, Wal-Mart went on a search for new countries, countries which are underdeveloped. Initially it searched out the BRIC countries (Brazil, Russia, India, and China), where it succeeded. Then it searched out South Africa, as a country which could give it access to others in Sub-Saharan Africa.

In the United Kingdom, the only thing that GMB, the trade union that represents the workers in Wal-Mart depots, could say about Wal-Mart's head is that he was "honest." After their six-month struggle, they won the right to a union—with collective bargaining that the government mandated. Wal-Mart gave them virtually nothing in 2006, after three years of working with Wal-Mart. But in 2012 there was a major settlement at Wal-Mart for 10,000 GMB workers. This settlement was achieved by the Trades Union Council. It is now expected that the workers in England will really have a union through which they can bargain collectively. The workers got a significant wage hike, instead of the 2 percent which the Wal-Mart "union" promised them, and which they rejected by 98 percent. And they will get the respect they have asked for. But of course, they will still be employees of Wal-Mart!

Mexico, until this year, was "the jewel in Wal-Mart's crown." But it was the bribery scandal there which might have been the reason that stopped Wal-Mart from expanding into more cities in the U.S. When the story broke in New York, and it was alleged that Wal-Mart in Mexico was the bribery capital of the world, New Yorkers had another reason for not allowing Wal-Mart into New York City. Wal-Mart has presumably given $24 million as bribes, to Mexican public officials, to enable them to build the more than 2,147 stores in Mexico. Wal-Mart, in addition, has always (unbeknownst to most of the public) had protection contracts, the worst labor laws that protect Wal-Mart from having legitimate unions. And Mexico is poor and a seat of corruption. But, Wal-Mart has already "conquered" Mexico, with its stores that cater to the poor. It has more stores than any other country, except for the U.S. It has restaurants, and a bank where they charge the people more than 75 percent in interest to take out a loan.

In Argentina there are people who work against the unions, people like Alfredo Oscar Saint John, "who served during the nation's bloody military junta" in cities where clandestine detention centers operated, during Argentina's "dirty war."

But in Brazil, where the president was formerly a union leader, and the government ministers also were formerly union leaders, everybody must pay their union dues. This is a country that is proud of it unions, Wal-Mart refused to participate in a traditional union event. It refused to give back to its workers a day's pay that is one of the union's regulations to support citizens' protection. It also refused to give its workers a portion of their profits for the year. Upon militant demonstrations at the stores, it finally did. As it reputedly does in Mexico, it finally gave them back a portion of profits to be spent only in Wal-Mart stores.

In Chile, Wal-Mart tried to destroy the union by choosing one out of many of the unions which shared Wal-Mart's "philosophy." After a year, the workers and the government booted out that union. They are waiting to see if Wal-Mart will try to destroy the legitimate one.

Wal-Mart has most recently focused on South Africa, a very poor country with an official unemployment rate of 25 percent—and 50 percent if counted correctly. However, three ministers of the government of South Africa were fearful that Wal-Mart would make dangerous use of its supply chain, and import products from China, to South Africa. These imports would compete with industries such as textiles and food, and put their South African competitors out of business. Just as in America, South Africans would inevitably see their unemployment rate go up, something they can hardly afford.

There was a heated battle fought by SACCAWU, the trade union of the South African Blacks who had fought against apartheid under the Botha regime. Indeed, three ministers of the government supported Wal-Mart's leaving the country. Despite the heated battle, the ministers and SACCAWU had with the Competition Commission, Wal-Mart won. Wal-Mart bought "the whole kit and caboodle" of Massmart stores. Wal-Mart plans to establish more than 90 new stores in the 12 countries where it has the rights to do so.

And as to India, Wal-Mart was hovering about its door, waiting to pounce on the country if the FDI restriction was lifted; it said it will build 100 stores. The Communists have not been re-elected in India, so India is free to permit FDI. But India has seen the emergence of its agrarian forces, who certainly do not want Wal-Mart or Foreign Direct Investment to bring in colossal supermarkets. India has had an ongoing struggle with its agrarian forces, from the Banata Janitra Party, who represent the almost landless poor. Although the government has argued that there is inflation, and that existing agrarian logistics can't get food to the people without losing 35 percent of it to spoilage and rotting. Yet the government, the Congress Party, points out that there is a fear of famine.

The antipathy toward Wal-Mart started when it used a successful businessman to get into India. The store formed a partnership with Bharti, a billionaire, "only" to supply Bharti's stores when they opened. When after six years this still didn't lead to Foreign Direct Investment in India, Wal-Mart used another approach. It managed to build its stores there, as suppliers to kiranas. But there are only 17 such "supplier" stores, not enough to let Wal-Mart become a power in India as of yet.

Wal-Mart was waiting for India to change its decision on FDI. Finally, in India the decision was made to accept Foreign Direct Investment in 2011 and, with it, Wal-Mart and other new stores. Suddenly, India retracted the decision, and said FDI wasn't possible— as of yet. While there are strong political forces, in a country that is democratic and still anti-corporate, the Congress Party won the battle, and India soon changed its mind. It actually opened India to FDI. The agrarian interests will not benefit at all from the policy. Wal-Mart planned to build the first new supermarket in 18 months. But then the opposition discovered an investment scandal, and Wal-Mart is being investigated. There is also an allegation that Wal-Mart invested $100 million dollars in the retail business of Bharti in 2010, two years before the Indian government permitted foreign direct investment in a multi-brand retail. Wal-Mart is not only investigated for this, but it is being investigated, under the FCPA, for the allegations that it gave bribes. But even with these two investigations going. Wal-Mart still lobbied in the U.S. on close to 50 issues before various government departments and agencies, and spent a total amount of $1.84 million on these activities.

And China is a country where the union is part of the government; the unions do the bidding of the state. China's industrial relations are like those of the United States—100 years ago. In the factories, which produce for export, there are sweatshops. In the sweatshops, the women work 13 hours a day and live 10 in a room.

Wal-Mart has chosen a female labor force in China's Wal-Mart stores, while men are the managers. In a society where women used to "hold up half of the sky," there is a young female labor force which has always been subservient. Their wages get lower and lower, despite the fact that they have, or don't have, a union. They are poor, and do not expect to work at Wal-Mart for long. Most will accept the low wages because they are planning to marry, or simply because they are happy to have a job, any job. But the turnover is especially high. This suits Wal-Mart, despite the ACTFU, as the wages get lower and lower.

And then there is Central America, which is even poorer than India. The people constantly fight to have their land, which has been stolen by fraud and power, returned to them. Many of the indigenous farmers who fight the "gringos" undergo brutal killings, and their women suffer rape. The government does nothing at all. Indeed, the killings are often linked to the government and to the drug war. And Wal-Mart does buy from the farmers, but only from a very few.

Wal-Mart in America and its hierarchy of young male managers have a horror of unions that is almost pathological. Wal-Mart has a penchant for believing that unions are intrinsically "bad." One young American manager, when I asked if he ever thought of doing something else said, "Wal-Mart—it's all I know." Perhaps it is because managers are trained to believe that a person who thinks a trade union may be good for people, has a very serious flaw in his or her character. Yet, in its foreign subsidiaries, Wal-Mart shapes men's responses and their behavior to the labor situation, and it lives with unions as it has to.

Wal-Mart Corporation as a whole has a singular way of dealing with unions. It seeks to destroy them or emasculate them, to make sure they can never interfere with Wal-Mart in any way. Or, if it says it bargains with a union, it is only pretending to do so. It only bargains from a position of absolute strength. All in all, it gives little to employees—especially in wages or respect.

There have been many studies showing how Wal-Mart could give all of its workers a better wage, a living wage, and still make a handsome profit. But there is no way that a company that makes over $8 billion in profit cannot do this. But Wal-Mart is ungenerous, even in its charitable works. The Walton family has given away only about 2 percent of its net worth to charity. Bill Gates is giving away 48 percent of his net worth, and Warren Buffett 78 percent of his net worth, according to Business Pundit.

These men have one way to treat unions. This is embodied in the company's handbook, "How to Make Wal-Mart Union Free." In that little pamphlet, which is used more or less around the world, and shows more or less what it can get away with, it demonstrates how it treats its associates.

It does so with disdain. Wal-Mart always instills fear, suspicion, and overall confusion in workers, as it tries to make them eschew unions. That is a mechanism to make them fear for their jobs, and make their meager benefits acceptable. Wal-Mart workers say they don't get any respect from their superiors, and such it is throughout the world.

Why is it so beneficial for worker to have a union? Having a union gives one an opportunity to have some power or influence over how the events of work happen to you in your life—higher wages, insurance, health protection, and pensions—all the things that make life more secure and comfortable, and reduce the stress.

In fact, currently, real collective bargaining negotiations between workers and firms usually press the union to decide on an annual wage increase, or to meet inflation costs when it can, according to the company's profits. But Wal-Mart does not give the workers access to its company's profits, as it used to. Wal-Mart also gives almost no annual wage increases. In fact, there's a wage limit, an average wage beyond which you cannot go, determined by the company. Anxiety and poverty seem to be the main "benefits" that Wal-Mart provides.

OUR Wal-Mart

On June 21, 2011 the workers at Wal-Mart, the associates, organized an alternative to a union, since it was impossible to start a regular union at Wal-Mart in the United States. The supporters of the Organization United for Respect at Wal-Mart ("OUR Wal-Mart") marched to the Wal-Mart headquarters in Bentonville. There were:

"nearly 100 Associates representing thousands of OUR Wal-Mart members from across the United States who came to the Wal-Mart home office in Bentonville, Arkansas, and presented a Declaration of Respect to Wal-Mart executive management." (1)

Since they are "organized" associates have now taken on a stream of protest. What has really mobilized them is the bribery scandal in Mexico, in which Wal-Mart is alleged to have bribed officials to ensure they got permission to open new stores. Wal-Mart is now under investigation by the Department of Justice and the Securities and Exchange Commission for this.

A woman who now works at Wal-Mart, Venanzi Luna, said, "I'm worried because, while I am working hard, now I'm hearing that they're risking our company by lying and cheating." She was so angry, and felt that she had to do something about it. So she started her own web petition, on change.org, with help from the UFCW, "calling for the resignation of Wal-Mart CEO Mike Duke and Chairman Rob Walton." Much to her surprise, the petition got 4,000 signatures the first day, and by this date it has almost 10,000. She said she wants a "thorough and independent investigation into what really happened." (2)

The Annual Shareholders Meeting was built around two issues. One was "dumping four board members who were involved in the Mexican scandal," and supporting a worker-shareholder resolution "to make executive compensation more transparent." The second was voting "No." Fifteen percent voted "No," on the re-election of the four board members: H. Lee Scott, former Wal-Mart CEO; Michael Duke, the current CEO; Rob Walton, the current chair to the Wal-Mart fortune;, the heir of Sam Walton and Christopher Williams, who chaired the audit committee during the purported bribery scandal. (3)

But even more important was action in New York City, where elected officials and labor leaders called a press conference at City Hall over this issue. There is a growing campaign against Wal-Mart, which had tried to place a store in Brooklyn and in Queens, in New York City. The store, a small store in Brooklyn, had already been approved by the authorities. But after the bribery scandal, the local community is having second thoughts about it. And in Watertown, Massachusetts, there was a protest to demonstrate the opposition to the construction of a Wal-Mart store.

A California pension fund is suing Wal–Mart—the goal of the plaintiffs at California's State Retirement System is not to reap big financial rewards, but to change corporate governance. The pension fund's CEO, Jack Ehnes, called the alleged bribery scandal, "The Fortune 100 version of Watergate." (4) And all over the United States now there are many other lawsuits appearing about Wal-Mart's alleged bribery in Mexico. The Wal-Mart workers in "OUR Wal-Mart," are angry too. They want Wal-Mart to be much better than it is today. They want a living wage—something as little as $12 or $13 an hour. They want to be full-time. They want a weekly schedule. And they want to be treated with respect. Maybe this scandal, horrific as it is, will help them get these things.

Wal-Mart recently had a "strike" at 28 stores in 12 cities, the work of OUR Wal-Mart and Warehouse Workers for Justice. It was more widespread than "the only other strike in the company's history." OUR Wal-Mart then planned a much bigger strike on Black Friday, the day after Thanksgiving—the biggest shopping day of the year.

As Matthew Cunningham-Cook says, globalization has changed the world:

"With the deregulation of trade in favor of multinational corporations, and the emergence of economic specialization, most major commodities are now produced with components manufactured all over the world. But with the automation of ports—as well as the deregulation of containerization in 1984, and the trucking industry at the end of the 1970s, the global and national supply chain transit costs have been reduced. The increasing mobility of production and distribution has spelled disaster for unions. Rather than relying on a stable pool of workers, the key to Wal-Mart's success has been getting low-cost goods to customers at precisely the right moment, according to microanalysis of market patterns. But that is what also what makes it vulnerable to work stoppages. (5)

Nelson Lichtenstein has also argued, "While Wal-Mart has resisted unionization wherever possible—the retail giant has been willing to abide by the laws of the country if the laws are there and they're going to be enforced." But U.S. labor laws have done little to restrain Wal-Mart from union busting. The labor campaign confronting Wal-Mart in the United States now plans a partnership with the global union federation UNI, the union affiliated group. Making Change at Wal-Mart has supporting a "Global Day of Action, "with participation expected from workers in Argentina, Brazil, Canada, Chile, India, Nicaragua, South Africa, the United Kingdom and Zambia." (6) When all the world where Wal-Mart operates learns about and participates in demonstrations of this nature, let us hope that Wal-Mart will finally stop its union busting.

Footnotes

1. "OUR Wal-Mart, Organization United for Respect at Wal-Mart," 2010.

2. "Wal-Mart Employees Call on Top Executives to Resign in Light Of Bribery Scandal and Cover Up," Making Change at Wal-Mart, May 3, 2012.

3. Roger Williams, "Unprecedented Number Vote for Change at Wal-Mart," Left Labor Reporter, June 8, 2012.

4. Anne D'Innocenzio, "California Pension Fund Sues Wal-Mart Leaders," USA Today, May 4, 2012.

5. Matthew Cunningham-Cook, "How Workers are Using Globalization against Wal-Mart," The Independent, October 25, 2012.

6. Wal-Mart Workers Will Rally in Ten Different Countries Tomorrow, Josh Eidelson, The Nation, December 13, 2012.

www.ingramcontent.com/pod-product-compliance
Lightning Source LLC
Chambersburg PA
CBHW031156270326
41931CB00006B/292